Praise for *Secret*

"*Secret Service Dogs* tells the incredible story of the fearless animals who put their lives on the line every day to protect the First Family and the men and women of the Secret Service who love them. It is a heartwarming and compelling read that offers an inside look at the incredible bond between these dogs and their handlers—a uniquely American story of bravery, loyalty, and love."

—Kate Andersen Brower, #1 *New York Times* bestselling author of *First Women* and *The Residence*

"A wonderful account and history of these unsung heroes at work every day to make the world safer. . . . An important addition to the works that shows how dogs really are man's best friend."

—*Library Journal*

"Goodavage compels readers with stories of the bonds between Secret Service dogs and their handlers. A must-read for the dog lover." —*Booklist*

"The latest treat for dog lovers by Goodavage." —*Kirkus Reviews*

"*Secret Service Dogs* offers an inside look at these animals; how they're selected, trained, and save the president from bad guys. . . . A collection of funny, dramatic, and heartfelt anecdotes."

—*Men's Journal*

"It has been said that the best nonfiction books are those that reveal a hidden world to the reader: a place they wouldn't otherwise be able to experience. Maria Goodavage's *Secret Service Dogs* is that kind of book—a well-researched and compelling read not only for dog lovers, but anyone interested in seeing high-level White House security operations from an insider's perspective."

—Gerald Petievich, former US Secret Service special agent and author of *To Live and Die in L.A.*, *The Sentinel*, and other Secret Service novels

"As a guide dog user and survivor of the terrorist attacks on the World Trade Center in 2001, I appreciate and understand the value of the teamwork and trust that bind a canine unit such as those portrayed in *Secret Service Dogs*. This book is a must-read not only for anyone who wishes to better understand dogs, but also because it is just a really good story. Maria Goodavage captured me right from page one. As Larry King said about my own book, *Thunder Dog*, 'This is a page-turner.' After reading *Secret Service Dogs* you will have a new and stronger appreciation for how to build a relationship with your own animal colleagues and friends. Enjoy. The read is well worth your time."

—Michael Hingson, #1 *New York Times* bestselling author of *Thunder Dog*

"Maria Goodavage takes us into a world that few know about and shows us just how special these dogs are. Although their work is serious, none of it could happen without the special relationships between the dogs and their handlers that come shining through."

—Gregory Berns, author of *How Dogs Love Us*

Courtesy of Marshall M.

SECRET SERVICE DOGS

★

THE HEROES WHO PROTECT
THE PRESIDENT
OF THE UNITED STATES

MARIA GOODAVAGE

DUTTON

DUTTON

An imprint of Penguin Random House LLC
375 Hudson Street
New York, New York 10014

Previously published as a Dutton hardcover, October 2016

First paperback printing, October 2017

The Library of Congress has catalogued the hardcover of this book as follows:
Names: Goodavage, Maria, 1962– author.
Title: Secret service dogs : the heroes who protect the President of the
United States / Maria Goodavage.
Description: New York : Dutton, [2016]
Identifiers: LCCN 2016025219 (print) | LCCN 2016037197 (ebook) |
ISBN 9781101984734 (hardcover) | ISBN 9781101984741 (ebook) |
ISBN 9781101984758 (paperback)
Subjects: LCSH: United States. Secret Service—literature. |
Police dogs—United States—literature. | Secret service—
United States—literature.
Classification: LCC HV8144.S43 G66 2016 (print) | LCC HV8144.S43 (ebook) |
DDC 363.28/3—dc23
LC record available at https://lccn.loc.gov/2016025219

Printed in the United States of America
1   3   5   7   9   10   8   6   4   2

Book Design by Nancy Resnick

To the dogs of the United States Secret Service,
who have been steadfastly and enthusiastically protecting presidents since 1976
and have never let politics stand in their way

A NOTE ON MISSION SECURITY

The United States Secret Service is not an agency that jumps at the chance to be the subject of a book. It is, after all, the *Secret* Service. It took nine months to secure permission to research and write this book, in part because of some sweeping changes within the agency, but also because of concerns about OPSEC (operational security).

With security missions as vital as the Secret Service's, I didn't want to do anything that would jeopardize OPSEC, but I also wanted to be able to tell the full and vibrant story of its canine teams. We came to an understanding that would safeguard OPSEC while granting me both unprecedented access and editorial control.

There were certain items I agreed not to disclose, including the names of explosives the dogs detect, certain tactics, and names of any of the dozens of venues that allow dog teams to train in realistic scenarios (including stadiums, arenas, parks, airports, and malls). In addition, I opted not to mention names of family members.

The Secret Service also asked me not to include last names of current employees—just first name and last initial, or a nickname.

FOREWORD

The United States Secret Service is constantly updating its protective methods and procedures, seeking to improve its ability to carry out its various missions and responsibilities. In the mid-1970s, I, as the assistant director for Protective Forces, along with my deputy Paul Rundle and members of our staff, maintained a continuous dialogue with the various Protective Units, discussing what they believed was needed to improve their protective posture. One subject that continuously came up was the use of K-9 units, in both explosive detection and emergency response. We had been receiving K-9 assistance from local law-enforcement agencies and, when appropriate, the U.S. military services. These requests always put a strain on the agencies, who had their own responsibilities and problems to deal with. The discussions finally came to a conclusion in 1975 when Director H. Stuart Knight agreed to our researching the possibility of having our own K-9 units.

We selected one of my staff members, Special Agent in Charge Bill Livingood, to be in charge of the research project and he began the task of determining just exactly what would best fit the requirements of the Secret Service. He interviewed local law-enforcement agencies using K-9 units, visited federal facilities where K-9 units were trained, observed their training methods, determined how they selected the handlers, and researched the type of dog best suited for our needs. Cost was always a concern, and this, being a new project, had to be included in the final analysis. Once Livingood's research was concluded, and approved by Director Knight, the K-9 program began on a very limited scale.

Dogs have been used for centuries to protect property and individuals. They have been used as trackers to locate escaped prisoners and find human remains. They have been used successfully by the military services in a variety of ways. Increasingly, canines were being used throughout the entire law-enforcement community, and as a result of Livingood's research, it was clear that the time had come for the Secret Service to include this addition to our protective umbrella. In July 1975, as I was about to retire, the K-9 unit within the Secret Service became a reality.

Maria Goodavage has become known as an authoritative author on the subject of K-9 utilization by the military and law enforcement. Her previous books, *Soldier Dogs: The Untold Story of Canine Heroes* and *Top Dog: The Story of Marine Hero Lucca*, give an insight into the effectiveness of canines under the most stressful conditions. In *Secret Service Dogs: The Heroes Who Protect the President of the United States*, she takes the reader into the selection process of these dogs, the training, their maintenance, and, most of all, the extremely close relationship and respect that develops and is maintained between dog and handler. In this interesting and informative book you will come away with a new understanding of the tremendous value these special dogs provide in protecting the leaders of our great nation, the United States of America.

Clint Hill
Assistant Director, Protective Forces (Retired)
U.S. Secret Service

CONTENTS

CHAPTER 1

A VERY STRANGE DAY

Marshall M. had been protecting the president of the United States for eight years and was ready for just about anything. Even terrorists, if God forbid they made it to the White House fence.

But when he woke up early on the morning of October 22, 2014, with his canine partner staring at him next to his four-poster bed, he didn't know what to make of it. Hurricane had never ventured upstairs without being invited. And yet here he was, on the third floor of their downtown Baltimore home, looking like a normal dog who wanted to go for a walk.

"'Cane, what's your deal, buddy?" Marshall croaked, squinting at his clock and his dog.

For the two and a half years they'd been partners in the United States Secret Service's elite Emergency Response Team (ERT), the only place Hurricane had wanted to be while his handler slept was near the front door. From there, the black Belgian Malinois could keep watch on the entire first floor, including the back door and the main windows. All roads led to Hurricane. His fur, the color of midnight, blended him into the darkness. Perfect for surprising an intruder.

Hurricane wouldn't move from his bed unless Marshall called him upstairs, and even then, he always seemed to be in a rush to get back to his spot. He reminded Marshall of a kid who wanted to finish watching his favorite TV show, although he imagined Hurricane's show was more like a live version of *The Wire*.

Marshall lifted his head off the pillow to get a better look at his dog. It was still dark out, but the street lamps bathed the room in an amber glow. As soon as Marshall moved, Hurricane trotted over to the top of the stairs eight feet away, then back to the side of the bed. Stairs. Bed. Stairs. Bed.

"'Cane, what are you doing? What's gotten into you?"

Marshall closed his eyes, hoping his dog would settle down. They'd be pulling a long shift later at the White House. No need to get out of bed at this hour. He heard Hurricane's paws pad the hardwood floor in a new direction. He looked and saw him standing on the other side of the bed, close to the window, over Marshall's gear bags and tactical boots. Hurricane gazed at Marshall with an intensity the handler found unsettling.

Marshall realized what his dog was trying to tell him.

Grab your gear and let's go.

Hurricane lived to work. The dog could tell by what Marshall was wearing if it was going to be a workday or not. If his handler came downstairs in civilian clothes, Hurricane usually stayed in his bed. But when Marshall greeted him wearing his black uniform, Hurricane jumped up, tail wagging, and shadowed him until they left for work.

Hurricane lowered his head toward his handler's gear bags and exhaled forcefully through his nose, making an odd grunting sound that always got Marshall's attention.

Marshall laughed. "OK, you little weirdo, we're not going to work yet. You need to go empty or something?" In their early days together he would say, "Go potty," but he quickly realized that didn't sound very badass. The dogs who protect the president don't "go potty."

They were out the door in less than a minute, even with leashing and muzzling Hurricane. Marshall slept in shorts and a tank, no matter what the weather. He kept a pair of size 12 slip-on Nike 7.0s at the front door and the back door. In an emergency, he could be on his way in seconds. As part of ERT, it was second nature to be ready for anything—even, it seemed, a dog with pressing bathroom needs.

Marshall headed left toward the park. Hurricane had other ideas. He jerked to the right, toward their white work van. He pulled so hard that he would have dragged anyone who wasn't as strong as his muscle-bound 235-pound handler. Marshall reeled him back with a word and a quick tug.

Hurricane usually marked every tree and rock he came across. But now he didn't bother lifting a leg until Marshall told him, "Go empty," in a firmer voice than usual. On the walk back home, Hurricane pulled the whole way, ending up back at the van. Marshall had never seen him so anxious to go to work.

The dog wouldn't relax at home as Marshall tried to go about his morning routine. Even their tradition of catching up on sports news together in the living room didn't settle Hurricane. Instead of reposing on the floor next to the couch, he paced the hall back and forth to the front door.

"You're so wound up, dog! Let's get you some real exercise," Marshall said, and ran upstairs to get dressed for work.

The vice president's residence (VPR) looks far more like a traditional home than the White House. The Queen Anne–style mansion's location, on the sprawling, tree-flanked grounds of the U.S. Naval Observatory, keeps it fairly hidden from would-be onlookers. By comparison, the White House is a fishbowl.

There's a secluded field on the grounds, and if no one is around, it's an ideal spot for ERT dog handlers to run their dogs. Even though the dogs are under exquisite control, handlers aren't supposed to let them out in public areas without a muzzle and leash unless they're working. But these are high-energy dogs, and they need to cut loose.

Marshall pulled up and eyed the area. On this misty October morning, it was deserted. Time for a half-hour game of fetch—on steroids. Marshall, a southpaw, had pitched for the Kutztown University baseball team for four years. Two of those years they'd gone to the College World Series.

He launched a black rubber Kong ball for his dog. Hurricane streaked out in its direction. The Kong jettisoned past him and landed seventy yards out. Hurricane caught it on the bounce and dashed back to him, wagging and bracing himself for the next throw.

Ever since he could remember, Marshall had wanted to be a pro ballplayer or to work for the Secret Service. Both had the team vibe and would provide plenty of athletic, adrenaline-charged moments. His arm didn't get him into the majors, but it proved convenient as a dog handler.

Soon after he entered the Secret Service at age twenty-three, he learned about ERT, the Service's version of a SWAT team. The challenging program takes guts, strength, speed, courage, smarts, and a level head. Many apply, but few make it through the rigors of the class.

Marshall spent two years patrolling around the White House, and made the Emergency Response Team on the first try. After three years on ERT, he was offered the chance to be part of the canine team. Marshall had never owned a dog but had worked alongside ERT tactical canines at the White House and was so impressed by their capabilities that he found himself wishing he could work with a dog.

He realized that if he became part of the ERT Tactical Canine Unit, his responsibilities would only increase. ERT canine handlers don't transition away from their tactical capabilities. Handlers are in the stack just like the other ERT techs, but they have a dog on top of everything else.

When he walked into the kennels on the first day of the ten-week class in 2012, the dogs—all Malinois—barked with a ferocity that jarred him. They growled. They whirled. Foam flew. Teeth flashed.

Except this one dog, all black. The dog Marshall had been assigned for his first day of training stood at the kennel door and stared at him.

"You want me to just walk in there?" he asked the instructor as he stood outside the kennel holding a harness, leash, and muzzle.

"He's all yours."

"Why is he all 'stealth' like that?" Marshall said with a chuckle, trying to sound like he was at least half joking. "Is that for a good reason or a bad reason?"

Marshall cautiously opened the door and took one step in. As the dog jumped toward him, Marshall braced for the worst.

In a flash it was over. The dog was standing on his hind legs, front paws on Marshall's chest. He wagged and looked into his new handler's eyes. The canine version of a hug.

Oh thank God! Marshall thought. He stroked the dog's head and neck as they took each other in amid the surrounding canine cacophony.

Marshall immediately knew this was the dog for him, and not just because Hurricane would be the only black dog in ERT— although he'd enjoy having a dog who stood out from the rest. There was something about him.

He vowed that by the end of the week, when the instructors matched handlers with dogs, Hurricane would be his. If that meant putting his thumb on the scale to increase the likelihood of getting him, so be it.

Throughout the week, handlers played a version of musical dogs, taking different dogs out of kennels each day and switching dogs when instructed. Whenever Marshall had the chance to partner with Hurricane, he took it. He also took it when he didn't have the chance, switching dogs back and forth with the deft hand of a magician performing a cup-and-ball trick until Hurricane was at his side again.

By the end of the week, instructors assigned him Hurricane. When no one was looking, Marshall tapped his chest. Hurricane jumped up and rested his front paws on top of his new handler's Kevlar vest. They had a few quiet words with each other before going back to training.

Almost everything they did together as partners in training came easily. Ridiculously so, Marshall thought.

"Why is everyone saying this is so hard?" he asked his dog one morning when they'd aced a few new commands.

All it took was one run-through for most tasks and Hurricane nailed it. In the first few days of training with their new canine partners, handlers used sliced hot dogs to reward their dogs and speed up bonding. Marshall's stash of sliced hot dogs remained robust, while other handlers ran out. All it took was one piece of hot dog and Hurricane knew what he was supposed to do.

The dog even learned advanced techniques in one try. The first time Marshall told Hurricane to stop biting a decoy in a bite suit—a "verbal out"—Hurricane let go immediately.

"I think I've got a real knack for this!" he razzed his teammates during a break as they went hunting for more hot dogs.

"You didn't do anything!" one heckled back. "You told your dog to do it and he did all the work!"

About halfway through training he found out what was behind his knack. Hurricane was not the young dog many of the others were. He was at least three and a half years old. And the Netherlands-born dog was titled in Europe—a champ in a popular police dog sport.

Most of the dogs the Secret Service purchased from its U.S. vendor in Indiana were about two years old with minimal training. The Service's trainers didn't want to have to untrain them on certain tasks in order to train them in their own techniques. Besides, highly trained older dogs were getting harder to come by as demand for them increased.

Marshall got to see Hurricane's European training papers once. They were in Dutch, but he Googled a few of the terms.

"His résumé is, like, a thousand times better than mine!" he said to a supervisor as he leafed through page after page of his dog's accomplishments.

Hurricane saw the supervisor look down at where he was resting on the floor. Not one to let an opportunity for affection pass by, the dog was instantly at his side, nudging his hand insistently. When the supervisor relented and gave him a quick head rub, Hurricane flipped onto his back, four legs sticking up.

"He's good at training people to give him love," Marshall laughed as the supervisor gave Hurricane the requested belly rub.

"Your dog has a very big 'off' switch. He's an anomaly," the supervisor said, shaking the black fur from his hand as Hurricane tried to persuade him to continue.

"I know! He's the best dog ever!" Marshall beamed.

Hurricane's friendly nature made the long commute from Baltimore bearable. On their way to and from the White House, Marshall often chatted with Hurricane.

"Man, that maniac cut me off! Can you believe that guy, Hurricane?"

Hurricane, the ultimate good listener, could *not* believe that guy.

Marshall usually smiled when he spoke to Hurricane outside the training arena. His tone was happy and friendly. He sounded like a father talking to a smart toddler. A smart toddler who could whup some serious terrorist butt.

At ERT headquarters near the White House, the shift got a briefing and assignments. The First Family would be in residence. Not that this information changed how they protected the White House, but it was important to know.

Marshall and Hurricane would be working on the north grounds of the White House, facing Pennsylvania Avenue. So would Mike J. and his dog, Jardan (pronounced jar-*dan*). The four had gone through canine school together and trained with each other more than any of the other guys and dogs. Jardan was more of a typical ERT dog. He had smarts and brawn, and was friendly enough as far as a SWAT dog goes. But no one ever accused him of being overly affectionate.

The handlers drove their vans onto the U-shaped driveway and parked close to the White House, Marshall on the east side, Mike on the west. For the next several hours they'd be keeping highly trained eyes (boosted by technology) on the fence line and surrounding area. Vigilance was key. Anything out of place, and someone would be notified, or they'd take action themselves. They didn't sit in their vans and peruse the grounds wearing more than forty pounds of full kit plus their weapons for nothing.

Marshall hoped Hurricane's half hour of chasing the Kong at the VPR would take the edge off the odd way Hurricane had been acting. Normally, the dog spent much of his shift chomping on his black Kong as Marshall kept vigil. Sometimes Hurricane napped in his open kennel in the back of the van, but at the slightest movement of his handler, the dog would jump up, ready for action.

But Hurricane still wouldn't settle. He bolted in and out of his kennel. He stood with his front paws on the console between the two front seats, ears forward and eyes looking in the same direction as his handler's. He hopped to the flat area in front of the kennel and just stood.

Marshall was focused enough not to let Hurricane's actions interfere with his attentiveness to the fence line. But this wasn't the same Hurricane he'd been with 24/7 for these last years. In a fleeting thought, Marshall wondered if the dog somehow sensed danger, like some dogs were purported to sense earthquakes ahead of time.

"Trust your dog," the instructors always told handlers.

But these were SWAT dogs, not psychic dogs, he reasoned. Hurricane was smart, but no soothsayer.

"Did you sneak out for some Starbucks before I woke up, 'Cane?" he asked as he gently elbowed him down from the console. The image of Hurricane jumping up and putting his front paws on the counter to order a cup of coffee made him smile. It lightened the moment. He realized his dog was probably just having one of those off days he'd heard others complain about. Chances were that everything would be back to normal tomorrow.

Still, when night fell, he found himself leaning forward an extra half inch, even more vigilant than usual.

CHAPTER 2

HIGHLY SKILLED OPERATORS

"They need you in the freight elevator! Down that hall and to the left. EOD's already there."

Kim K. and her explosives detection dog, Astra, hustle past tables resplendent with croissants, elegant pastries, cheeses, and thinly sliced melons and pineapples in the lower lobby of the Grand Hyatt, Washington, D.C. The lithe Malinois doesn't so much as glance at the upscale continental breakfast as she streams through the room largely unnoticed.

The cavernous elevator is waiting, doors wide open. Kim surveys the situation. Not exactly an emergency, but a job that has to be done. The cargo—stacks of folding chairs and bottles of juice—needs to be swept for explosives before it can be cleared and brought onto the floor. The president will be here later, and nothing can come into the area without being checked by a dog team.

"Seek!" she tells her dog.

The smell of fresh-brewed coffee permeates the air. But to Astra it's just olfactory white noise, no impediment to the rock-and-roll scent of explosives. With a little direction from Kim, Astra inspects the contents of the freight elevator. She's fast, but thorough.

In twenty seconds, she's done. An explosive ordnance disposal (EOD) tech stays on to check that nothing got past Astra.

Kim and Astra have been here since 4 A.M., working with other dogs and handlers from the Secret Service Explosive Detection Team. The dogs have already inspected every bit of the ballroom where the president will be speaking at 4 P.M., as well as the food prep area, the restrooms, the lobby, and the halls where the president will be walking to get to the dais.

They head over to a handler and his German shepherd, Max, waiting near the magnetometer. Everyone attending the Women's Leadership Forum has to pass through it. The main mission of the dog teams now is to inspect the equipment brought in by members of the media.

It's only 7 A.M., and the trickle of early guests and media is becoming a steady flow. A photographer sets down a bag filled with gear. Since Astra is already sniffing some high-tech recording equipment, this one's for Max, waiting a few feet away.

When Max's handler points to the bag, Max lets out the kind of excited cry some dogs might use when begging for a pork chop. Max is hungry to do his job. He pulls hard on the leash. The photographer unzips the bag and its interior compartments.

"Seek!" the handler tells Max.

Three rapid sniffs and the job is done. As an EOD tech continues the inspection, Max stands in front of his handler, tilting his head and staring at a small pouch attached to his belt. It contains Max's paycheck: his rubber Kong.

Max likes to be paid frequently in Kong-chewing sessions, but it's getting busy, and his handler can't make deposits to his account as much as Max would like. He pets his dog's head instead. Several feet away, a videographer is laying out his equipment on the carpet. Max sees it and lets out a whistle-like cry of joy, pulling toward it to do his job. He knows the check is in the mail.

Wherever the president goes, there will be dogs. They'll be there no matter what the country or state. They'll be there regardless of the political climate, the danger level, the weather, or the hour.

Most of the time, presidents don't see their canine protectors. The dogs who sniff out explosives arrive at a destination well before the president arrives and typically remain in the background while the president is present. The dogs who protect the president physically—the ERT dogs—tend post covertly.

Though not usually seen, dogs are an integral part of the Secret Service's many circles of protection for the commander in chief and vice president. The canine teams can also protect members of the First Family, the vice president's family, and often visiting heads of state from other countries. Before presidential elections, dogs may be part of the entourage of candidates who are granted Secret Service protection.

Handlers, like others in the Secret Service, don't let political preference get in the way of their jobs. They protect just as diligently no matter how much they agree or disagree with the administration or presidential hopefuls. And since dogs are completely nonpartisan, it's never an issue for them either. Republican, Democrat, it doesn't matter as long as they get their Kongs and some praise for a job well done.

Secret Service canines work at some functions attended by former presidents (formers and their spouses are under lifelong agency protection) and at certain events designated as National Special Security Events by the Department of Homeland Security.

Every vehicle that enters the White House complex gets searched by a dog. The average Secret Service explosives detection canine will search 7,020 vehicles per year.

After a car is ushered through the initial checkpoints, on E Street NW at either the Fifteenth or Seventeenth Street NW kiosks, the driver turns off the engine and pops the trunk. Depending on the weather and how busy it is, dogs will be waiting for vehicles in their handlers' vans or on the pavement. A large strip of pavement was recently painted white so paws wouldn't suffer during hotter months.

One of the dogs walks over and sniffs inside the trunk. His handler then guides the dog around the vehicle. If the dog doesn't alert, the car moves on. If it's a bigger vehicle, like a truck, human inspectors will then give it a thorough check under the hood, in the cab, in the truck bed or cargo area, under the vehicle— anywhere someone could be hiding something bad.

The president could look out the windows of the White House and see the canines who work there 24/7. But looking out windows for long periods isn't on the agenda of most presidents. To get an up-close view of what Secret Service dogs do to protect them and their families, presidents head about twenty miles northeast to the Secret Service's main training ground, the 493-acre James J. Rowley Training Center (RTC), in Laurel, Maryland.

The businesses that line a few streets in a corner of RTC seem to need someone to help them improve their curb appeal. Among the bland names of the gray edifices: "Italian Restaurant," "Gun Shop," "Hotel," "Office Building," and "Bar and Grill." The place looks like a dreary leftover downtown from the 1970s—a lifeless casualty of a mall moving into a nearby suburb.

But wait. Someone is shouting on L Street! A gun fires. More yelling. Oh no, man down!

"This is a very bad place for the Secret Service," says Special Agent Bill G., canine program manager, as he takes a visitor on a driving tour of Rowley Training Center. "We always get attacked."

BOOM! In the middle of the street a block away, a fiery flash. Secret Service personnel sprint in, weapons drawn. Not wanting to get in the way, Bill drives off from the tactical village before the end of the drama is revealed.

Down the street from the village stands a mock White House. Very basic, far too small, no grandeur whatsoever. White House architect James Hoban would cringe to see this interpretation. It's just four plain white walls with about a dozen small windows in the front and a U-shaped driveway. If it were a model in a new home development, no one would choose it. But it works well enough for the Secret Service to practice some basic protection scenarios.

Nearby, two aircraft—stand-ins for Air Force One and Marine One—sit on the "tarmac" outside a one-building airport. Air Force One is actually just the front half of a plane, known around here as "Air Force One-half" and Marine One is an old military helicopter with a flat tire. Nobody's flying those birds anywhere, but they're good for practicing protection work.

Next on the tour is a blacktop driving pad, where protective operations drivers practice the kind of maneuvers that could help save the president in a dire event. There's nothing going on here during the tour, but painted lines show where they perform their high-octane feats.

RTC is home to another tactical village, multiple firearms ranges, a raid house for nabbing counterfeit suspects or other ne'er-do-wells, a faux courtroom, and buildings that house gyms and classrooms. Woods, meadows, and fields provide important training grounds for scenarios that might unfold in more natural settings.

From Perimeter Road, if you turn onto Canine Way, you'll come to what most VIPs who visit here consider the highlight of a tour of RTC: the canine training area. This is ground zero for Secret Service dogs and handlers. They all start their training here and come back frequently for the intensive year-round training required by the agency. Most of their training is in the field, but this is home base.

It's not much to look at. There's an old concrete kennel that will be razed for a state-of-the-art kennel when funding is approved. It's next to the canine offices and a fenced training yard with an obedience course consisting of matching beige ramps and tubes and other equipment used in canine agility.

It's here that VIPs get to witness demos of Secret Service canines in action. The training staff frequently hears from members of Congress, athletes, actors, and other notables who tell them that of all the demos put on for them during the RTC tour, the canines are their favorite.

President Barack Obama was the most recent chief executive to watch the dogs through the training yard fence. Michelle Obama had visited previously to learn about how dogs help protect their family. Other presidents, vice presidents, and their spouses have visited RTC over the years and seen demos by bomb dogs as well as the more badass ERT dogs.

A canine program instructor or experienced handler often starts off explaining the blanket of protection the First Family gets from the dogs and handlers.

And then it's showtime:

A handler wearing a full protective bite suit is the bad guy. He runs as best as he can in the stiff, heavy getup in the training yard. His movements, while encumbered by the unwieldy gear, are purposefully haphazard: a jog to the left, a jog to the right, a sprint forward and then some zigging and zagging.

On the other side of the field, a dog barks and wags as he heels so close to his handler that he's lightly touching his leg. No leash binds them. The handler—rugged and muscular, as all ERT handlers are—shouts police warnings to the bad guy.

"Police! Police canine! Get down on the ground or I'm going to deploy my dog!"

Those words tend to quickly bring real-life suspects to the ground. But not this guy. Another warning. And another. The dog barks steadily. There's no question he means business. But this man isn't giving up.

The handler gives his dog a command in German, and in a flash the dog tears down the field. When he's within six feet of leaping for the bite, the bad guy comes to his senses and throws his hands up in the air.

Is it too late? Will the bad guy forever regret his belated decision to give up?

The dog's handler shouts another German command, and the dog now inches from the suspect whirls around and gallops back to his handler. Once at his handler's side, the dog does a quick one-eighty and is back in heel position again, ready for whatever is next.

The dog was probably aching to bite the bad guy, but even more, he wanted to please his handler. The result is a textbook "call off."

Later the dog gets to sink his teeth into the bad guy's bite suit. The suspect yells and tries to push the dog off and makes it look like he's fighting the dog. But the dog hangs on. Dogs with prey and fight drive find this extremely satisfying.

The handler yells: "Stop fighting with my dog! Suspect, freeze!"

Eventually it seems to dawn on the bad guy that he can't win, and he freezes. With one word from the handler, the dog lets go immediately. Someone explains to the president that this is known as a "verbal out."

These are challenging skills to master. Many canine teams attempt them, but few perform them as exquisitely as the dogs and handlers of the Secret Service ERT. They're among the nation's best.

Every few years, three ERT handlers and dogs attend the K-9 Olympics at Vohne Liche Kennels (VLK) in Denver, Indiana. They usually clean up. ERT handlers who want to go have to compete with one another for months to claim one of the three coveted spots and represent the Secret Service.

The in-house winners for the August 2015 K-9 Olympics all had call offs of zero feet, among other impressive victories. This meant the handlers called back their dogs just as the dogs were leaping, ready to bite. The dogs turned their heads away and changed direction, maybe bumping the guy in the bite suit, but nothing more.

Of 110 military and other law-enforcement canine teams that participated in the patrol portion of the Olympics, the Secret Service teams took first, second, and fourth place individually, and first place overall. They won eleven out of twenty-eight trophies— a handsome showing by most standards.

But there were no high fives. They were not happy. They beat themselves up over what they could have done differently, and their instructors beat themselves up, too.

"We can always do better," bemoans lead instructor Brian M. "We put huge pressure on ourselves. We should be ecstatic, but it wasn't good enough."

Brian, a fellow instructor, and the three dog teams missed the big K-9 Olympics barbecue to train on a new task, hoping the dogs would learn it quickly, which they did. When they arrived at the barbecue, the roast pig was barely more than a skeleton. All that was left to eat was corn on the cob.

The previous time Secret Service dog teams attended the Olympics, in 2010, they took first, second, and third place individually, and first overall. They won sixteen out of twenty-five trophies. They were a little easier on themselves but still talked for days about what they could have done differently, and in the weeks that followed, worked to improve what they saw as their deficiencies.

They're quick to note that in the end, it's not about winning games. It's about the mission, about the significance of whom and what they're protecting. It's something Brian thinks about around the clock.

"Every day after work, on the long ride home, you wonder: Are we more prepared today than our enemy?"

Compared with many military dogs, Secret Service dogs are specialists. Most military dogs perform two jobs: They sniff out explosives *and* they do apprehension/patrol work. These dual-purpose dogs are known as PEDDs, patrol explosives detection dogs. They're the backbone of the military working dog world.

Today's Secret Service dogs do one job or the other. A dog like Astra is not going to take down a White House fence jumper. And a dog like Hurricane won't be snorting around elevators for explosive devices. Neither dog has time for another job because of their rigorous training and work schedules. And there's another thought process behind having single-purpose dogs.

"Rather than have a dog and handler be good at everything, we want them to be great at one thing," Brian says.

Specialization is everywhere these days. Just ask your general practitioner, if you can find one. If anyone has a good reason to specialize, it's the dogs who protect the POTUS. Mistakes could have dire worldwide consequences. Being focused in one area creates the kind of expertise that can save lives. You wouldn't want that general practitioner to be your brain surgeon.

The four-legged specialists are almost always immigrants, starting out life in another country, and with another language, often Germanic.

Secret Service dogs, like most military dogs, are usually born and raised in European countries known for their long history of police dog sports like KNPV and Schutzhund. Countries such as the Netherlands and the Czech Republic have been breeding dogs who excel in this kind of work for many decades.

The Secret Service has a contract with a U.S. vendor, which procures most of the dogs in Europe and ships them back stateside. The vendor for all but a couple of years since 2000 has been Vohne Liche Kennels, which also hosts the K-9 Olympics. The northern Indiana facility has contracts to buy dogs for hundreds of federal, state, and local law-enforcement agencies, and to train dogs for departments worldwide.

Secret Service canine crews visit VLK frequently to select new recruits. The Service has a reputation for being extremely choosy.

The dogs the agency selects will train hard and work hard. And at the end of the day, they'll get to go home with their handlers. Military dogs don't have that luxury and, unless they're deployed in a war zone, spend their nights in military kennels.

The Secret Service won't allow the number of dogs in its current programs to be published. There are concerns about operational security if the wrong people know an exact number. While there are enough dogs to get the job done well all over the world, more canines are in the pipeline as their roles continue to expand.

The elite canine specialists selected by the Secret Service will spend their career in one of the following job categories:

Emergency Response Team (ERT) dogs—The Emergency Response Team is the Secret Service's version of a SWAT team. It began in 1992, and dogs were added in 2003, partly in response to the 9/11 attacks and concern about possible threats from bombers. ERT dogs function as part of the Tactical Canine Unit, sometimes called the ERT Canine Unit.

ERT dogs are super-high drive, smart, energetic, and courageous. They're trained in advanced SWAT tactics to physically protect some of the world's key leaders.

You can call them intrepid or heroic. Just don't call them attack dogs.

"*Attack* is a curse word for us," says Sergeant "Stew," an ERT Canine Unit supervisor and a former handler. "We 'attack' no one. These aren't vicious attack dogs. These dogs are highly skilled operators that can slow their minds during stressful situations and think."

Many police-type dogs trained in aggression work are dogs you wouldn't want to mess with even on a good day. But the Secret Service will only consider canines who are fairly social with people and other dogs, since they're around so many people, and since they have to work and train with other dogs all the time.

ERT dogs are an option of less-than-lethal force. Instead of being on the receiving end of a bullet, an offender might end up on the receiving end of a dog bite. Not much fun, but better than the alternative.

All ERT canines are Belgian Malinois. Many people mistake Mals for German shepherds, but Mals usually have shorter hair, slightly different coloration, and tend to weigh less, which makes it easier to carry them when a mission calls for it. Malinois are known for being intense and energetic, with fewer hip dysplasia issues than shepherds.

There are no female ERT canines. Brian says that while the males are typically bigger and stronger, "the female dogs are just as good as the male dogs. The aggression we're looking for comes from the mind, and females have it in similar levels to the males, sometimes even more."

He says the problem is that if a female Secret Service dog goes into heat during class, the male dogs' focus will fly out the window. Since the class for ERT is only ten weeks long, and a typical heat cycle is two to three weeks long, that's a large portion of class to have distracted dogs. (Detection dog classes are seven weeks longer, so if a female goes into heat, it won't be for such a significant chunk of class. Eventually the female explosives detection dogs get spayed, but not until the Secret Service is as locked in as possible about selecting them for keeps. Male dogs, per military tradition, are usually not neutered.)

Costs for Secret Service dogs run in the thousands of dollars, with ERT dogs tending to be the most expensive. Law-enforcement agencies and military special operations canine programs are always looking for great dogs with this kind of drive. There aren't usually enough to go around, so they command a higher price.

Most of the dogs have been trained in rudimentary aggression work, but they're otherwise green. If time allows, canine program instructors, who all double as trainers, work with the dogs for a few weeks more before the ERT canine course begins.

ERT dog handlers have usually been on the team without a dog for about three years before they can apply to be handlers. Their teamwork and tactics have to become muscle memory before they add a living, breathing creature to their arsenal. (There are not currently any women in ERT, although there was one years back. ERT leaders say it's a matter of the grueling physical standards. So far there have been no female ERT canine handlers.)

The bulk of ERT work is at the White House, inside the fence. The ERT motto, *Munire arcem,* translates loosely to "Protect/fortify the castle." The team had come up with the idea for the motto in English, and Stew had it translated by someone who spoke fluent Latin.

For Stew and other members of ERT, the meaning of the motto goes beyond its normal translation: "It may sound crazy, but to us, those two little words mean, 'Defend the castle/fortress against those who attack.'"

ERT dogs can also protect the vice president's residence. ERT canines may travel to protect the POTUS and VPOTUS, depending on the mission and situation. But most ERT dogs are not on the road much. When compared with their canine colleagues who sniff out explosives, they are positively homebodies.

Explosive Detection Team (EDT) dogs—These bright, focused, driven, patient dogs are able to detect every known explosive. Their repertoire is constantly changing and expanding to keep a few steps ahead of those who might seek to do harm.

EDT dogs are officially part of the Explosive Detection Canine Unit. These super sniffers are always stationed at the two main entrances to the White House complex for vehicle checks. But their job designation also takes them far from the Executive Mansion. EDT dogs hunt for deadly explosives around the world.

They precede the president and vice president almost anywhere they go, and work until they leave.

Unlike military working dogs, they're not marching into war zones rife with improvised explosive devices (IEDs), with every step potentially being their last. EDT dog handlers contend with a different challenge.

Most will never find a true explosive device. But their mind-set must be that it could happen anywhere, anytime. Deployed military dog teams have intensive and relatively short rounds in war zones, but EDT handlers and dogs will spend several years seeking out explosives day in, day out. It may be lower stress, but it's over a far longer stretch, with little downtime.

Secret Service dogs have found explosive devices. But you will not have heard about these "finds." The Secret Service will officially say only this about the subject:

"We confirm the presence of finds/hits historically, but we decline to discuss further details in interest of operational security."

It could give the agency a public image boost if these finds were publicized. But it's not even a question at headquarters: No amount of publicity is worth compromising OPSEC.

EDT dogs don't get much public attention. They work mostly behind the scenes. They aren't stationed within camera distance of the White House press corps as the ERT dogs are, or in the thick of the tourists around the White House.

This doesn't bother the dogs, who are content with a Kong and praise from their handlers. But some EDT handlers wouldn't mind it if their dogs got a little more public recognition for the important work they do.

Secret Service EDT training assistant Kevin H., a former handler, makes the best of it. When he gets together with his ERT handler friends, he likes to point out one benefit of being EDT:

"ERT has 18.1 acres of land," he ribs them. "EDT has the rest of the world."

Personnel Screening Canines (PSCs)—Despite their name, these dogs do not screen job applicants for human resources. If you've taken a tour of the White House in the last several years, chances are that you were sniffed by one of these dogs and didn't know it.

PSCs are all Explosive Detection Team dogs. The PSC gig is something many, but not all, EDT dogs do. Dogs who are too high energy to be sniffing for explosives in a small section of one room won't make the cut. These dogs have to be cool.

A PSC dog and handler stand behind a louvre screen in the first room visitors enter in the security process at the White House as strategically placed fans gently blow each person's scent toward the dog. The slightest whiff of explosives can lock down part of the White House.

Personnel Screening Canines Open Area (PSCO) aka Friendly Dogs aka Floppy-Eared Dogs—The official name for these dogs is an awkward mouthful that doesn't quite match its acronym. Canine staffers have taken to using the other two names, which more accurately describe these affable sniffer dogs. "Friendly Dogs" is the one they tend to use.

Friendly Dogs are the canines you'll have the best chance of seeing while walking around the streets that flank the north and south grounds of the White House. They're most often found strolling along Pennsylvania Avenue. You'll recognize them by their floppy ears (with one notable exception, whom we'll meet later) and black harness or vest.

If you're still not sure if a dog near the White House is a mere passerby pet or a real-deal Secret Service Friendly Dog, look at the other end of the dog's leash. If you see a uniformed dog handler, perhaps wearing a black shirt with the words U.S. SECRET SERVICE POLICE K-9 emblazoned in yellow across the back, it's a good bet that you're in the presence of a Friendly Dog.

But tempting as it may be, don't pet this dog! The dog's harness warns against petting for a reason. As approachable looking as they are, while they're on the job they're hard at work, and their handlers don't want anyone to distract them.

Like EDT dogs, these dogs sniff out explosives. The difference is that the odors are coming off moving people, not stationary objects. Even the indoor Personnel Screening Canines do their job only when a White House visitor has stopped. But Friendly Dogs track the vapor of an explosive as it moves.

Friendly Dogs go for walks for a living. Rain, shine, sleet, heat, snow, ice—regardless of the conditions, they spend their workdays weaving among tourists near the White House fence line, focused on their mission. If someone smells "suspicious," a dog will zip behind the person and follow the scent trail until it's clear to the dog's handler if something needs to be done.

The Friendly Dog program began in 2014 to expand the circle of canine protection at the White House. These days if someone with an explosive device is going to try to get to the Executive Mansion, he or she will have to contend not only with human Secret Service personnel, but probably with an enthusiastic floppy-eared moving-scent hunter as well.

The agency could have used typical police breeds like Belgian Malinois and German shepherds to do the job. But while some of these dogs can be robustly friendly, they tend to part a crowd when walking through it. This is especially true at a place like the White House, which attracts visitors from around the world, including areas where pet dogs may not be woven into the fabric of everyday life.

For vapor-trailing dogs to work most efficiently, it helps if people don't try to avoid them. Labrador retrievers, springer spaniels, and other breeds (and mixes) of floppy-eared dogs don't usually have the same scattering effect as Malinois, who are decidedly unfloppy in every possible way.

The Friendly Dogs are so appealing that it can be problematic. Some tourists see the dogs as a reminder of home, or a warm memory from bygone years, and want to pet them. Others have loads of questions. A few try to get training tips or give advice.

Handlers may answer a few quick questions but always stay focused on their dogs, who are not distracted by questions. After that, a Secret Service officer will usually take over the conversation briefly so the handler and dog can continue their work.

Friendly Dogs are bright, focused dogs with exceptional noses and an abundance of energy. They work intensely for varying amounts of time, and they take frequent breaks, trading shifts with other dogs waiting to take over. Downtime is important so they can recharge and get out of weather that's not ideal.

It's also a time for handlers and dogs to reconnect in their vehicles and have a little chat about this and that. After all, the canines don't get the name Friendly Dogs just because of their ears.

The Secret Service was created in July 1865 to thwart counterfeiting—a Civil War–era scourge that threatened the broken nation's financial and banking system. Despite its inception less than three months after the assassination of Abraham Lincoln, the agency began with no mandate for presidential protection. It wasn't until 1901, after the assassination of President William McKinley, that safeguarding the chief executive became part of the Secret Service's responsibilities.

Financial crime investigation continues to be a core mission of the agency. In 1997, the Secret Service added a Dutch shepherd named Mike to the Miami field office. The dog's job: detecting counterfeit money, in a pilot for what would become the Canine Counterfeit Detection Program.

The program was established to help root out counterfeit U.S. currency coming from Colombia, a major source of fake U.S. banknotes. It was hailed as the world's first use of canines for this purpose.

The doggy dollar detective, as some alliteration-loving Secret Service staffers dubbed Mike, did a bang-up job. In just a one-year span after the program was well established, his work resulted in $5 million in currency being seized and twenty smugglers arrested. The program was so successful that the Secret Service helped implement a similar canine program in Colombia.

As part of a counterfeit crew, Mike and his handler would have worked closely with Secret Service agents, since it falls to agents to investigate financial fraud.

But wait! Aren't handlers agents? Isn't almost everyone in the Secret Service an agent?

Actually, no. Most people don't realize that there's a vital component of the Secret Service called the Uniformed Division (UD). It employs more than 1,300 officers (compared with the 3,200 agents in the Secret Service).

The UD is considered the police or security division of the Secret Service. It began in 1922 as the White House Police Force and changed names and missions over time. Dog handlers are part of the Uniformed Division. Canines have been playing an integral role in the Secret Service since 1975.

Uniformed Division officers are charged with protecting the White House complex, the vice president's residence, and the main Treasury Building and its annex. Chances are that most of the Secret Service "agents" tourists see in the vicinity of the White House are UD officers.

UD officers also protect foreign embassies in Washington, D.C., as well as heads of state visiting the United States. They travel the nation and the world in support of the protectees. But the job is based in Washington, D.C., which makes it appealing to people who want a firm home base. Many who choose to go UD instead of becoming an agent do so for this reason.

Besides the Explosive Detection Team, several specialized units fall within the UD, including the Countersniper Team, Emergency Response Team (with its own canines), Motorcade Support Unit, Crime Scene Search Unit, and bike patrol. Officers can apply to be part of these units once they put in enough time on their initial basic duty.

Agents have an entirely different career path, starting in field offices for several years and then getting assigned to a presidential protective detail, vice presidential protective detail, or dignitary protective detail. Or they may alternate between protective assignments and financial crime investigations.

If you'd like a quick way to tell UD officers from agents, you can sometimes look to their attire. Officers usually wear uniforms, and agents often wear suits. But there are many exceptions to both. It's not always easy to distinguish the two at a glance. Agents wear whatever the situation dictates. If a president is walking on the beach, an agent may wear a polo shirt and khakis. Depending on the assignment, UD officers may also wear a more casual attire that helps them blend in, especially when in foreign countries.

But there's one type of UD officer you can distinguish from a long way off, no matter what they're wearing.

They don't walk alone. Their partners are short and furry. And although it's hard to tell at a glance, these canine partners tend to be great listeners—a helpful talent, considering the weight of the mission their handlers bear.

CHAPTER 3

ON-OFF SWITCH

During a checkup, a doctor asked ERT dog handler Jim S. what he does for a living. He told her in a few words. She paused for a moment.

"Oh, that makes sense," she said.

"What do you mean?"

"When you came in here, you checked around corners and looked everywhere."

"I did?"

The Marine veteran was surprised, but not really. He knew that living in a state of increased vigilance around the clock is common in his profession.

And when you're part of a team that's responsible for the safety of the president of the United States, you have to do a lot of fumbling in the dark to find your "off" switch. Many end up just leaving it on.

With a mission this vital, there's simply no room for error.

"If you let down your guard on the job, it can change the history of the world," says Bill.

It's a burden Secret Service dog handlers take extremely

seriously regardless of their specialty. Tactical dog handlers on the White House grounds, handlers whose dogs sniff for explosives around the world, and those who walk their floppy-eared dogs up and down Pennsylvania Avenue all share one unspoken mantra:

Not on my watch. Or my dog's.

"What is really on our shoulders is almost unbearable to think about," says ERT dog handler Luke K.

Jim, now an instructor and ERT canine training sergeant at RTC, reminds his students about a lesson they learned in basic ERT school.

"Bad guys can try one hundred times and they only have to be successful once. We can't let that happen. We have to be successful all one hundred times. We have to win every single time."

No pressure there. Fortunately most of the guys on ERT are hardwired for challenges. Many were on sports teams in college. Some were military. They all know teamwork. They know winning. They may have lost some football or baseball games along the way, but losing is no longer an option.

Some things don't change, though. They train intensively. Confronted by every type of enemy and scenario in training, they sweat in full bite suits in 110-degree heat, get shot at with "sim" rounds (essentially paintball rounds designed to be used in their standard weapons systems), get knocked down like bowling pins by dogs, and apprehend some of the most heinous bad guys imaginable, maintaining absolute control of their dogs at all times.

Brian is always thinking up new ways to train, and to test his team.

"We put the dogs and handlers under a lot of stress to know they'll perform when it's critical," he says while walking toward the training yard. "I have to get in the mind-set of the bad guys and all the crazy stuff they can do—as bizarre as you can think."

A gray plastic garbage can sits upside down in the middle of the yard. "What's *that* doing here?" would be the reaction from most people. But not ERT dog handlers. They assume someone with bad intentions is hiding under it.

Within seconds, several muzzled, barking ERT dogs charge up to the garbage can. Their handlers let them sniff it and lunge at it one at a time. One dog knocks it hard and the plastic can topples, revealing a "bad guy" who had managed to squeeze himself under it. The dogs go crazy trying to get him, even with their muzzles on. He eggs them on as the handlers take turns letting their dogs approach.

In the fray, there's a mishap with the bad guy's dental work, and one of his crowns pops off. Barely skipping a beat, he spits it out, shoves it in his pocket, and continues the fun and games.

Brian can't publicly divulge most scenarios and tactics used by dogs and handlers. But the goal is that dog teams and the rest of ERT work together as a unit that can thwart anything that might head their way.

"We have to assume Paris is coming here," he says, referring to the deadly series of coordinated terrorist attacks in the French capital in November 2015. "We can't simulate the real thing but we do our darndest.

"The team has to be able to perform perfectly when and where it really counts. I can think of no bigger stage than the White House."

No ERT handlers really want to have to act on that stage; they want to avoid drama if possible.

"If nothing goes on, it's a good day," says handler Shawn S.

"The less exciting the better. Because what entails a bad day when I'm working is a *really* bad day."

But when something happens, every tactical canine handler believes he needs to be there with his dog to help put an end to the threat. After all, every handler's dog is *the best dog*. And with all the training they've done, the ERT handlers want a chance for their dogs to shine: To end a threat. To protect the First Family. And to be able to badger the other guys who weren't lucky enough to be there.

"It would be like the winning touchdown at homecoming, only way better," says handler Larry C., who played defensive back at Winston-Salem State University in North Carolina. "You train and you train and you train and you train and it's game time. No one wants to be left saying, 'Damn, I wish that was me and my dog!'"

Larry's dog isn't just the best dog. "Maximus is like my own child," he readily admits. "If he gets to be a dog that apprehends someone, a lot more people would know how great my son is."

The bonds between Secret Service dogs and handlers run deep. They're together almost 24/7. The lives of the world's top leaders depend on the dogs and handlers being able to read each other better than most long-married spouses.

"We know if they are mad, if they're sad, if they've done something mischievous, or when they are sick," says Stew.

"On the other hand, they know the same about us. What's the saying? 'Lord, help me to be the person that my dog thinks I am.' It's so true.

"These animals will gladly run into a hail of gunfire—giving their life—to do their job. All they ask in return is for you to throw the ball with them, pet them, and talk to them in an embarrassing high voice like they're the best toddler in the world."

Working and living alongside a canine partner can make the load feel a little lighter as well, helping alleviate some of the stress of the mission. Most people who have dogs as pets attest to their stress-busting benefits. Numerous studies point to these positive correlations.

In war, the effect a dog can have on troop morale is profound. Men and women in units with military working dogs report feeling happier and more relaxed when they get to spend a few minutes with a dog, or even if a dog is simply part of their unit. Military dog handlers find great comfort in their dog's companionship.

Secret Service EDT handler Sergeant Sal S. believes dogs also play a key role in helping "humanize" handlers.

"The entire Service is pretty much alphas," he says. "The dog gives you the ability to be more sociable and really show that gentle side of you when it's appropriate."

In 2005, Sal brought home a handsome 110-pound German shepherd named Daro. They'd just finished EDT school together, and he was excited to add the gentle giant to his house. He made sure no one would be home at first so the dog could acclimate without his family around.

Daro entered the house behind Sal. They got to the stairs and Daro stood beside his handler.

"Climb!" Sal told his dog.

Daro walked up to the top of the stairs, turned around, lay down on the cream-colored carpet, looked toward Sal, and sighed. From then on, that was Daro's spot. It was the perfect vantage point for watching the front door. Daro enjoyed his post so much that Sal and his wife vacuumed around him so they wouldn't disturb him.

His wife gave Daro the nickname James Bond. Daro was every bit a gentleman. When walking through doorways on searches, Daro always paused to let Sal through first.

After you, Sal could almost hear him saying.

But when searching for explosives, the dog has the right of way. "No, after *you*," Sal would tell him.

Sal marveled at Daro's finesse when eating or drinking. "He may as well be wearing a tuxedo," he used to tell his children.

One day the children decided to marry Daro to their pet dog, a black German shepherd named Luna. The groom cut a dashing figure in the tux they imagined him wearing.

Daro was even James Bond on the job. No matter where he and Sal went, how long they worked, or how challenging the conditions, Daro searched for explosives in a calm, methodical manner. Nothing ruffled him. He was the epitome of suave.

In March 2009, the Service assigned Sal and Daro to protective duty in Prague. Daro got a physical and the vet gave him the green light. Two days later, Sal woke up at 4:30 A.M. for their trip. He'd already packed their bags, so he headed over to rally Daro out of bed.

"Come on, boy, big day ahead!"

Daro didn't move. Sometimes he was a deep sleeper. Sal tried again.

"Hey, Daro! Rise and shine!"

Still nothing. Sal walked closer to see what was going on. It wasn't like James Bond to sleep through his wake-up call.

He leaned in and looked at his partner for a few seconds. Daro wasn't breathing. Sal touched Daro's chest gently with the palm of his hand and was hit by the sickening realization that his dog was dead.

But Daro couldn't be dead, he insisted to himself. He had been playing like a puppy the night before, and nothing was wrong. Sal scooped up his dog and ran to his work van with him. Daro was heavy and unwieldy and Sal understood for the first time what the term *dead weight* meant.

He raced to a local emergency veterinarian. He felt lost, out of his body. Nothing was familiar. Nothing except Daro. So he talked to him. They always talked in the van.

"Hang in there, James Bond, I'm getting you help. You're going to be OK."

Maybe he's just sick, really sick, he told himself. It was a coma or something. He clung to that one thought to keep from going over the edge of a dark abyss.

He's Daro. He's going to make it. The vet will bring him back.

He ran in with Daro in his arms, and within seconds the dog was on a steel table.

"Please step aside," a tech told him as the veterinarian and four others surrounded his partner, trying to revive him. It didn't take long before someone delivered the news he knew was coming.

"I'm so sorry, there's nothing we can do."

His heart tightened and the edge of the abyss gave way.

The next day Sal was transferred from canine to the Foreign Missions Branch, which provides exterior security to hundreds of diplomatic facilities.

"I know it's hard, but you're needed there," a UD supervisor told him. "You're not needed in canine without a dog."

As the days without Daro passed, Sal couldn't shake the raw

emptiness, a kind of bottomless sadness he had never come close to experiencing. And he was angry, at himself and everyone. How could he have not known that Daro had a lower intestinal cancer that was silently snuffing out his life? How could the vet have missed it? Why couldn't he have at least had a chance to say good-bye?

He had to take some time off. He could barely eat or sleep.

"Daro was my whole world," Sal told a neighbor. "We were together pretty much every minute of the day. Where there's Sal there's Daro. Where there's Daro there's Sal. There were two. And then they became one."

The stairs at home were the worst. At first he thought he saw flashes of Daro in his usual spot at the top of the stairs, but when he looked, it was just a gaping, lifeless space.

Handlers and instructors tried to talk with him, but he wouldn't return their calls. The Secret Service's Employee Assistance Program (EAP) phoned, but he didn't want to talk to them or anyone.

Eventually his canine friends had enough. They came to the house and insisted he let them in. They tried their best to get him to talk about what he was going through. Before they left, he promised to see someone at EAP.

He did it for himself, his family, his job, and for Daro. The dog wouldn't have wanted to see him like this. After several visits with a counselor, the grief began to lift.

"Of course it took you so long to talk about it," the counselor told him. "Daro broke ice everywhere you went. He was the channel you used for communication. How would you communicate your emotions without Daro?"

A fellow handler suggested Sal and his family hold a red-balloon ceremony. He told him how it had helped him with his grief about his own dog.

A few weeks after Daro passed, Sal, his wife, and his children stood in a circle in front of their house. Each held the string of a red helium balloon. They took turns sharing a favorite memory of Daro in a few words, saying what they would miss about him.

"What I'm going to miss the most," Sal said when it was his turn, "is when Daro would say, 'After you,' and I would tell him, 'No, after *you*.' There will never be another gentleman like him."

When they were done, they all released their balloons at the same time and watched them ascend. Sal took a deep breath for the first time since Daro died. He felt as though sunshine had finally broken through the thick gray clouds.

That October, Sal was back in canine school with his new dog, Turbo. Working without a dog had felt all wrong. He realized he belonged in canine and applied for an opening in a new class.

The Secret Service has an unofficial "one and done" policy for handlers. The idea is that others who want to try dog handling should have a chance. (Many would like this to be revisited, since highly experienced handlers can mean the best protection.) But there are exceptions to this policy, and Sal was glad to be one.

At first he was concerned his new dog would remind him too much of Daro. No chance. Turbo is nothing at all like his predecessor.

Turbo eats and drinks with reckless abandon. He moves in a herky-jerky fashion, and in training, when he alerts to the odor of an explosive, it's like a Scooby-Doo double take.

And he never says *after you*.

Sal's wife gave Turbo the nickname Snoop Dogg. Sal jokes that if the dog could wear gold chains around his neck, he would.

But what Turbo may lack in good graces, he more than makes up for as a working dog. He quickly gained a reputation as a phenomenal detection dog. Sal still misses Daro immensely, but he's grateful to be working beside another excellent dog, even one who's a little rough around the edges.

"When you're protecting the president," he says, "nothing feels as good as working with your best friend at your side."

Larry doesn't mind night duty outside the White House. He feels a sense of pride that he and his dog, Maximus, are protecting members of the First Family as they sleep. He hopes the president sleeps a little more soundly knowing the dogs are right there, ready to explode out of their vans at the slightest hint of trouble.

As his Malinois relaxes in the back of the van, Larry sits in the driver's seat, clad in full kit, and maintains a keen focus on his sector. Nothing's going to get past him.

Friends and family sometimes ask him how he can stay awake, much less hyperaware—especially during the night shift.

"It's easy," he says. "You see this family walking around in the news, and you have people who cry because they have a chance to meet them. But you also have people all across the world who want to do away with them. You're the ones protecting them. You don't get lax, because you can't get lax."

By itself, passion for the work can't keep away the fatigue of late shifts and long hours. When Larry feels himself getting tired or less focused, he pulls out some items from his bag of tricks. One of his favorites is a set of thirty-five-pound dumbbells. For the former college athlete, they're light, but doing curls with them at 3 A.M. is the equivalent of a cup of coffee.

Sometimes he lifts the weights in the driver's seat of his van, and sometimes he lifts them as he stands just outside the vehicle, with Maximus looking at him with a "What the heck are you doing?" expression.

Larry is an extremely fit forty-four-year-old—one of the older guys on the team. He loves working out and wants to be in top physical condition for the job. When he has time during a workout at the ERT gym, he likes to fit in one thousand push-ups—twenty sets of fifty. "I try to make them know I still got it," he says.

On the south grounds of the White House on the same shift, Marshall keeps vigil in his van. When he starts feeling slightly tired, he takes a few gulps from his Monster Energy drink. He buys them by the case, regular flavor, in the black and green. One of his favorite ways to keep his mind in the game while watching his sector is to go through possible scenarios and figure out how he'd react.

Since Marshall is facing the direction of some of D.C.'s famed monuments on this night, he creates this one:

"What if an explosion goes off down by the Washington Monument and then I see gunfire? Where am I going to position myself, what am I going to do? Where am I going to put the dog? Where am I going to be at for the best place to cover? And then as that's happening, a guy goes over the north fence. Do I pull back, go forward, come to one side, what am I going to do differently with Hurricane?" The next day, he might talk to some of the guys about it before training and see what they'd do.

Unlike their human partners, Maximus and Hurricane don't need to create scenarios or swig caffeine, or even worry about keeping on high alert. They can chew their Kongs in the backs of the vans and sleep when they want to. At the least rustle of the handlers they're so tuned into, they're ready to fly.

Marshall marvels at Hurricane's ability to chill out when his "on" switch isn't needed. Sure, the dog is usually energetic. He's a Malinois, after all. But the dog's propensity to be mellow and loving transforms him from a formidable presidential protector to a happy goofball as soon as Marshall lets him know it's OK to relax.

Although Hurricane loves hanging with his handler, he's not a one-man dog as far as affection is concerned. He's more of a "you look at me and I think you're the greatest" kind of dog.

Give him so much as a glance while he's off duty, and he'll wag on over and push his head toward you until you pet him. And don't even think about stopping. He is not shy to lean in, wag, look you deep in your eyes, and ask for more. He might even train you to rub his belly.

Because Hurricane knows he's guaranteed affection and attention when he gets a bath or visits the vet, he enjoys these activities that many other dogs—even pet dogs—would prefer to avoid.

"The hardest part of going to the vet is trying to get him to stop doing everything he can to be petted," Marshall says. When vets feel Hurricane's body during exams, the dog pushes himself into them with his head so they'll love him up.

Like all Secret Service dogs—even the Friendly Dogs—Hurricane is required to wear a muzzle at veterinary hospitals. He makes Darth Vader–like sounds under his black leather muzzle as he seeks out belly rubs from the staff.

The vet techs love him and have figured out a way to get him to stay still: When they need to, they squirt a little bit of canned cheese near his mouth under the leather muzzle. He momentarily forgets about his looking for affection as he licks away the tasty treat. The staffers get the job done, Hurricane gets a little more love, and off he goes, wagging contentedly down the hall alongside Marshall.

Stew's old dog Nero had a similar switch. Stew has a couple of Yorkies at home. The diminutive dogs have no fear and would growl at Nero when he came near them while they were eating. Nero wouldn't argue or force the issue. He just walked away slowly to give them their space.

"You have no idea, little dogs," Stew would laugh. "He could crush you in a second."

But he knew Nero wouldn't have.

"He wasn't mean," says Stew. "He was loving and sweet. But if I flipped on the light switch, he became SWAT Dog!"

In stark contrast, Marshall and Stew and most other ERT handlers have personal SWAT switches that stay on most of the time. ERT guys could light an entire city with all their "on" switches. It's a common phenomenon in law enforcement.

Hypervigilance is essential for their own survival and the safety of others. Their job entails suspecting the worst at all times. This mentality can easily bleed into off-hours. Their vigilance takes no holiday.

"I go to church and they say 'Let us pray' and I can't close my eyes," says Stew, a former Marine sergeant.

When Marshall goes to the movies, he sits in specific spots he feels will give him the best ability to react to an incident. If he can, he buys tickets in advance so he can pick the seat. Otherwise he arrives early. He's looking for a seat that will give him an excellent vantage point and let him respond to the entry and exit points, if necessary. It's easier to enjoy the movie if he knows he'll be able to react appropriately to protect his friends and other innocent people if something happens.

Like many in law enforcement, he often carries a weapon off duty. He was doing this well before the recent spate of movie theater shootings.

He doesn't even let down his guard in the house of God. He's always scanning for problems. Friends ask him why he carries in church. He has a great story.

"My first year patrolling," he tells them, "I helped with the arrest of a man with a gun close to the White House. It was the first time I drew my gun and I actually ended up wrestling the guy down while his gun laid right next to us on the ground in front of a hundred people. I'd never forget that man's face.

"Well, a year later, I was at church in the middle of the week at daytime mass. I scanned through the crowd as I always do, and who do I see but him. I couldn't believe it. He had a weapon last time, who knows if he had another one. Maybe he would've seen me and remembered and freaked out.

"Nothing happened that day. He didn't even see me. But it was good to know I was ready for whatever came my way."

Stew frequently reminds his handlers of the "C word" when they meet at ERT headquarters near the White House.

"Complacency is cancer and it will get you or someone killed."

All Secret Service dog handlers know that nothing can be assumed to be safe until it's thoroughly checked out. Luggage, packages, vehicles—and even rodents.

Alarms (not heard by the public) frequently go off on the White House grounds. They're exquisitely sensitive. Sometimes they get set off by bad weather, or by the squirrels who seem to find the vicinity of the White House intoxicatingly attractive. Even if a Secret Service officer or agent sees a squirrel tripping the alarm and reports it via a Service radio, ERT is going to proceed as if it were a lot more than a squirrel. The officers approach with guns and dogs, in whatever tactical advance the situation dictates.

"Some of the guys who aren't on ERT think we're completely insane," says Jim. "But we perceive things a little differently than the average officer does. It's a tactical mind-set. We're going to do what we have to do before we call it clear."

They do this for every alarm breaker, for any possible penetration without an alarm, and for anything that doesn't seem normal.

"That's how we have to be, because the one time we're relaxed and we don't take the time to check it the right way is going to be the one time that somebody gets past us," Jim says. "And that's not going to happen."

Stew recalls one night when an alarm went off. It would be easy to assume it was probably the fox that had been seen in the area earlier that night. But ERT wasn't going to assume anything.

It turned out not to be a fox. It was a fence jumper, and he was running on the south grounds. The team quickly apprehended him, with the help of a barking dog whose handler threatened to release him if the guy didn't give up.

"What the dogs and handlers do is overkill," says Bill, "until it's not."

CHAPTER 4

A FIRM GRIP

You could set your watch by President Ronald Reagan. His reputation for punctuality gave Secret Service dog handler Tony Ferrara some comfort as he stood at the end of a row of fifteen handlers and dogs in front of the hay barn at the president's California ranch.

At first the dogs—German shepherds and Belgian Malinois— sat patiently at their handlers' sides. But after several minutes, composure turned to restlessness. Some whined and fidgeted. Ferrara's 110-pound Dutch shepherd, Bart, pulled and barked toward his four-legged colleagues as if he wanted to eat them. Ferrara took a few steps in the other direction to move Bart away from temptation.

Horses snuffling the ground for hay behind the dog teams glanced up to look at the creatures who were disrupting their peaceful morning routine. They flicked their ears and snorted, and went back to their breakfast.

It was October 29, 1988, less than three months before Ronald Reagan's two-term presidency would end, and just ten days before the nation would elect its next president. Someone had decided this would be a good time for photo ops with the Secret Service dog teams that had protected the president and Nancy Reagan on their 688-acre ranch atop the Santa Ynez Mountains northwest of Santa Barbara. Although Reagan would receive Secret Service protection for the rest of his life, he wouldn't be getting this kind of massive canine protection after he left office. It needed to be documented for posterity.

Right on the dot, the president strode up a dirt path, flanked by a couple of Secret Service agents. He wore khaki riding clothes with rich brown leather boots and a matching belt, and he was smiling.

As he approached, a strange thing happened. The dogs all settled down. They stopped barking and sat quietly, looking toward the chief executive. Ferrara wondered if the sudden attentiveness of the handlers had dumped down the leash to affect their dogs, or if Reagan's presidential presence had a calming effect.

Reagan said a few words of thanks to the group, then walked to the first handler and shook her hand. The photographer took a photo. Down the row of handlers Reagan proceeded, shaking hands as the photographer captured the image.

Then came a gap of about six feet. The president looked past the gap and saw Bart giving the evil eye to the other dogs. Ferrara kept a firm grip on Bart's coiled leather leash. Bart had never snapped at anyone unless he was supposed to, but Ferrara wasn't taking any chances.

Reagan walked toward them and shook Ferrara's hand. "He doesn't like those dogs, does he?" Reagan asked with a grin.

"There's a few things he doesn't like, Mr. President," Ferrara said. "German shepherds, bad guys, and Democrats."

Reagan burst out laughing, his eyebrows drawn together in an expression of easy joviality. Still shaking his right hand with

Ferrara's, the president grasped Ferrara's elbow with his left. Ferrara relaxed and felt an undeniable warm connection. But he didn't for a second loosen his hold on Bart's leash.

Secret Service director H. Stuart Knight had no idea of Wilson (Bill) Livingood's love of dogs when he called the special agent in charge of protective operations into his office in 1975 and asked him to form a canine unit.

With incidents of domestic and international terrorism on the rise, the agency had done some research to find out how to best detect explosives. Dogs came out on top of the list.

The Service had been piecing together canine protection for presidents by calling in military and local law-enforcement canine teams wherever the president went. There was no standard of training, and dogs weren't always available. This patchwork quilt was no way to protect the president. It was time for the Secret Service to develop its own canine program.

Livingood was thrilled that the job of starting a canine unit fell to him. Early in his Secret Service career he had watched the nation plunge into "a deep, deep sadness" after the assassination of President John F. Kennedy. He would support anything that would diminish the chances of such a national disaster again.

If it involved dogs, all the better for the lifelong dog lover.

When Livingood was a radioman on a Navy minesweeper after high school, he managed to convince the captain to allow him to keep a puppy he had adopted while onshore. She looked like Dagwood Bumstead's dog, so he named her Daisy. She became the darling of the crew. Everyone loved her. Everyone except one gruff boatswain who always grumbled about her.

One day in rough seas, Livingood heard an alarm go off while he was at work in the radio shack.

"Man overboard, man overboard!" a voice announced.

Then a pause.

"Correction. *Dog* overboard!"

Horrified, Livingood bolted out and ran to the edge of the vessel. He looked down and saw that someone had jumped into the swells and already had a hold of Daisy. He was shocked to see that of all people, the hero was the boatswain. The crew deployed a motorboat and picked them up.

After thanking him profusely, Livingood asked why he rescued her.

"I thought you didn't like her," Livingood said.

"Bill, I love this dog," the boatswain told him. "I just couldn't admit it because that's not how I am."

After the Navy, Livingood went to Michigan State and majored in criminal justice. During summers he had a job on a small police force. The animal warden in the area had a reputation of being cruel to dogs, so Livingood and some of his cop friends would scoop up whatever strays they came across and find their owners, or find homes for them if they didn't have owners. He found it rewarding to pair up dogs who needed a home and people who needed a companion.

And now here he was, being asked to pair up the Secret Service with a whole new breed of program. How hard could it be?

The Metropolitan Police Department of the District of Columbia (MPD) seemed like the logical agency to approach to help launch the Secret Service's canine program. It was widely regarded as an outstanding department and was accepted as a leader in K-9 training. Bomb dogs were fairly new to the department, but MPD's patrol and narcotics dogs had a stellar reputation.

MPD offered to provide dogs for the Secret Service, and to train the dogs and their handlers. For the Secret Service, it seemed like the perfect answer, with one-stop shopping in its own backyard.

In the summer of 1975 the Service announced six open positions for handlers. Job applicants had to meet an unusual requirement right off the bat. They had to be married. The logic behind this was that if an officer was sick, someone else in the house could care for the dog.

More than one hundred applied. After a taxing interview process that involved wives of the finalists, six Uniformed Division officers were selected. Four had been dog handlers in the military.

William (Bill) Shegogue (pronounced *shay*-go) had trained as a combat tracker dog handler when he was drafted in 1968 during the Vietnam War. He loved the job and longed to work with dogs again. He was instructing a firearms class at RTC when he heard the news over the loudspeaker.

"Congratulations, Billy Shegogue, you are now the proud owner of a dog!"

His students cheered.

In early December, Shegogue and the other five handlers reported to the MPD training facility at Blue Plains in southwest D.C. to get their dogs. Training wouldn't start until after the holidays, but the trainers wanted the dogs and handlers to acclimate to each other.

For some it would be a happy holiday.

For others, it would be memorable.

The dogs, all German shepherds, had been plucked from

shelters or donated. Their temperaments ranged from assertive to ballistic.

Shegogue's dog, Diamond, tried to bite him a few times over the holidays. Despite his previous work with dogs, he couldn't get a handle on how to stop it. He looked forward to starting class in January and smoothing Diamond's rough edges.

But even in the hands of the professionals, Diamond's biting continued. Through basic obedience, detection work, and patrol training, nothing anyone did helped the dog. He was likely to bite any time he was anxious. When searching buildings, if the dog couldn't find the bad guy hiding behind a closed door, he'd turn around and bite Shegogue for good measure. He never broke the skin, but it hurt like hell.

Shegogue described the pain to his wife. "It feels like you put your hand down on the table and took a hammer and hit yourself with it really hard."

After five weeks of this, MPD took Diamond back and gave Shegogue his next dog, Keeper. He hoped the dog would live up to his name. Keeper had been donated by a married couple. Word was that Keeper hated the husband and wouldn't let him get near the wife.

Shegogue quickly discovered that the dog didn't like most people. Only Shegogue and one other handler could touch him. And they had to be careful.

One afternoon Shegogue tried taking a candy wrapper out of Keeper's mouth. He ended up with his thumb split wide open and his thumbnail hanging off in a grotesque fashion.

He had a description of a new sensation for his wife. "You start with a number two pencil and smash it down on the ground, break the tip off, round it out, and stab yourself with it multiple times."

Keeper did well on the patrol work, where he could use his

innate talents of running and fighting and biting. But explosives detection work was of no interest. No matter how much Shegogue and the trainers encouraged him with praise and rewards, Keeper put in minimal effort.

The only part of explosives detection he seemed to enjoy was what happened the moment he detected the scent. MPD trained what's called an "aggressive alert." Anything with the word *aggressive* suited Keeper.

In an aggressive alert, the dog signals the handler to a find by vigorously pawing and scratching at it. In effect the dog is trying to dig up his reward, which in training would magically bounce up from the area. It's a technique traditionally used in narcotics detection.

Shegogue's classmate Cliff Cusick had trepidation about the aggressive alert for explosives. It seemed obvious to the former Air Force sentry dog handler that a dog digging at a volatile substance could easily trigger an explosion, even if a handler pulled away his dog immediately.

"It defeats the entire purpose, doesn't it?" he asked a classmate.

But Cusick had too much going on to find time to challenge the status quo. He was on his third dog in four months of training and needed this last dog to work out if he was going to graduate.

Cusick had loved his first dog, Rajah, a stunning German shepherd who'd been donated by a wealthy woman from Virginia. Everything was going beautifully until gunfire acclimation training. The noise of the firearms frightened Rajah so badly that he once bit Cusick in the leg as he panicked to escape. A dog who had that kind of fear wouldn't do well in a life-or-death situation without a great deal of work, if ever. It wasn't a problem MPD trainers had time to fix.

Cusick's next dog had an ear that had been half chewed off or had met some other unfortunate fate. He felt bad for the dog, whose jagged ear hadn't yet healed and attracted flies. The dog had some other issues, and MPD took the dog back and gave Cusick a new dog by the name of Devil. Or more accurately, Devil #6, as they'd had five other Devil dogs before this one.

Devil was donated by an MPD officer whose career had become too busy to give her dog the attention and training he needed. The dog was highly aggressive, but in the end, he made it through the program.

On April 30, 1976, the first canine class of the United States Secret Service graduated. The six uniformed handlers posed with their dogs on an outdoor staircase. In the front row, lined up close together alongside their handlers, were canines Bullet, Tony, Danny, and Duke.

On the step above them stood MPD trainer Dave Haskins. The men held him in high esteem and knew they were going to miss seeing him daily. He and the other trainers had done their best with the dogs they'd been given. Three of the six dogs looked like they were going to do great things in the Service. Not bad, considering.

Two dog teams in the photo had physically separated themselves from the other dogs and from each other by several stairs: Cusick and Devil way at the top of the staircase, as far as possible from the others. And Shegogue and Keeper, with a wide cushion between Devil in the back and the rest of the dogs in front.

Anyone watching may have thought the handlers arranged themselves this way to make the photo look more interesting or symmetrical, unaware of the melee that would probably ensue if they'd been closer.

Like new graduates anywhere, Shegogue wondered about his future. Where would he be in a few months or years? Would this dog get better at detecting explosives? What if Keeper missed something and the worst happened?

He stashed these thoughts away and tried to enjoy their big day.

Shegogue and the MPD trainers had to face reality after Keeper had been on the job for three weeks. Keeper was not, after all, a keeper. No one could get him to show interest in explosives detection. Shegogue gave back his dog and reluctantly stepped out of the world of dog handling, since no other dogs were available.

The dog found another home, and Shegogue found himself back at the Foreign Missions Branch, standing post in front of embassies without a canine, often on the midnight shift. He went from having little supervision as a dog handler to having layers of it.

Soon after, another dog from the class washed out.

And then there were four.

A third dog wasn't doing so well either, but the handler didn't call attention to him. He didn't want to end up pulling night duty standing post by himself.

Livingood and Senior Special Agent Thomas Quinn were already painfully aware that the canine program was in need of extensive changes if it were to survive. As the dogs were washing out and others were pawing at explosives during training, the agents made phone calls and spoke with law-enforcement leaders and with military canine training facilities around the country to get information about what others were doing.

Their research led them to Lackland Air Force Base in San Antonio, Texas. It seemed to have just the kind of program they were looking for. Livingood and Quinn visited Lackland, headquarters for training most of the nation's military dogs and handlers.

They liked how the dogs alerted with a passive response rather than one that could cause an explosion. Instead of digging at explosives, the dogs simply sat and stared. And the quality of the dogs impressed them. These weren't dogs scraped together from whatever free resources were available. They were high-quality dogs, primarily German shepherds, procured from breeders in Europe and the United States.

Back in D.C. the men worked out a deal. The Air Force would supply the dogs to the Secret Service and train the handlers and the dogs in an intensive course at Lackland, followed by more training in the Washington, D.C., area.

Shegogue and the other dogless handler got sprung from post duty. They flew with four new handlers to be part of the first Secret Service canine class at Lackland. He figured he was in for a smooth ride this time, at last.

And then he met Coley. The dog had already bitten several handlers before Shegogue got him. "He's a good dog, really," he was assured.

The problem seemed to be that Coley didn't like to be told what to do. As Shegogue worked with the dog on obedience the first few days, Coley conveyed his message as best as he could.

Every so often, the dog spun around and put his teeth on Shegogue's groin area. He didn't clamp down. It was just a warning: *No one tells me what to do.*

Shegogue knew he needed to nip it in the bud before the dog decided to take it to the next level. He didn't want to have to call his wife with a description of a new and particularly awful kind of bite pain. He had a feeling it would involve more than pencils and hammers.

Within a week, with the help of the trainers at Lackland, he and Coley had come to an understanding. From then on, Shegogue had no doubt his canine partner was exactly what the dogs of the other Secret Service handlers were to them: the best.

Coley was proving excellent at obedience and looked like he was going to be a fine patrol and explosives dog as well. He didn't like coming off the bite once he got hold of a bite sleeve, but that would give Shegogue something to work on when they headed back home for more training.

The next class of six handlers that flew down to Lackland included Cusick with Devil, and two other handlers from the original MPD class. Their dogs needed to unlearn the aggressive alert and replace it with the passive alert, among other new skills.

The canine unit grew by increments of six teams every several months, and soon there were enough dogs to work around the clock, rotating to different areas each shift. Every day brought something new. No one stood post for eight- or twelve-hour shifts. Boredom was rarely an issue as they pulled four-hour blocks at the White House and on the streets or wherever they were needed.

The Secret Service hired their favorite trainers from Lackland to work at Rowley Training Center. The program grew and became more self-sufficient. It was becoming robust enough that the Secret Service would soon be able to end its training relationship with Lackland. But there was still one more class to go . . .

Shepherd, shepherd, shepherd, shepherd . . .

Malinois.

Five dogs, five handlers. They had spent six weeks together at Lackland getting to know each other, for better and worse. And now back at RTC, the handlers were about to learn which dogs the trainers had picked for them.

The program had never selected a Malinois before. The breed wasn't that well known yet in the United States. A Malinois named Marko had caught the eyes of the Air Force trainers, who could see he was strong, tough, energetic, and driven.

"Who's going to get Marko?" the Lackland trainers had asked before the dog handlers had gone back to RTC.

"Not sure yet," a Secret Service instructor responded.

"Watch out, or Marko will kill him!"

Handler Freddie McMillon knew this was no joke. He had developed an ongoing internal dialogue with Marko during their encounters.

Dog, don't chew me up. You don't need to eat me alive. Let's work together on this.

McMillon wanted to say the words but only thought them as he willed himself to open the kennel door whenever he was assigned to take out Marko. He didn't want any whiff of doubt to trail in with him.

The barking and whirling of the other dogs didn't bother him so much. But Marko's icy glare gave him cold feet. McMillon could almost hear what Marko was trying to tell him with his look: *I dare you to bring your ass in here!*

The handler was always relieved when it was someone else's turn to take out Marko. The dog was a biter, out of control, and tireless.

And now was the moment of truth. The instructor began the matchmaking announcements.

"Denny, you've got Mutz."

"Billy, you've got Bear."

Oh no, just three of us left. Please don't let me get Marko.

"George, you've got Abus."

Uh-oh. Give Marko to Marty, give Marko to Marty . . .

"Marty, you've got Fritz."

Noooooo!

"And Freddie, you've obviously got Marko. Don't worry, you can handle it. That's why we chose you for him."

He wanted to believe him, so he decided to get this relationship off to a strong start. After the announcement, he walked over to have a chat with Marko at the kennel.

Marko glared, as always. McMillon knew what he was trying to tell him.

Look, I don't know what your intentions are, but I'd advise you not to come any closer.

"OK, OK, you can look at me like that but your ass has to eat, and guess who has the food?" McMillon said to him, out loud, standing tall and trying to make himself look sturdier and more in control than he felt. He made sure his body language conveyed that he was trying to tell Marko something important, something he needed to know.

The first day, when everyone fed their dogs, McMillon showed up but brought no chow. The same happened the next morning. Later in the day McMillon approached the kennel. He had kibble in his pockets.

"OK, Marko, are we going to be friends or what? This is going to be a good partnership. They said to me you'll be a great detection dog. We already know about your patrol side."

The dog stared, but it wasn't the usual defiant pose. McMillon entered the kennel without incident but stayed near the door just in case.

He took some kibble from his pocket and cupped his hand toward Marko. The dog ate it hungrily. After several fistfuls, McMillon still had some food in his pockets when something unprecedented happened. Marko wagged his tail. McMillon kept feeding him, and his dog's tail kept wagging.

"I got you, boy," he said to Marko, and smiled.

He and Marko became closer every day. He saw in the dog the kind of hard-core dedication and energy and determination he valued in himself.

By the end of the months of training, Marko was calling him Dad.

Several years into the canine program, the Secret Service hired Ray Reinhart to be an instructor. He had put in nearly twenty years as a K-9 handler with Prince George's County, Maryland, and was ready to bring his brand of instruction and training, and his passion for K-9s' capabilities, to the Secret Service.

He knew firsthand what great dogs could do. His German shepherd, Rommel, had saved his life on three occasions.

"There was a bank robbery," he'd tell his classes. "And two of the assailants took off. K-9 was the first one called. We were searching in some high sage grass. Suddenly Rommel stopped and bristled. I couldn't see anything but I let him go and he bolted and got the guy in the arm—the arm that had been holding the gun he was about to shoot."

Rommel got steak that night.

"Did you know Rommel was a water dog?" he'd ask his students.

"A water dog? I thought he was a German shepherd," someone would inevitably say.

"No, he was a water dog. You could turn him on and you could turn him off just as easily. I'm hoping all your dogs will be water dogs."

Reinhart handled every facet of training: criminal apprehension, explosives detection, obedience, agility, and article searches.

When problems needed to be solved, students knew the solution would likely bear Reinhart's unique, creative stamp.

"You gotta experiment," was his philosophy. "It's not all in a book."

Members of the media had set up for their nightly newscast on the north grounds of the White House when they noticed a Secret Service dog staring, utterly riveted, at something in the distance. The Malinois, Rudy, lowered his body as if ready to bolt after an intruder.

"Wow, is he intense!" one of the reporters yelled over to the dog's handler, Henry Sergent.

"What's he fixated on?" another asked. "Is he getting ready to go after someone?"

"I hope not!" Sergent said, half joking.

Rudy charged forward, pulling his handler with him. Sergent wasn't worried about a fence jumper. Dozens of other Secret Service officers would have seen someone jump the moment it happened. But he couldn't fathom what his dog was doing. It was certainly nothing he'd ever done before.

They approached a tree and Rudy locked onto something in the branches. Sergent finally saw the intruder. It was a squirrel. Rudy stared, not barking, not even breathing. Sergent gave the leash a tug and Rudy left reluctantly, but kept looking back.

After that, Rudy was a dog obsessed. Whenever he worked on the White House grounds, hunting down squirrels was his sole mission. He was in luck. Squirrels have been calling the area surrounding the White House home for a long time, enjoying whatever bounties the gardens and trees provided and the safe haven from cars and people. They were everywhere.

Sergent didn't know what to do. He turned to Reinhart.

"I've got an idea. It's crazy, but it just might work," Reinhart said with a chuckle.

The next day Reinhart met Sergent on the south grounds. He was carrying a bag with a toy stuffed squirrel he had bought. He'd named it Rocky. That morning he had made a small incision in Rocky, pulled wads of stuffing out of him, and infused the squirrel with hot peppers and Tabasco sauce. He tied a string to Rocky and stood behind a tree.

Sergent walked toward Rocky with Rudy. Reinhart pulled the string. The squirrel skittered across the grass with Rudy hot on its trail. Sergent let Rudy have a go at him. The dog grabbed the squirrel in his mouth and shook it. Hot sauce oozed out like blood. Moments later, he spit it out and was shaking his own head.

After a bowl of water and some TLC, Rudy and Sergent went about their rounds as usual. Squirrels would dash across the White House lawn and dart up trees for the rest of Rudy's career. But they were far too spicy for his tastes.

Sergent had a hard time finding a dress that fit his sturdy six-foot-five frame. The one he ended up with didn't match his purse, but he wasn't going to fret about it.

The mustachioed dog handler slipped the dress on out of sight of the congressional representatives and other VIPs who'd gathered at the RTC dog training yard for a demonstration of the canine program.

He tapped on the edge of a large baby carriage, and Rudy jumped in. The dog sat dutifully while Sergent tied a white baby bonnet to his head. They'd practiced enough times that Rudy didn't bother trying to push it off with his paws. He knew the drill. Rudy lay down and Sergent covered him with a blanket.

"Break a leg," said Reinhart, who had coached them through the scenario on numerous occasions.

On cue, Sergent strolled out in front of the audience, pushing the pram. Everyone broke out in laughter at the sight of this unusual-looking mother out for a peaceful stroll with her baby.

Suddenly a man sprinted out from the audience toward the mother and child. In an instant, the bad guy had grabbed her purse and was running away.

But the mugger had picked the wrong mother. She uttered a couple of words the audience couldn't quite hear, and out of the baby carriage sprang her enormous, furry baby. The baby/dog charged the purse snatcher. Rudy's bonnet flew off as he leapt at the mugger's arm (which was covered with a bite sleeve) and apprehended the bad guy.

The audience exploded in cheers. The purse was returned to the happy mother, who pushed the carriage back to where they'd started. Rudy wagged and trotted beside Sergent.

After the demo, a few audience members walked over to talk with Sergent and meet Rudy. Someone asked how the dog could go from attack mode to happy pup so quickly.

"He has an unbelievable on-off switch," Sergent answered. "He can do attack work like he's the Tasmanian Devil, then he goes right back and can be next to a group of little kids who hug him, and he doesn't blink an eye."

Reinhart smiled. Water dogs were definitely in abundance these days.

After eight years on the job, it was time for Shegogue's dog, Coley, to hang up his badge. He was getting tired too easily—more than a dog his age should. The vet had diagnosed him with cardiomyopathy. It could be treated with pricey medications, which would make him feel much better, but he'd need to take it easy.

Coley became the first dog to retire from the canine unit. There was no precedent for how to handle it, but Livingood, Quinn, and the others who helped start the program had long ago determined that dogs at the end of their careers would be retired to their handlers, as most other law-enforcement dogs are.

(Dogs in the military didn't have the same happy ending. At that time, they were usually euthanized. A fine thank-you for their devotion to the job. And devastating for their handlers.)

Coley had done great work. In addition to his normal duties, he had even apprehended a suspected rapist near the White House. The Secret Service decided the dog would retire with full medical benefits. It would pay for all his medications and any treatments he might need. (That's not how it works today. Medical bills are the adoptive handler's responsibility.)

The old guard was stepping down. Cusick's dog Devil had passed away three years earlier, in 1981. Cusick disappeared from canine because of the "one and done" policy. Shegogue knew this would be his fate, and he wasn't looking forward to it.

But Shegogue and Cusick were lucky, rare exceptions. Each got to be a handler again, although not until after they put in some years without a dog. Cusick got a sweet dog named Buddy. And Shegogue's new partner was Barry.

They were both great dogs. The best dogs yet.

Forty years after he helped start the Secret Service's canine program, Bill Livingood is sitting in an Alexandria, Virginia, restaurant with his assistant and a guest and extolling the virtues of Dunkin' Donuts.

"It has to be the law enforcement in me," says Livingood. "I could just about live in Dunkin' Donuts. Their coffee is the best. I'm a cake donut fan. I usually get the glazed cake donut. It's dense and sweet—like me!"

His assistant shakes her head but can't help laughing.

Livingood retired in 1994, after thirty-three years in the Service. The next year, he became the sergeant at arms of the House of Representatives. As the House's chief law-enforcement and protocol official, he was responsible for maintaining security on the House side of the Capitol complex, as well as on the floor of the House.

He held the office for seventeen years, many fraught with deep challenges. The 9/11 terrorist attacks, the shooting of Representative Gabrielle Giffords, and the anthrax mailings all happened on his watch.

"An example of class and humility, Bill has led us through the unthinkable," Speaker John Boehner said at an event for Livingood's 2012 retirement.

As important as his role in Capitol safety and security was, most Americans might only know him as the man who introduced the president before a State of the Union address and escorted him to the podium.

"Mr. Speaker, the president of the United States!"

These eight words gave Livingood butterflies every time he had to say them, although it got easier with time.

At the Alexandria restaurant, he leans in toward his lunchmates and lowers his voice, not wanting to disturb a couple having a romantic meal at the next table.

"As a police officer I don't mind going through a doorway when there are bad guys on the other side. That's easier than standing up in front of all these cameras and introducing the president, even though it was an honor. I was just nervous. If I messed up, millions would see.

"I practiced and practiced. I practiced while I was driving. I tried to practice when no one was around. And my press secretary—I had a press secretary in my office because I had ten or fifteen press calls a day—she said, 'Don't tell them how many times you practice!'"

His assistant remarks that he really is more comfortable behind the scenes.

"It's true," he says. "Like when they asked me to form the canine program. I've done a lot of things in my career, and that was extremely special and gratifying.

"There's no telling the difference that these brave men, women, and dogs have made. They love what they do so much, and they work so hard."

In fact, as he spoke those words in late August 2015, the dogs and handlers of the United States Secret Service were gearing up for one of the busiest months in their careers, and in the history of the Secret Service. It would put all their training and dedication to the test.

CHAPTER 5

SLEEP TIGHT, POPE FRANCIS

Tuesday, September 22, 2015, 10 P.M. In the main courtyard of the sprawling Herbert C. Hoover Building, through its grand arches, and past its majestic black gates, Loren S. is briefing three dozen Secret Service officers and other federal security experts about their overnight missions to secure the area for Pope Francis.

A dog barks. Another one echoes. Their handlers quiet them.

"Dog handlers, you're going to be splitting off on different floors here, two teams of dogs and EODs get two floors each," says Loren, a Secret Service physical security specialist. "Later, when you get to the African American history museum, be careful with your dogs. There are a lot of chemicals, solvents, scaffolding, and limited lighting."

There are hundreds of rooms to check in the Hoover Building alone. The dog teams will be sweeping only the offices along the papal parade route on Fifteenth Street NW. But the building is more than one thousand feet long. That's a lot of sniffing.

Loren wraps up his talk with a few words about vigilance.

"Remember: It *is* the pope. He is loved by many, hated by some."

The security teams filter out in various directions. Dog handler Jon M. gets instructions that he and his dog, Rex, are going to sweep the fourth and fifth floors.

"OK, Rex, let's do it!" Jon says. His ninety-pound Malinois, who had been sitting patiently during the briefing, comes to life. He jumps up and wags his tail. There's a distinct bounce in his stride as he heads into the building alongside Jon. When he sees elevators, he pulls toward them, tightening the leash.

A building security specialist laughs when he sees the dog's response to the elevator.

"He loves elevators," Jon explains. "They mean a lot of things to Rex. They can mean he's going to work. They can mean he's going outside for a break. Either way, it's all good!"

On the fifth floor, Jon meets up with the rest of his team: two Army EOD techs, a couple of security officers who know the building inside and out, and another dog and handler.

As they discuss how the dogs will efficiently hopscotch each other down the corridors and secondary corridors of offices, something catches Rex's interest. He stares across the hall at another dog, a black Labrador retriever accompanied by her DHS police handler.

She is young, shiny, and calm. Her name is Lola.

Rex fixes his gaze. His right ear angles slightly forward toward her, but his left ear flops off to the side. Some find this endearing, but Lola doesn't even seem to notice him, much less his cute left ear.

This doesn't discourage Rex. The Explosive Detection Team dog may not have found a bomb, but he seems to have found a bombshell.

Lola's handler tells Jon that he wants the two dogs to keep their distance. Jon nods in agreement and doesn't mention that Rex is one of the nicest, friendliest, most unflappable dogs he'll ever meet. All anyone has to do is look at Rex with a smile and he's likely to come over and lean on them. He may even try to climb on their lap if they're sitting down.

He may also try to lick their shoes. Rex has a thing about shoes. Any kind of shoe. He may lick a shoe being worn by someone if he has nothing else interesting going on. But if he finds shoes with no one wearing them—coveted *empty* shoes—he stops and breathes them in as if they're a rare and mesmerizing bouquet.

In Jon's experience, offices like these will have plenty of empty shoes under desks. He'd have to watch that the footwear didn't slow their progress. They were going to be pulling an all-nighter as it was.

Their work tonight would be just one small part of the advance work for Pope Francis's six-day U.S. tour. The wildly popular "People's Pope" had landed late that afternoon at Joint Base Andrews and would be making his first public appearance of the tour the next morning outside the White House.

The pope is expected to attract hundreds of thousands, if not millions, of onlookers as he greets crowds in the nation's capital, New York, and Philadelphia. Everyone who attends his parades, masses, and other events will be subject to a security screening.

Keeping the pope safe will be a massive intergovernmental undertaking. The U.S. Secret Service is taking the lead for this DHS-declared National Special Security Event—a significant event that could be a target for terrorism. The Service is coordinating with the FBI, U.S. Coast Guard, National Park Service, FEMA, and dozens of other federal and local agencies to make sure the pontiff's visit doesn't turn into a global nightmare.

September is always an exceptionally busy month for the Secret Service. Protecting the approximately 140 world leaders who gather every September in New York for the United Nations General Assembly (UNGA) is a tremendous undertaking. Everyone who works for the Secret Service knows that September is not the month to request vacation time. It's all hands on deck every year.

This September, with the arrival of a beloved pope plus a high-profile U.S. visit by Chinese president Xi Jinping, schedules are going to be even more daunting. But for the energetic dogs of the Secret Service, it's a walk in the park. Sometimes literally.

While Jon and Rex hunt for explosive devices in the Hoover Building, Secret Service dogs are letting their noses guide them around places like the Ellipse, the Washington Monument, and other grassy park areas in the secure zone. (Outdoor duty is convenient, because when nature calls, the answer is just a tree trunk away.)

It's going to be a long night for everyone. Many of the Secret Service EDT dogs and handlers are on the schedule from 9 P.M. until early afternoon. If lucky, they may be able to clock out after the parade, around noon. But there won't be much downtime. Some will have to drive to New York early the next day to help with pope security setups or UNGA, and then it's off to Philadelphia.

As tireless as Rex usually is, he isn't used to pulling all-nighters. If he starts getting tired while he's in detection mode, he may not be as vigilant in his searches. That could be a problem. He has to stay alert and focused, and unlike the humans around him, he can't rely on coffee and Red Bull.

Jon plans to let him nap in the van whenever the crews break. But if Rex starts flagging during a search, Jon knows how to recharge his batteries. It's easy with Rex. All Jon has to do is let him rest for a minute or two while he pets him or lets someone else pet him. The loving attention revives Rex, and he's good to go.

But as they start their night, it's obvious Rex won't need a recharge for a long time. He pulls Jon down the corridor, wanting to work, wanting to find something. In this situation, pulling ahead is just what Jon wants him to do. The partners have a lot of ground to cover in a relatively short amount of time. The searches need to be fast, but not so fast that accuracy is compromised.

Even with Rex leading the way, Jon can easily guide his dog. They pause in the main corridor as a building security officer unlocks a door to a suite of offices. An EOD tech says something about how enthusiastic Rex is to work.

"I'm really lucky," Jon tells him. "All he wants to do is make me happy. Right, boy?"

Rex looks up at him and then whips his head back to stare intently at the door, as if willing it to open.

When they enter, Rex moves like liquid. He pours into the large office with multiple desks, quickly covering all areas. He misses a spot Jon thinks he should cover.

"Check back!" Jon says, guiding the leash in its direction. Rex streams toward a corner with a trash can and, finding nothing of interest in it, glides back, ready for the next office. An EOD tech follows and does a quick check.

Office after office is unlocked before Rex. In some offices, computer cables dangle and loop and connect to other equipment in a way that would be easy for a fast-moving leashed working dog to snag. But somehow he avoids entanglements.

Whenever Lola passes on the other side of the corridor, Rex slows and gives her a look. But she continues to convey a "Talk to the hand, dog!" message.

Rex pants, his long Malinois tongue hanging straight down like it's weighted at the tip. Jon knows it won't affect his detection capability, because Rex usually pants while he's in working mode. He's a phenomenal explosives detector, mouth open or closed.

Suddenly, behind a desk in a small office, Rex's mouth closes and he draws in deep, rapid breaths. What's this? Could this be a suspicious device?

He's not sitting to alert his handler—yet. Jon looks unconcerned. He knows his dog's every move and expression. "I'm with you more than I'm with my wallet," he sometimes tells him.

Still, Jon steps up to look at what could be of such interest to Rex. He can't take any chances.

Under a table covered with papers he sees what has caught his dog's fancy. It's not an explosive. It's a short row of footwear: low black pumps, purple running shoes, and floral rain boots. Rex inhales over and over, transfixed. Jon lets Rex sniff a little more before moving him along—a small reward for his hard work.

All would-be bombers, but especially shoe bombers, are out of luck when Rex is around.

About ninety minutes into the sweep, Rex is still going strong, but the leash is slightly looser than it was earlier. Jon stops at a watercooler. He fills a little clear plastic cup and leans down to offer it to Rex. Rex sticks his big snout in it and slurps it up. He licks Jon's face for good measure. Jon offers an ear rub, Rex accepts with enthusiasm, and they bound down the hall to continue their work.

The neoclassical Hoover Building is home to the U.S. Department of Commerce, with more than 3,300 offices. By some clever space-saving arrangement, the main corridors often lead to locked doors that open to secondary corridors with suites of offices tucked along the side. Everything has been going smoothly, with the building's security staff able to unlock locked offices, so there's almost no delay as the dogs approach.

But at one of these suites, a row of four windowless offices is locked, and there doesn't seem to be a key. Someone apparently didn't get the memo about leaving certain doors unlocked tonight.

Security is able to pick a couple of locks, and Rex inspects, followed by EOD. Just two offices to go. It would be easy to assume they're fine and move on. But assuming is not something that's being done here.

Security and EOD discuss their options. An athletic-looking security officer walks into the office next to a locked room and stands on the desk. He jostles a couple of large white ceiling tiles out of their frames. In an impressive show of strength he pulls himself up through the rectangular opening and, in a flash, jumps down into the locked office through a tile he removed on that side. He lands on his feet, like Superman coming to save the day, and unlocks the door from the inside.

Rex and Jon don't move in for the sniff yet. There's one more office to unlock. This time an Army EOD tech gets to work. He's shorter than the security guy but agile as a cat. His strategy is to enter from the outside along the corridor, since there's already a table in place. More ceiling tiles get displaced, up he goes, and then down he leaps into the office. He unlocks the door.

Rex goes in and sniffs around, then the EOD tech gets to work. No sign of explosives.

But if the people who work in those offices come back in a couple of days and see their uprooted ceiling tiles and chalky particles on their gray carpet, they may wonder.

Wednesday, September 23, 2015, 1 A.M. The Washington Monument glows with a buttery hue against the overcast amber sky. Only law-enforcement officers and people with approved ID badges remain in the area. Secret Service cars and other police vehicles are parked everywhere, whether in real parking spots or improvised temporary ones.

The papal parade starts in ten hours. There's much to do before people start arriving en masse in a few hours for the parade and an earlier ceremony for ticketed guests at the South Lawn. There are magnetometers to be brought in, buildings to finish securing, screening areas to be set up, and a long list of other security measures to complete.

A Secret Service dog chases a Kong near the Ellipse during a break. It flies by her but she manages to leap and catch it, returning it to her handler for another round.

By now Rex is making his way around the construction inside the National Museum of African American History and Culture. Other EDT dogs are still searching buildings along the parade route.

If Pope Francis isn't suffering from jet lag, he should be fast asleep at the Apostolic Nunciature of the Holy See to the United States—basically the Vatican's embassy—in the nearby Embassy Row neighborhood. Among the agencies guarding both him and the building as he slumbers is the Pontifical Swiss Guard, one of the world's oldest armies.

Secret Service ERT dogs and handlers are posted in strategic pope-protecting areas as well. If the pope could see a demo of the way they train, he would surely sleep extra soundly knowing they have his back.

———

Wednesday, September 23, 2015, 5:30 A.M. Small clusters of people walk swiftly along G Street NW toward where the pope will be making his appearances later in the morning. It's still dark, with hours to go before the 9 A.M. arrival ceremony or the 11 A.M. parade. But to these early birds, getting up at zero dark thirty and racing others to the starting line is a small price to pay to see this pope.

About two blocks from the White House, they'll pass a row of homeless men and women sleeping near an entrance to Macy's. They're laid out close together, side by side. Some nestle in sleeping bags, others are wrapped in blue camping tarps or just sheets of plastic.

A leather-skinned man wriggles his torso out of his tarp and props himself up on his elbows. He blinks a couple of times and settles in to watch his own private parade.

Wednesday, September 23, 2015, 5:35 A.M. The tickets for those lucky enough to be attending the White House arrival ceremony state that the gates open at 5:30 A.M. But the line is already a long snake, serpentining along Pennsylvania Avenue, past the Treasury Building, and curving down Fifteenth Street NW. Hundreds have already passed through an initial checkpoint, but now the line is stopped.

A man holding a powerful megaphone and a twelve-foot-high triple-decker sign blasts his message to his captive audience before the first checkpoint. His sign declars that THE POPE IS THE HEAD OF A CULT! and JESUS IS "THE HEAD" OF THE CHURCH!

He drives home his views of the pope through the megaphone.

"The man is evil to the core! He's a sodomite and a pedophile!"

Not the kind of speech you'd expect to start your day at a pope celebration, but the White House area is known for attracting protestors who don't mince words.

People do their best to ignore him. They glance ahead, to where the fortunate ones who got here even earlier are lined up farther from this guy.

"Look, Michael," a woman in line says to her companion as she points across a barricade. "They even have dogs on the other side!"

He looks up, grateful for any distraction.

A couple of black Labs bounce along Pennsylvania Avenue beside their Secret Service handlers. One dog walks far from the crowd, wagging his tail in a relaxed, easy manner. The other sticks close to the crowd-control barriers and seems to be sniffing for something while trotting along.

"I wonder what they're doing," he says.

"I imagine something important. They look very presidential."

Wednesday, September 23, 2015, 10:30 A.M. Marshall and Hurricane stand post near the gleaming white popemobile. The modified Jeep Wrangler is parked in a heavily protected area off the South Lawn. Gone is the crushing crowd that had gathered on the lawn to see the pope with President Barack Obama. Many have rushed out to try to nab a spot along the parade route.

The rear of the popemobile, where the pope greets his fans, is completely open on the back and sides. Pope Francis, ever surprising his protectors with impromptu interactions with people in the crowd, is not one to go around in a bulletproof "glass sardine can" as he has called a traditional popemobile. "Let's face it," he said in a newspaper article. "At my age, I don't have much to lose."

In the center of the popemobile's regal red carpet is a comfy-looking white swivel chair. With the exception of the papal crest it bears, it looks like it would be perfectly at home on a high-end fishing boat. The chair doesn't get much use, since the pope enjoys standing during parades.

Marshall knows that Pope Francis will soon be climbing into the popemobile for the big parade. He has watched over many luminaries in his Secret Service career, but the pope is his rock star. Seeing him up close like this would be a moment he would never forget.

Marshall takes his Catholicism very seriously. Like his father, he was born on Easter Sunday. His mother went into labor at church during Easter services.

At his house, a foot-tall crucifix is poised above a main door. On a wall near another door hangs an intriguing picture of Christ. If you look at it one way, it's a soulful rendition of Christ's face. If you look at it from a slightly different angle, the image transforms into Christ on a cross with angels flying above.

But as close as Pope Francis will be getting to Marshall on this red-letter day, Marshall will not see him. His job isn't to look at the protectee. It's to look away, at everything else in his sector. If trouble is going to come roaring in, it's likely to come from anywhere but the protectee.

As much as he would want to turn around and see the pope, as much as he would love for the pope to give him and Hurricane a nod and a smile, he'll have to settle for just being within his realm. The "complacency is cancer" mind-set of ERT is muscle memory for Marshall. Turning around is completely out of the question.

Tuesday, September 29, 2015. The pope is safely back at the Vatican, his whirlwind three-city tour a huge success. President Xi has flown home to Beijing. A few days remain for the United Nations General Assembly, and security is running smoothly.

Marine One lands on the South Lawn of the White House. President Obama and the First Lady disembark. On his way to the White House, the president stops to speak with a group of reporters.

"I wanted to make a special commendation of our Secret Service," he says over the noise of the helicopter. "When something goes wrong, when there's a fence jumper, everybody reports on it.

"The Secret Service had to manage the pope's visit, President Xi's visit, and a hundred something world leaders in an unprecedented fashion during the course of the last several days, and they did so flawlessly.

"And Joe Clancy, the head of the Secret Service, and the entire team and detail and professional services, they all deserve a huge round of applause for being such great hosts and keeping everybody safe," Obama said. "So I just wanted to make sure everybody heard that. All right? Thank you, guys."

For the next few days, canine program instructors at RTC make sure handlers know about the president's words of praise, grateful he tried to bring positive attention to the Secret Service.

There's been a whole lot of negative attention of late.

CHAPTER 6

WORTHY OF TRUST AND CONFIDENCE

E mblazoned in brushed-metal letters across a gleaming metal-paneled wall at Secret Service Headquarters are these five words:

WORTHY OF TRUST AND CONFIDENCE

It's the Secret Service's longtime motto. "It's what we are looking for as candidates go through the hiring process, and ultimately, it's the expectation we have of everyone in the Secret Service," says an agency spokesman.

The motto is also written on Secret Service ID credentials, which state that the bearer "is commended as being worthy of trust and confidence."

Occasionally the motto takes a hit, but in the last few years it has taken a beating. Scandals involving prostitutes in Colombia, DUI agents at the White House, and an officer charged with soliciting a minor for sex are just a few that have made headlines.

Then there are the security breaches: a knife-wielding fence jumper who made it into the White House, a man pretending to be a member of Congress who found his way to President

Obama in a secured area, a drone that landed on the White House lawn.

Articles and news reports have taken to describing the Secret Service as "the beleaguered agency" or "the scandal-tainted agency." A bipartisan congressional investigation resulted in a 439-page report in December 2015. Its title: "United States Secret Service: An Agency in Crisis."

The report noted that Secret Service morale was "at an all-time low."

A longtime dog handler was recently sitting in a diner where the news was on TV when a story about a Secret Service scandal came on.

Not again.

He felt a knot in his stomach. He looked down at his food and hoped no one would notice his uniform.

"It's embarrassing. People see these stories and it taints everyone in the Service," he says. "They don't see that the vast majority of us take our responsibilities extremely seriously. We devote our lives to the Service. They don't see the birthdays and Christmases and first steps and recitals we miss. They don't understand the tremendous dedication almost everyone has."

It's some comfort to him that no dog handlers have been involved in the scandals. "And much to everyone's relief, no dogs have been implicated either," he jokes. "They keep their noses out of all that."

Secret Service dog handlers have responsibilities others in the Secret Service don't. After a shift, most can't or don't go out with other officers, because they need to get their dogs home. When traveling, if they go out to eat, it's usually with other canine handlers. Takeout is a popular option among handlers on the road. They often bring it back to their hotel rooms and relax with their canine partners.

"It's a totally different animal when you get a canine," says former Secret Service dog handler Daryl G., now an EDT training assistant. "When I first came on, the trainer said, 'You got a kid now. You don't have any kids? You got one now.' Because it's 24/7."

It's hard to get into too much trouble chilling in a hotel room with your dog. Daryl's dog, Boky, was fond of pulling toilet paper off the roll when Daryl wasn't looking. And when the dog was young, he tore the sheets off the hotel bed a couple of times when Daryl was washing up. Daryl found him gnawing on the corner of the mattress. No visible damage, just some dog slobber. He washed it off and remade the bed.

Kind of a pain, but hardly the stuff of *Washington Post* headlines.

Trust and confidence are mainstays of the Secret Service canine world. Dogs have to trust their handlers. Handlers have to trust their dogs.

It's this way across the board in the world of law-enforcement K-9s and military dogs. But in the Secret Service, the life of the president of the United States may depend on this all-important bond between dog and handler.

Some dogs arrive from their European kennels hungry for a best friend.

"They haven't always had the best experience in life so far," says ERT handler Luke K. "They want to be part of somebody's pack. A lot of these dogs, as soon as you get them, they're ready to be your partner."

His dog, Nitro, was not one of these dogs. He didn't want to listen to anyone. He did things his own way or no way at all. Regimented training cut through some of this. But it was the time

Luke put in with him away from the job that really forged the dog's trust.

"I talked to him all the time. I still do. Even though he doesn't understand what I'm saying, he knows my voice, the inflections," Luke says.

It took a year for Nitro to finally let his handler roll him over on his back for a tummy rub. Luke had finally won his dog's trust.

Handlers work to do whatever it takes to maintain the trust and confidence their dogs have in them. It's one thing to earn their trust. It's another thing to keep it.

After Rex's long overnight duty for the pope's visit to the capital, he didn't go right to sleep when he got home. Tired as he was, it was time for his usual game.

"Get your toy, Rex!" Jon said with an enthusiasm that came naturally despite his fatigue.

Rex has many toys. But there's one toy, *the* toy, he must have every day after work. It's a hard nylon bone with big knuckles on the end. It helps him unwind, like a canine version of a martini and a pair of slippers. Jon, who is a newlywed and has no children yet, calls Rex's bone his "Binky."

Rex immediately located the knucklebone and dropped it at Jon's feet. Jon threw it for him a couple of times and Rex settled in for a good chew.

The tradition was once in jeopardy, when Jon threw the bone while they were outside and lost it in the bushes. Handler and dog looked everywhere and couldn't find it. Rex eventually gave up and stared at Jon with an expression that went beyond disappointment. It was more like crestfallen shock.

"I came back empty-handed and it took the wind out of him. It made me sad. I know it's pathetic to say, but I literally got sad," Jon recalls. "I'd really let him down."

The pet supply store was still open, so Jon drove over and managed to find the same toy. Only he'd forgotten that it comes with green rubbery material that covers the straight middle part of the bone. Rex had worked his way through that covering over time and would certainly know a fraud.

Jon couldn't face disappointing his dog. Rex had trusted him, and he had thrown his happiness away. The green rubber had to go. Besides, he didn't want to have to watch over Rex as he chewed through it, trying to pick up every single shred so Rex wouldn't eat them, as he had tried to last time.

When he got home, he brought out a razor to slice through the rubber. It barely made a dent. This was some hard rubber. It took more than twenty minutes, but at last Jon had fashioned it to look just like the one he lost.

He brought it to Rex and hoped his dog would be OK with Binky version 2.0. Rex looked at the bone, looked at Jon, grabbed the bone, and wagged his tail. And all was once again right in his world.

"If you think about it, these dogs never lead you to anything good," says lead instructor Brian M. "You have to be able to trust your dog. So we train and we train and we train."

The Secret Service's federally accredited dog training is rigorous, with year-round validation testing of skills. Being a handler in the Secret Service canine program is like being a student who ends up with that teacher who gives hard tests and throws in pop quizzes.

The difference is that the Secret Service's tests can happen day or night, and the test venue can be in rain or snow or blistering heat.

For ERT handlers, tactical abilities, speed, and strength are always being challenged. Handlers have to meet intensive physical demands on a monthly basis. Dogs are evaluated in much the same way.

Detection dogs need to be able to work safely and efficiently in realistic environments, often surrounded by masses of people. The greater Washington, D.C., area is where they do most of their training.

The Service works with dozens of venues so handlers and dogs can be exposed to as many different environments as possible before they'll face them in the real world. No one wants the first time a dog sniffs for explosives in a football stadium to be the first time a dog has experienced a football stadium. It's equally important for the handlers to know how to navigate different complex scenarios.

The names of the venues the Secret Service uses can't be published, but among the places that welcome the canine teams, apart from football stadiums, are convention centers, airports, train stations, baseball parks, arenas, rental car parking lots, and shopping malls.

Exposure to the world outside RTC starts early in training.

One blazing summer afternoon, a class of Friendly Dogs is enjoying the cool atmosphere inside a large shopping mall. The dogs and handlers are about halfway through their seventeen-week training. Since Friendly Dogs will be working among the throngs in front of the White House for a living, it's important they hone their skills in crowded settings.

A sign at both ends of the practice area lets mall-goers know that these are dogs in training. Most shoppers go about their business, but some stop to watch.

"What's she doing?" a young girl asks her mother as a shiny black Lab walks around with his handler and sits every so often.

"Aw, she's so pretty. She must be tired of shopping, honey. See how she's sitting?"

"I'm tired of shopping, too," the girl announces, sounding all too happy to have solidarity with the dog.

But this Lab, a male named Lappy, is anything but tired. He's gaming the system. He has been rewarded for sitting after tracking an explosives scent that a Secret Service "plant" is carrying, and for alerting to a backpack or briefcase containing a scent he's been trained on. So Lappy figures that if he sits a whole bunch, he's apt to get his reward more frequently.

Trainers call it cheating. They're used to it. It's a phase most detection dogs go through. Lappy is the new kid in the class, so he has some catching up to do.

His handler's previous dog, Jack, had to be returned to Vohne Liche Kennels because he was scared of slick surfaces. It's a surprisingly common problem. To some dogs, especially those not exposed to it early in life, walking on tiles or shiny hardwood or marble is said to feel like walking on moving ice, or a wobbly treadmill. They dig in, or retreat.

Pet-dog owners with time and patience can help their dogs overcome this fear. The Secret Service usually tests for this issue before buying a dog, but sometimes the problem doesn't show up until the dog is in a different setting. Instructors will try to help the dog, but time is of the essence.

Even though Friendly Dogs don't work on slick surfaces at this point, there's a strong possibility their roles will expand. Jack's issue wasn't something that turned around quickly, so he made the long trip back to Indiana, and Lappy replaced him.

Cheating is a much more fixable issue, although some handlers have to be on the lookout for it throughout a dog's career. If Lappy's handler needs any encouragement, he just has to ask Jon.

"If Rex wasn't cheating, he wasn't trying," he'd tell him. "And trust me, he tried to cheat all the time. You've just got to stay on it. They come around."

Secret Service dog handlers want to be worthy of trust and confidence in the eyes of the president. They want the president and other protectees to know they've got their sixes, and to never doubt it for a moment.

They don't often see the president up close. But when presidents spend time at their vacation residences, chances for crossing paths increase. Activities like horseback riding, hiking, hunting, fishing, and walking in nature all take a president outside, where the Service's ERT dogs and handlers post.

In the past, dual-purpose dogs were the ones with this duty. Former handler Freddie McMillon and his dog, Marko, used to work at George H. W. Bush's estate in Kennebunkport, Maine.

Bush (generally referred to as "Bush 41" in the Secret Service) hosted many VIPs at his stunning seafront compound. British prime minister John Major, Canadian prime minister Brian Mulroney, and Israeli prime minister Yitzhak Rabin were among his guests over the years.

McMillon says sometimes the president didn't want to talk with these world leaders inside. For whatever reason—McMillon suspected the president wanted more privacy—there were times that Bush and a VIP guest walked away from the main house and ended up in the area he and Marko were watching.

Whenever that happened, McMillon would turn his back to them to watch out for anyone approaching. He'd also turn off his ears to their discussions the best he could.

"The president trusts you enough to be out there talking about important world matters in front of you," he says. "You have to live up to that trust and just keep doing your job."

He and Marko were also regular fixtures at Ronald Reagan's Rancho del Cielo. The canine teams were the front lines of defense on the large California property.

"If the bad guys got through us, that means we were all dead out there in the field," he says. "We'd give our lives to make sure nothing happened to the president."

Like Bush, Reagan hosted world leaders at his vacation residence, known as "the Western White House." While they never walked out to McMillon's distant post, as Bush's guests later would, McMillon sometimes enjoyed a little interaction with Reagan when the president went horseback riding.

"On occasion he'd stop and he'd talk to me. Just nice talk, asking how I'm doing, how's my dog, how's the family and kids, stuff like that," he says.

"The agents didn't like it but what could they do? I couldn't ignore the president. I'm from Brooklyn and if you talk to me, I talk to you!"

McMillon enjoyed knowing that the president was aware of Marko. "He knew we were out there looking out for him and Nancy. Marko wasn't going to let anything bad happen to them."

One day the president came out to greet his Secret Service canine protectors and take photos with them, as he had done with the group of Secret Service dog handlers that included Ferrara and Bart.

Marko sat calmly at McMillon's left side. The president approached and stuck out his hand to shake McMillon's. As McMillon reached out to the president, he saw something horrifying from the corner of his eye.

Marko was staring right up at the president, and baring his teeth.

McMillon didn't want anything to go down the leash to Marko and make him think Reagan was dangerous. Any wrong move on his part—even unconsciously tightening up because of his dog's reaction—could cue his dog that this guy reaching out to him was a foe, not a friend.

"I could see Marko was saying, 'Should I or shouldn't I?'" he says.

Pulling the dog tight when he was like this could have prepped him for fight mode. He did the only thing he could do.

He relaxed.

Then he told Marko, "Stay," and dropped his hand to his side, making the leash loose. He was confident of Marko's obedience and knew he would listen. Marko stayed, still staring up at the president as Reagan and McMillon shook hands.

If you look carefully at the photo capturing the moment, behind the president you'll see the face of another dog handler. He's looking down at Marko. He doesn't look as confident as McMillon about the situation.

"He's got that 'OMG!! Fred, watch your dog!' expression going on," McMillon says with a laugh as he looks at the photo decades later.

"I think a lot about what could have happened. Without the trust Marko and I had in each other from all the training and time we put in, this could have had a very different ending."

The top of the Secret Service Explosive Detection Team ply their trade at some of the best homes in the world. Before the president or vice president attends a fund-raiser or other function at someone's residence, an explosives dog team or two will have done a thorough sweep of the home first.

No matter how rich or famous, the homes' owners (or more likely, someone who works for them) must open their bedrooms, bathrooms, closets, pantries, and sometimes dresser drawers to dogs and their handlers.

Most have no problem giving dogs access to even the most private areas of their houses. They know it's something everyone who has hosted the president has done. Friends in these circles communicate to other friends what to expect.

"They are extremely professional, a well-oiled machine," says a key staff member of the home of a West Coast couple that has hosted presidents and vice presidents several times. "The handlers are considerate, quick, and thorough, and the dogs are beautiful to watch."

When friends ask about her experiences with the Secret Service, she lets them know that the agency comes out about a week before an event and sets up phone lines, looks for windows and other areas that may need to be blocked, and performs other preparatory security work.

A few hours before the event, the dog team arrives. Hectic as it can be before a presidential fund-raising dinner, the staff has to leave. The cooking staff plans for this, so there won't be any culinary disasters during their absence. In this couple's case, the canine team's sweep of their five-story house—from wine cellar to upstairs specialty kitchen, plus the gardens—takes well under an hour.

This staff member and the couple are usually in the house during the sweep. Two of their own security staff accompany the dog team and the EOD techs who go along. The couple stays in a bedroom, and she stays in her office.

"It's very interesting watching the dogs. They're hyper in a good way, so energetic. You can tell they love what they do," she says.

When the sweep is done, the house and property are considered secured, and everyone coming back in is screened by Secret Service personnel and magnetometers.

"The dogs are the highlight of the process. We'd have them back in a heartbeat," she says.

Barbra Streisand might not feel the same way. According to a memoir by former Democratic National Committee chairman Terry McAuliffe, in the late 1990s Streisand was to host a brunch for the Clinton Library at her Malibu Hills home.

When she learned on the morning of the brunch that Secret Service dogs needed to do a sweep of her property, she refused. "Barbra did not like dogs," McAuliffe writes in *What a Party!*

> "Let me make it simple: No dogs, no Bill Clinton,"
> I said. "Please, Barbra. This is important for the presi-
> dent for his library and his legacy . . ."

She kept arguing, talking about how the dogs were going to get into her shrubs, which she meticulously maintained herself.

McAuliffe managed to convince her by telling her he would personally walk around with the dogs. He did, but they worked swiftly, and he couldn't keep up with them.

> Later, I was in the big tent we'd set up, checking on
> some things, when I heard Barbra screaming my name.
> I walked out into her beautiful garden to see what the
> commotion was all about.
> "Look what I stepped in!" she said.

When Brian M. learned about this story more than fifteen years later, he shook his head and looked down at the floor of his shared office at RTC.

"That's mortifying. That would never happen today. That should never have happened then."

A Secret Service dog handler who overheard the story chuckled and chimed in.

"Shit happens," he said. "You just have to clean it up, always."

Former Secret Service dog handler Cliff Cusick recalls the time he and his dog Devil went to Mississippi for President Jimmy Carter in 1977. One of his jobs was to have Devil search the home of a couple who would be hosting the president.

"Well, the lady finds out that the dog's name is Devil, and she was a very strict Southern Baptist and she would not allow it," he says.

"She said, 'You are not coming in my home with the devil.' She was serious as a heart attack. She was adamant that the dog was not allowed."

He tried not to be put off that someone wouldn't want his dog to check out the house just because of his name.

"It's OK, Devil, don't take it personally. Some people just have trust issues," he told his dog as they moved along to search the outside grounds instead.

Barney was not a bad dog. It's just that sometimes he wasn't a very good dog. George W. Bush's Scottish terrier was known for his dislike of strangers. At a place like the White House, there's no shortage of those.

"Barney guarded the South Lawn entrance of the White House

as if he were a Secret Service agent," Bush said in a statement after Barney died in 2013.

Not quite. Secret Service agents don't bite people to protect presidential interests. Barney did. Within the space of two months in 2008, he bit the public relations director of the Boston Celtics on the wrist and drew blood, and he bit the hand of a Reuters White House reporter who tried to pet him.

Jenna Bush Hager, daughter of the former president, didn't wax sentimental about the family's dog in a 2013 *Today* show segment.

"Barney was a real jerk," she said matter-of-factly, temporarily stunning the hosts into near silence except for a couple of shocked "wows."

Barney was far from being a Cujo. He had friends around the White House, held on-screen appeal via his eleven "Barney Cam" short films, and greeted heads of state.

But Secret Service dog handlers say Barney wasn't fond of their dogs. Handlers are always vigilant about the locations of the pets of the First Family while on the White House grounds. Radio communications between handlers and White House staff prevent any surprises while a First Dog is taking a walk or running out for a bathroom break, or when an EDT dog is doing a sweep inside the White House after tours.

"Be advised the family pets are on the south grounds," a White House staffer might say.

"Copy that," a handler will reply.

It's a fairly foolproof system, but Barney, apparently, was no fool. On a few occasions, he charged unexpectedly in the direction of some ERT dogs on the White House grounds.

"We'd have to pick our dogs up on our shoulders," says Stew.

"Barney was dog aggressive. Our ERT dogs are not dog aggressive."

ERT handlers have exquisite control over their Malinois, but they couldn't take any chances. They're entrusted with keeping the First Family safe, and in this situation, that also meant keeping Barney out of harm's way. Barney blasting out of nowhere and surprising a Malinois with a bite was an event that had to be avoided.

ERT canine handlers routinely lift their dogs on their shoulders in case they have to use the maneuver in real life. Avoiding Scottish terriers wasn't one of the situations they practiced for, but any port in a storm.

Barney never sank his teeth into an ERT dog. But he did manage to put the bite on an EDT canine once. The dog, Oscar, didn't care much for other dogs. While sweeping the White House for anything that shouldn't be there after the day's tours were completed, Oscar's handler heard the distant sound of something troubling: Barney. And by the sound of his barking, Barney was closing in quickly.

The handler wasn't sure how Barney had come to be in the same place he and Oscar were working, but it didn't matter. He had to act quickly to protect the president's dog. He crouched down and scooped Oscar into the crook of his arms, then stood up, lifting Oscar high off the floor.

But not high enough. The stampeding Barney jumped up and grabbed hold of Oscar's tail. This surprised Oscar, who was already somewhat discomfited by being held aloft so suddenly in his place of work. The Malinois wriggled and writhed and tried to escape from his handler, who had to summon his strength to keep the dog from tearing after Barney.

Luckily for Barney, other officers almost immediately arrived on the scene and were able to grab the First Dog before all hell broke loose.

Secret Service EDT assistant trainer Leth O. recalls another near miss with Barney. An EDT dog was doing a sweep in the White House, and Barney ran up to the dog. "He wanted to fight," Leth says.

The handler didn't pick up his own dog. Instead, he picked up Barney—a brave move for anyone not in Barney's inner circle.

According to Leth, when the president heard about the incident, he called the handler to his office. Was he in trouble? Should he not have touched the First Dog?

The handler's concerns were allayed when the president thanked him for what he had done and presented him with a special presidential coin. It bears the presidential seal on one side and, on the flip side, says "George W. Bush Commander in Chief" around an image of the White House.

"This handler helped win the president's trust and admiration, and it was a boost for us all in a way," says Leth. "It's not every day a president shows his appreciation so directly to dog handlers."

He was Jesus Christ. Marilyn Monroe and John F. Kennedy were his parents. He was about to announce his run for president. And he planned to kidnap one of the Obama family's Portuguese water dogs.

Scott Stockert made these bizarre claims when he was apprehended by Secret Service agents in a Washington, D.C., hotel in January 2016.

The last claim did not surprise them.

They'd received a tip from the Minnesota Secret Service field office that the North Dakota man was headed to the White House to kidnap Bo or Sunny. When they searched his Dodge Ram 1500, they found a 12-gauge pump shotgun, a bolt-action rifle, hundreds of rounds of ammunition, a machete with a twelve-inch blade, an eighteen-inch billy club, and a few other related items not found on the typical visitor to the nation's capital.

He was arrested on gun-related charges and will be on the Secret Service's radar for a long time.

While dogs of presidents are not on the list of Secret Service protectees, they are part of what some call "the First Family bubble." If anyone tries to harm the dogs when they're anywhere near the First Family, the Secret Service would be on it.

If someone tries to mess with the president's dogs at the White House, there's a good chance that at least one of their canine cousins who work on the Emergency Response Team would be called upon to help apprehend the perpetrator.

There's nothing like having a relative on the police force to make you confident that someone's got your back.

CHAPTER 7

SHUTTING DOWN THE WHITE HOUSE

It's a strange fact of life if you're a Secret Service bomb-dog handler. You, and you alone, may have to make a decision that could prevent the president of the United States from leaving or reentering the White House. Or you may cause the president to have to immediately move to another area in the White House.

Your decision could interrupt meetings with heads of state or cabinet members. It could delay sensitive negotiations. It could keep the president from attending important functions.

If your dog sits while sweeping an area, or has a change of behavior associated with finding an explosive, you don't call the boss and say, "Hey, here's what happened . . ." and figure it out together. It's completely up to you. This is your dog, and you should know your dog well enough to know if this is something that needs to be acted on.

While dog handlers don't decide what the course of action within the White House will be, once they make the call that a dog may be "on odor," the effect could be profound.

"It's a really big responsibility," says Hector H., deputy special agent in charge at Rowley Training Center. "Within five minutes of a dog alerting, the whole side of the White House near a potential blast area could be closed down."

The Secret Service won't say the extent to which a handler's call has ever changed anything inside the White House. It's safe to say that most of what is often referred to as "shutting down the White House" takes place on a much smaller scale, primarily outside the White House fence.

Sometimes a dog alerting to an odor closes off Pennsylvania Avenue on the north side of the White House for a while, or E Street NW along the south. Or the alert may shut down one of the vehicle checkpoints along Fifteenth or Seventeenth Street NW.

At the very least, some or a lot of people are going to be inconvenienced. Tourists may not be able to enjoy the coveted view of the White House they may have traveled halfway around the world to see. And staff who park at the White House complex may be late to work.

All because a dog plants his rear on the ground, or responds to an odor in a "Hey, this may be of interest to you" manner.

This is where trust comes in. The "trust your dog" mantra of the canine program isn't just a homey three-word catchphrase. If a dog or handler doesn't test well during the monthly verifications that look at different aspects of their skill sets, they won't report to their assigned job. Instead, they'll train on whatever the deficit is, sometimes working one-on-one with a Secret Service canine program instructor who helps both the dog and the handler.

Until recently this was called remedial training. But the name wasn't a hit with some around the training center. They changed the name to "personalized training." The dogs didn't care either way.

Teams will do as much personalized training as needed. It can take a day or a few weeks. Only when the dog or handler or both are back up to standard will they be able to head out to the real world on the job again.

Since the dogs who are at the White House, on the streets, and traveling around the world have been deemed good to go, and since handlers know their dogs' foibles (if Jake, for instance, always whips his head around and stares if he smells pizza), most feel confident in making the call. They try not to think of the ramifications.

"You have to go with what your dog is telling you," says Barry Lewis, former Secret Service dog handler, instructor, and unit commander. "Don't ever think, 'What's going to happen?' or 'How will this look if it's nothing?'

"What would you rather have? Some people inconvenienced or something happen you don't even want to think about?"

It's rare for Secret Service dogs to alert. Luckily, the places the dogs have searched throughout the canine program's history have been almost entirely free of explosive devices.

That's not to say dogs haven't found them. Some former handlers who have spoken about this off the record indicate otherwise. The Secret Service confirms that there have been finds but won't go into detail, citing operational security.

The Secret Service invests time and money in the explosives detection program because there is no technology yet that can beat a dog's nose. As David Petraeus once famously said, "The capability they bring to the fight cannot be replicated by man or machine."

Figures vary widely on how much better a dog's sense of smell is than a human's. The general consensus is somewhere between 10,000 and 100,000 times better.

It's hard to imagine what this would be like. The research of Stanley Coren, a neuropsychology researcher and psychology professor well known for his books on the intelligence and capabilities of dogs, is a useful guide.

> Let's say you have a gram of a component of human sweat known as butyric acid. Humans are quite adept at smelling this, and if you let it evaporate in the space of a ten-story building, many of us would still be able to detect a faint scent upon entering the building. Not bad, for a human nose. But consider this: If you put the 135-square-mile city of Philadelphia under a three-hundred-foot-high enclosure, evaporate the gram of butyric acid, and let a dog in, the average dog would still be able to detect the odor.

This kind of olfactory sensitivity is necessary for the job of sniffing out explosives, but it also occasionally leads to alerting that seems to amount to nothing. What dogs may actually be reacting to in these cases is residual odor—the ghost of a substance that had once been present. It doesn't necessarily mean it was part of an explosive device. It could be a harmless related substance.

Think about golfers who track through fresh fertilizer from the golf course and walk into the clubhouse. The dog doing a sweep for a protectee visit may or may not go into full alert mode. It depends on many factors, including the concentration of ammonium nitrate (a chemical compound that can be used to make improvised explosive devices) in the fertilizer and the amount of time that has gone by.

If the dog alerts on the rug of the golf clubhouse and nothing is found—this happened during the George W. Bush administration—it might appear to onlookers that the dog is embarrassingly wrong.

But don't call this a false alert. It's not false if a dog smells something that she's been trained on. Of course, no one knows what a dog is really alerting to in a case like this. The Secret Service calls these, appropriately enough, "unknown alerts."

This is where it would come in handy if dogs could talk. Many handlers whose dogs have had an unknown alert have wanted their dog to be able to tell all.

"I have wished Rex could say, 'Well, I think I smell X, but I'm not entirely sure,' or 'Yes, this is definitely the scent of X, Jon,'" says his handler.

Rex would be polite like that if he could speak. Some of the other Mals with more attitude (like Turbo, aka Snoop Dogg) might be inclined to say something like, "Hey, all you people looking at my handler like you doubt our abilities. Just because you can't smell it with your terrible sense of smell doesn't mean the odor I have been trained for years to find is not here in a big way! A little trust, please?"

It can be awkward for handlers whose dogs alert and cause streets or checkpoints or the White House itself to be on lockdown, only to have nothing found. But there's no way around it.

During their long career together, Lewis and his Dutch shepherd, Marco, did tens of thousands of searches—from vehicle searches at checkpoints to protectee sweeps. The dog alerted only four or five times. Nothing was found during any of the searches.

"You don't like to hear people complain about a dog shutting down Seventeenth Street or the White House and thinking a dog made a mistake," Lewis says. "I didn't want anyone trying to do harm. But the few times Marco sat, I have to admit I really hoped something was there.

"It wasn't for the glory. I wanted people to know how valuable these dogs are, and how much good they're capable of doing."

An older red Cadillac pulled up to a White House complex checkpoint. The driver, a pass holder, was admitted through the first security gate. He drove ahead and stopped for the next check.

No stranger to the routine, he popped his trunk and waited.

Jon and Rex approached the car and Rex began his inspection. On average a Secret Service EDT dog will perform more than seven thousand vehicle searches per year. Handlers know exactly what to expect their dog to do on a typical search. Dogs usually hold to their own established pattern, starting in one particular area and ending in another.

Rex had a timeworn favorite way of searching, and it didn't involve starting at the trunk. Until this day.

When the dog got close to the car, he beelined straight for the trunk, which was open a few inches after the driver had popped it. Rex leaped up and stood with his front paws on the bumper— something he rarely did.

He shoved open the trunk with his head. This was definitely not in Rex's normal script. Rex is not a dog who opens anything with his head. If he's at home and wants to go into the bedroom, but the door is open only wide enough for him to stick his head through, he'll sit there until someone opens the door enough to fit his whole body.

Jon let his dog continue his inspection. Rex reached into the trunk with his nose and put his front paws inside the trunk. Jon hadn't ever seen Rex act like this.

The next moment, Rex pulled his front end from the trunk.

Before his front paws were on the ground, his hindquarters hit the pavement.

It was a very big, emphatic sit.

EDT dog language for, "Hey, Dad, found something!"

Jon felt a surge of adrenaline. The hair stood up on the back of his neck.

"Good boy, Rex," he said, and gave his dog a quick scratch on the head. He set to work searching the trunk. It was empty except for a large, eight-disk CD changer. He found only some dry cleaning in the passenger area of the car.

By now, several Uniformed Division officers were on the scene. They shut down the checkpoint and cleared the area of cars and people. The other checkpoint would now take on the burden of the traffic, which would mean longer waits for people trying to get in and more congestion on the streets near the White House if it backed up enough.

But what's a little traffic and some people being late for work when it comes to a possible explosive device near the White House?

They had the driver get out of his car. Jon and his sergeant asked him a series of questions. The driver, a regular there, was surprised and baffled at how his morning had taken such a sharp turn from normal. Officers from MPD arrived with bomb technicians and checked the vehicle thoroughly.

In the end, MPD found nothing. Jon figured it was probably residual odors of something perfectly legit that was no longer there. Rex's definitive alert left little doubt in his mind that the dog had smelled one of the many explosive substances he was trained to detect.

The driver was eventually allowed to proceed with his business, the checkpoint was reopened, and everything went back to normal.

Everything, that is, except Rex. He worked with even more spring in his step than usual for the rest of the day. He had received an unexpected paycheck, a bonus of sorts. He didn't get his Kong; that part of the paycheck is reserved for training. You don't throw a Kong in a situation where there could be a real explosive. But even better, Rex had been praised by his best friend for doing his job so well.

"Rex may be a dog, but Rex can count," Bill G., the canine program manager, says from his end of a conference table at Rowley Training Center.

Rex is lying at Jon's feet. His ears twitch when he hears his name. He gets up, trots to the other end of the table, and stands there wagging and looking at Bill until he pets him.

Bill continues explaining something common to humans and the dogs they work with. It has to do with expectations.

Let's say you're a dog handler training at a football stadium. You know you're there to find odors of explosives with your dog. You're fully expecting your dog to find something. You check all the seats in your quadrant. You search near the concession stands. You have your dog check the trash cans. You open doors to storage areas and try to find something.

This is training. There's got to be *something*.

But this is Secret Service training. There may not be anything.

Having a "find" every so often isn't what happens in the real world. Dog teams on the job often have to search for long periods. They do a high volume of searches. The Service doesn't want the dogs to lose interest. So they often train them with "blanks"—no odors of explosives.

Handlers don't know if there's going to be anything, so they can't unintentionally cue their dogs.

If a dog comes to expect an odor every ten minutes, or at every third trash can, the dog will start figuring out the math and will play the game, sitting at regular intervals or at every third trash can. No smell? It doesn't matter. The dog contends that if it worked before, it should work again.

Bill explains that blanks are a critical element in training Secret Service dogs. These dogs aren't like their brethren in the military, who may find IEDs all too frequently when on deployment. Secret Service detection dogs need to know there will be days and weeks when even in training, they're not going to find a thing.

When they do detect an odor they're trained to find, it will be that much more exciting to them.

"I don't like it so much. It's not fun for me, because you want to find something," Jon says. "Of course Rex wants to find something. Winning to me is when we find something. Same for Rex."

Rex hears his name and trots back to Jon's end of the conference table. He puts his paws on his handler's lap and leans into his chest, wagging.

Jon puts his arms around his dog while he explains that he appreciates the logic behind blanks. He gets a regular paycheck, which is inspiration enough to keep searching every day, day in and day out, with the great possibility of not finding anything outside a training venue. But Rex gets paid only when he finds something.

He doesn't want his dog to be used to frequently finding odors in training and expect that in real life. But what's a dog to do when he can go his whole career and alert maybe a handful of times in real life? How does he keep inspired? Those on-the-job paychecks may come only every couple of years, if that. A dog may as well be self-employed.

The answer to this problem is something called motivational training.

The Secret Service declines to say much about it. But what happened to Rex with the red Cadillac—and the subsequent bounce in his step—is something canine trainers can re-create themselves, wherever a dog may be working. It can happen any time. The White House, however, will not be shut down.

"Let's just say we make sure the dogs know the game is always being played," says Bill.

In the early days of the canine program, dogs searched not only every vehicle that drove into the White House complex but most items that were delivered, according to former handler Henry Sergent, who is now chief of the TSA National Explosives Detection Canine Team Program.

"The dogs went through everything from paper goods to donuts," he says.

Ah, the donuts . . .

He remembers that in the late 1980s, the Old Executive Office Building was home to what was known as the "blind stand" because it was operated by people who were legally blind. Each morning at least two dozen donuts came in with them for resale to staff. It fell upon the Secret Service dogs to inspect them with their Uniformed Division officers.

"Yes, it's true, basically police and dogs inspecting donuts," he says.

Donut duty always seemed to put a little extra pep into his Malinois, Rudy. If a dog could sign up for a gig at the Secret Service, you'd have to imagine there would be a lot of paw marks on the list for the job that entails sniffing donuts.

The dogs were trained to find explosives hidden among food items. Secret Service dogs who were presented with a bag of hamburgers in training had to be able to focus enough to alert if the odor of an explosive was also in the bag. Their desire for their reward needed to be stronger than the aroma of cooked beef.

To the dogs, detection was and is all a fun game. They don't know the danger of what they're seeking. They just know that when they find what they're supposed to, at least in training, their handlers get happy and give them praise in high-pitched voices, and throw them Kongs. With the right kind of training, a dog will stay on course no matter what kind of tempting morsels may be around.

Donut duty was a good gig. It was a great gig.

Then one day, a dog ate a donut.

And the gig, like the donut, was gone. Just like that.

It was decided an officer without a dog could probably be just as effective with a visual inspection alone. If the other dogs gave dirty looks to their colleague with donut breath, it would be understandable.

The White House hosts hundreds of thousands of visitors a year. Thousands of people from all over the world tour the "People's House" every day it's open to the public. The majority of those who make it onto the tour have had to go through a lengthy process to be here, and there's also an element of luck.

Most would-be visitors have to request the tour, which is self-guided, through their congressional representative's office. This is usually done via an online form. Citizens of other countries need to go through their embassy in Washington, D.C. Requests must be made at least six weeks ahead of time (three weeks is stated as the minimum on some sites, but it's almost unheard of to get ticketed that quickly these days) but no more than six months out.

There is no such thing as a same-day ticket. Rarely is there even a same-month ticket. This fact disappoints many Washington, D.C., visitors who haven't done their homework. After asking around for the ticket office (nonexistent), they often end up at the nearby White House Visitor Center. It's the next best thing to a tour of the president's house. And it has something the White House doesn't: restrooms for the public.

White House tour applicants older than thirteen will undergo a background check. With all the tour applications, this can take a few to several weeks. But passing the check doesn't guarantee entry. There's a first-come, first-served policy, and spaces fill up quickly, depending on the time of year.

The people in line to enter the White House on any given day have put in some real effort to be here. The items they've had to leave in their hotel rooms or cars include purses, backpacks, strollers, makeup, video recorders, laptops, tablets, food, beverages, tripods, and selfie sticks. The list of permitted items is far shorter: wallets, keys, cell phones, compact cameras, necessary medical items, and umbrellas without metal tips.

Having large pockets is a big plus on a White House tour.

Once at the entry point on Fifteenth Street NW just south of the Treasury Building, ticket documents are checked and visitors queue up near the south side of the White House.

It's fairly standard for it to take more than an hour from arrival to walking into the White House, but visitors who have come this far are usually in a good mood. Some of the more observant may notice the comings and goings of a dog or two from a modular-type building.

"I wonder what they're doing," a woman in line in early December for the White House's special holiday tour says to her companion.

"Probably drug dogs. They don't allow drugs here, obviously. Do you think they're shepherds?"

"Probably."

As they wend their way closer to the small outbuilding, the same woman who spotted the dogs sees a sign with a picture of a Belgian Malinois.

"Look! Canines working to keep you safe," she says as she reads it aloud. "Please do not attempt to touch or pet these animals while they are working."

"It doesn't look like a German shepherd," her companion says, using her chin to point to the photo, despite the lack of anything in her arms.

They move along and then up several steps into a room that seems fairly empty except for a couple of Secret Service Uniformed Division officers. Each visitor is asked to step in, one at a time, and place her feet on yellow outlines of shoes. The first woman stands where she is asked and moves on when given the OK. The second does the same. They're both in and out of the room in under thirty seconds. If they're like most people, they probably didn't notice much except a couple of officers in a relatively empty room.

But if you have keen situational awareness, you'll notice a great deal more. There's a slight breeze coming from somewhere overhead. You look up and see fans. That might strike you as odd, since it's a chilly day with no need for fans.

You look to your left and see a third Secret Service officer. This one is standing behind a louvre screen with just his head and shoulders above it. Listen and you might hear a *click–click–click–click* on the floor near the officer. If you glance over and look through the screen slats at the right angle, you might spot the source of the clicks. It's a dog, toenails tapping the floor as she walks about doing her job. On this shift, the dog is a Personnel Screening Canine (PSC) named Brenda.

You're given the nod, and as you walk into the next room, which has a magnetometer and a couple of screeners, you wonder what that was all about.

The room you were just in is called the White House Visitors Entrance Canine Checkpoint. The fans keep the airflow going toward the dog rather than out the door or anywhere else. The dog's handler gives the dog a command and the dog sniffs for explosives odors from behind the screen. (Keeping the dogs out of plain sight helps visitors who might have a fear of dogs and makes the process go more quickly for other visitors who might want to pet the dogs or talk to the officers about them.) If the dog doesn't have a change of behavior or an alert, the handler signals one of the other officers and you're good to go.

But what if Brenda or one of her PSC pals detects an odor she's been trained to alert? If she sits, you don't want to be behind that person. Once a dog alerts, everyone else behind that person gets pushed back out, often all the way to the park they entered.

The person the dog alerted to is escorted to another room for further screening and questioning. Once all tests come back negative and the information checks out, the person is cleared and tours resume. This could take as little as twenty minutes or more than an hour. It all depends on how well the person cooperates and how quickly Technical Security Division personnel are able to get to the bottom of the situation.

A chemical engineer and a landscaper are among some of the people dogs here have alerted to. Everything checked out fine.

Maybe under the "additional information" section of the White House ticket document, where a bullet-point list includes advice about dressing for the weather and making sure visitors eat and hydrate before arrival, there should be this helpful tip:

• Wear laundered clothes, clean shoes, and take a really good shower.

After the tour, you exit out the north side of the White House. If you're very lucky, you might see an ERT dog and handler while they're taking a brief walk. The handlers are unmistakable with their athletic physiques, their weapons, and their badass black uniforms. Their dogs also exude confidence and strength.

If it's your unbelievably lucky day, you might even spot Dale Haney, the superintendent of the White House grounds, walking a genuine presidential dog. The horticulturalist has worked here since 1972. The *New York Times* credits him with tending to every First Dog since Richard Nixon's Irish setter, King Timahoe.

On this early December day, as visitors trickle out of the White House after the festive holiday tour, someone spots what looks like a black sheep on a leash. Word quickly gets around that this is Sunny, the Obama family's all-black Portuguese water dog, often referred to as Bo's little sister.

"It's the president's dog!" someone says, and points.

"Oh my God, the First Dog!"

Cameras and cell phones train on the dog as a crowd gathers to watch her walking with Haney. After a couple of minutes, Haney walks Sunny in the direction of a group of visitors and introduces her.

He asks a ten-year-old girl if she'd like to hold Sunny's leash. The girl beams. She takes the nylon leash—blue with stars—in her hand and pets her.

"She's so soft," she says. Her extended family is with her, talking excitedly while snapping pics. Most don't speak English. One translates and tries to explain what's going on. The girl looks out shyly at the gathering crowd while Sunny sits. The dog is calm as a rock.

This is far from an everyday occurrence. A First Dog sighting like this is rare.

But not to worry. If you love dogs, you have one more chance to spot one before you stray too far from the White House. As you walk down the curved drive and out the gate, if you head left on Pennsylvania Avenue, you might see a dog you'd never associate with the Secret Service.

"What's that?" you might ask.

You would not be the first.

CHAPTER 8

WHAT'S THAT?

The stainless steel dog trailer full of new canine recruits pulled into the kennel parking lot at RTC. Highway dust from the thirteen-hour drive from Indiana—including two bathroom breaks for the dogs—dulled the sheen of the trailer, but the excited barking of the dogs was anything but muted.

They wanted out.

Instructors and handlers gathered to see what kinds of dogs two canine staffers had picked out at Vohne Liche Kennels for the brand-new Personnel Screening Canines Open Area (PSCO) program, aka the "Friendly Dog" program, aka the "Floppy-Eared Dog" program.

These would be the first Secret Service dogs to scent vapor trails coming off people, rather than fixed objects—an additional layer of defense for the White House or anywhere they might work. The future Friendly Dog handlers had been in classroom training for a week and were anxious to meet their potential partners.

Steve M., a canine program instructor, stepped out of the truck and stretched the kinks out of his back.

"I think we got some good ones here," he said. He and another instructor began bringing the dogs out of the trailer one at a time.

He introduced the staff to several Labrador retrievers, a couple of springer spaniels, and a cocker spaniel. They all seemed fairly affable, despite the long journey. Most stopped barking once out of the trailer.

These dogs had the hallmark floppy ears that were supposed to help prevent tourists from moving away from them in a crowd, as often happened with Malinois and other pointy-eared law-enforcement dogs whose reputations and looks tend to be more intimidating. Most wagged amiably. It was an altogether different group of recruits from the dogs that normally charge out of the trailer.

And then there was a dog who fit no category.

Part terrier, part border collie, most likely—a shaggy, scraggly morphing of the two. His fur looked like a black-and-white shag rug that someone had regrettably thrown in the dryer on extra hot. A cowlick partway along his back added to the chaos.

His muzzle was mostly white, with black mottling from his skin showing through in patches. White hairs intruded on the black fur that covered most of the rest of his face, giving him the appearance of an older dog.

To top off the look, hanging three inches down from each side of the dog's mouth were long, coarse tendrils of fur with a rusty orange hue. Brian thought it looked like a canine version of a Fu Manchu mustache.

He stepped back and silently surveyed the dog, from his pointy black ears—*ha ha, so much for floppy-eared dogs*—to his white-tipped tail.

What's THAT? he thought, but didn't say it aloud.

"Well, pretty is as pretty does," he uttered through his chuckles.

"This is Roadee," Steve smiled and told the group. He knew the impression the dog must be making. "I think he may have real potential."

Steve, a master sergeant in the United States Marine Corps Reserve, spent his nine active-duty Marine years as a dog handler and trainer. When he thinks a dog has what it takes, the dog usually does.

Bill strode up from the kennel office.

"You've gotta be kidding me!" the agent said, laughing and shaking his head.

Roadee looked up at him, eyes narrowing slightly, ears tipping backward, mouth firmly shut. His expression left little room for interpretation.

You wait and see, pal.

The handsome Labs and peppy spaniels made the rounds with the handlers during the first week of Friendly Dog training. Ziggy, a mellow, smart yellow Lab, was the dog most of the handlers wanted to work with.

Roadee wasn't part of the rotation the first few days. He was like the kid who never got picked to be on a team at school. He sat in his kennel and watched as the other dogs paraded in and out. He'd go on walks, but that was it.

No one wanted to interact much with him. When someone would pet him, he would get so excited he'd unleash his bladder. One of the springers, Dyson, had the same issue, but he was being worked and trained most days despite this.

Then one day, after it became evident that a couple of the other dogs didn't have the right stuff, Roadee was brought out of his kennel. It was more a matter of protocol than the belief he could be a bona fide member of the Secret Service. They couldn't return him to Vohne Liche Kennels without at least giving him a fighting chance.

A good bath and solid diet had made him look a little less rough around the edges. He bounced out of his cage, jumping around at the end of his leash and wanting to work.

It quickly became clear that Roadee had more previous training than the other dogs. Maybe too much.

While most of the other dogs were green and just beginning on obedience and some scent work, Roadee already knew the ropes. When instructors tried him out on basic scent work, he would alert.

In fact, he would alert to almost everything he was asked to sniff. It didn't matter if it had an explosives odor or not. He would sit. It was one alert after another. If he went out on the job like this, the White House would be under constant lockdown.

The instructors realized he had played this game before and he knew how to get paid. They set to work encouraging him, with positive reinforcement, to make more honest choices.

With the exception of his cheating ways, he quickly proved himself to be a top student. He was a fast learner and had the kind of high energy needed for the job.

Most of the handlers didn't mind too much if they were assigned Roadee for the day. They just didn't want him for keeps.

They couldn't imagine dealing with his "glee pee," especially at home, much less out in public in front of the White House gates where he'd be sniffing out passersby for potential explosives. Sometimes all it took was a look from someone and he'd let loose a stream.

Even though he looked better than he did when he emerged from the kennel trailer, the handlers didn't think he had the appearance of a Secret Service dog whose mission was to protect the president of the United States.

The handlers had all been in the Secret Service for years, mostly in jobs other than handling dogs. Ending up with a canine partner who looked like he lived down the alley from Oscar the Grouch wasn't something they'd envisioned when they signed up for this duty.

By the end of the second week with the dogs, the instructors had decided on the matches. They would be announcing them later that day. But just for fun, that morning they asked the handlers to rank their choices.

Ziggy was the first choice of most of the handlers. He had proven to be a super quick study, and with his happy, chilled-out personality he'd be a welcome addition to any household.

Only one person even put Roadee on his list. Josh B., the long-time handler of an EDT dog who was about to retire, realized Roadee's potential.

"The only thing going against him besides the pee thing is his looks," he told one of the other handlers in his class. "If he looked like Ziggy, I might put him as number one." Instead, he put Roadee as number three out of three.

The handlers all ranked their choices, handed them to the instructors, and went out for a few more hours of training

They were outside at Rowley Training Center working the dogs when a flashbang went off somewhere in the distance from unrelated Secret Service training. It wasn't terribly loud. Most of the dogs didn't seem to notice.

But Ziggy did.

He immediately appeared to deflate and lose all his confidence. He tucked his tail between his legs, and when he could be convinced to walk, he barely moved. It took exuberant motivational praise to even get him back to a normal walk, and after a few minutes he'd slow down again and his ears would pull back tight against his head.

This kind of reaction was not what they had expected. Ziggy had been exposed to loud noises during testing in Indiana and had not come undone. But no matter how perfect Ziggy was in every other way, they all knew that this was the end of any potential Secret Service career for him. They couldn't have a dog who shuts down at the sound of a blast doing the kind of work he would be doing at the White House. Cars backfire. Fireworks go off. Demonstrations get loud. Kids pop balloons.

Ziggy would be heading back to Indiana. He wasn't alone. He'd be joining Teddy, Jerry, Max, and Harley for a return trip. Because the program was new, it would take a little time to figure out what to look for in ideal canine candidates.

With the first choice of the handlers now gone from the list, they gathered in the classroom for their meeting with Steve and another instructor to learn who would be at their side at the White House and in their homes for the next several years.

"All right, five of you guys put Ziggy first, but as you know, he's going back," the other instructor told them.

The instructors went through one by one, adding dramatic pauses between. Halfway through the list, Josh knew he would be making a phone call after the meeting to give his wife a heads-up.

"I'm bringing home a dog today," he told her later. "He's a little rough looking but I think he'll grow on you."

Josh's retired Malinois, Ciela (pronounced *seel*-ah), was the kind of dog who commanded respect wherever she went. Never mind that her ears are so big that Josh jokes that if Batman had a dog, Ciela would be it. Even in retirement, she's a regal dog with a don't-mess-with-me air. When she was still working, people generally kept their distance.

If onlookers said anything, it was usually about how beautiful she was. Only one time did someone make a negative comment about her looks. It happened the first week Josh had her out on the job.

"That's a canine?" the woman asked. "*Man*, that dog is *so* ugly!"

Josh didn't know what to say. He was just as mad as if she had insulted his child. He said nothing.

Ciela was an excellent EDT dog. She alerted once at the White House in 2014, her last year on the job. She dove under a car, stared up, and wouldn't budge until Josh called her off. It was a dramatic alert that shut down an entry point. A bomb team took it seriously but couldn't find anything.

They had worked together since 2006, and she had never thrown that kind of change of behavior outside of training. Josh was sure she had detected an odor she was trained to find, but the cause of the odor was no longer visible. She wasn't a dog to tell fibs for rewards.

She alerted twice at the vice president's residence as well. One alert was for a car parked near the helicopter pad. The other was, of all things, for a rope that hoisted the American flag up and down. Nothing suspicious was found either time, but Josh once again had no doubt she had smelled something in her vast odor repertoire.

Josh and Ciela had traveled extensively for the job. They'd been to Germany for the G8 summit, Copenhagen for the failed U.S. Olympics bid, Israel when Cheney was vice president, Italy for a vice presidential vacation, Costa Rica, Canada, and all over the United States.

Secret Service dog teams sometimes work with military

working dogs and handlers. For the UN General Assembly, Secret Service dogs usually work close to the inner perimeter, while military dog teams tend to be a little farther out.

On one joint assignment in Florida, Josh ran across a Navy dog handler sitting in his white Ford Explorer. A big sign on the window warned: CAUTION: MILITARY WORKING DOG.

Josh walked up and introduced himself.

"You got a German shepherd in there?" he asked.

"No," the Navy dog handler said. "A Jack Russell terrier."

Josh laughed at the joke.

The handler rolled down the window and a scrappy Jack Russell terrier jumped up, put his paws on the door, and stared at him.

"This is Lars," the Navy handler said.

"Oh my God!" Josh said, busting up. "You weren't kidding!"

The handler had been through this kind of reaction many times. He just nodded and smiled. It was a feeling Josh would come to know all too well.

Karma is a cruel mistress.

On the lower windshield of Josh's work van is a sign warning POLICE K-9 VEHICLE in English and Spanish, over the Secret Service's logo. The head of a German shepherd appears to be looking at the warning words from the right.

Josh and Roadee don't usually get out of their van at work in front of many people, but they face plenty of double takes on the job at the White House fence line. People point, they smile, they ask lots of questions. It makes Josh's role particularly challenging, because he has to guide Roadee through the crowd, maintain a focus on what Roadee is up to, and be completely aware of any important changes of behavior that could indicate he's onto the scent of an explosive device.

When Roadee is working, he's serious about his job. He pulls ahead, tracing the scent of everyone near, hoping that someone, somewhere, will bear an odor he's looking for so he can get his coveted tennis ball reward—if not then, then afterward.

Many tourists ask Josh if he and his dog would pose for a photo—sometimes just to prove to their friends that this dog really exists and works for the Secret Service. He politely declines requests that would entail him stopping.

He'll try to answer questions when he can, but he doesn't let anything get in the way of doing his job at 100 percent. He's as serious about his work as Roadee is about his.

If there are too many questions, or if Josh can't stop to answer, one of the nearby Uniformed Division officers will take over. Most know Roadee's story. The same questions come up every day, and they're happy to answer whatever they can so Roadee and Josh can do their jobs.

The questions usually start within thirty seconds of Josh and Roadee walking from the van to the fence line. It doesn't seem to matter if it's crowded or relatively empty. There are always questions:

—"What kind of dog is *that*?" or for the less tactful, "What's *that*?!"

Josh tells them about the border collie–terrier mix theory. It usually satisfies people, but there are some who set to work figuring out just what kind of terrier must be at work in his gene pool to end up with this unique look.

—"I didn't know you guys use rescue dogs!"

"No, we go through a vendor. He looks like a rescue dog, but he's not." He wishes he knew more about Roadee's history and wonders how someone who breeds working dogs chose to create a Roadee.

—"I thought you used canines!"

"This *is* a canine," he'll say with a patient smile. Just like the Navy handler did all those years back.

—"Wow, that dog's old!"

"He's only four," Josh may reply. He knows that won't usually be the end of the conversation, which usually continues with, "But his face has so much white!"

—"He's so scraggly!"

There is no answer for this one as far as he's concerned. Maybe just a "Yup."

—"She's pretty!"

"Thanks!" He doesn't usually bother explaining the gender thing.

—"Does he bite?"

"All dogs can bite."

—"Is he a good dog?"

"He's a great dog."

—"Can I pet him?"

Even though DO NOT PET is emblazoned on Roadee's harness, this is one of the more common questions. "Sorry, he's working" is the simple answer.

There's another reason the tourists should not pet Roadee. This is one explanation Josh never shares with them.

Visitors to Josh's house, which is down a winding country road far from Washington, D.C., are never greeted by Roadee. It's not that he's antisocial. It's just that Josh and his wife like to minimize Roadee's little accidents.

They don't want to tell company, "Please don't pet him." It's easier, and the dog is more mellow, if he's off on his own until visitors have been there for a while.

When Josh's parents stop in, Roadee is so thrilled to see them that it doesn't even take them petting him to set him off. All they have to do is talk to him when they walk in, and a yellow stream hits the rug. Josh asks them to give Roadee the cold shoulder for a while after arriving, but it's hard to ignore their scruffy grandchild.

Josh's father was also in the Uniformed Division of the Secret Service, serving in almost every capacity for thirty-two years. Josh always knew he wanted to follow in his father's footsteps, but he chose to start his career on an entirely different path. He majored in illustration at Syracuse University and became a webmaster in Virginia.

After four years of office work, he was ready to make the transition to the Secret Service. He briefly considered applying to become a Secret Service agent instead of a Uniformed Division officer, but that would have meant uprooting from his large extended family to transfer elsewhere. Agents usually start in field offices away from D.C.

Once he settled on UD, he hoped to eventually become a canine handler. "I thought it would be the coolest thing," says Josh, who grew up with dogs.

Josh never envisioned himself in the canine world with a partner like Roadee, but the dog has proven himself a dedicated champ. He's well respected at RTC, where he's sometimes used to demonstrate how to do the job with focus and gusto.

Those traits follow him home as well. But at home, focus and gusto aren't the coveted attributes they are on the job, and can quickly get out of hand.

A large yellow foam sponge rests on a counter in the kitchen.

In its current state it looks like a giant piece of cheese with a corner that has been chewed away by a hefty mutant rat.

By coincidence, Roadee's nickname is Splinter. When Roadee's scraggly chin hairs and Fu Manchu mustache have not been groomed for a while, he bears a striking resemblance to Splinter, the wise martial arts mutant rat who mentors the four Teenage Mutant Ninja Turtles.

Two days earlier, Josh had been using the yellow sponge for some tile work on a kitchen backsplash. He went out to talk with a neighbor for five minutes while Roadee was sleeping. When he walked back in, he discovered that Roadee (alias Splinter) had shredded a large chunk of the yellow sponge (alias cheese) to tiny bits. There were not enough shreds to account for the loss, so Josh knew he would be scooping the collateral damage for the next couple of days.

"Oh my God, five minutes, Roadee? Five minutes and you get into this?!" Josh knew it was his own fault, though. He doesn't usually let down his guard with his feisty crime fighter for a second.

Ciela has the run of the whole house. She has been trustworthy since Josh's first days with her. Roadee, however, lives the home life of someone who is not to be trusted.

He's not as free-range as Ciela. He gets to go around most of the house as long as he's at Josh's side, but his room is a spare room in the finished basement. It's a spartan room, with only a couple of dog beds and a couple of plastic kennels the dogs can use as dens. The idea is that Roadee can't get into too much trouble there. Ciela often joins him.

One night after Josh and his family returned from a restaurant, he headed to Roadee's room to check on how he was doing with the new cover his wife had put on one of the beds. He got to the room and walked back to the stairs.

"Honey, can you come down here, please?" he called up to his wife.

He didn't want to face this on his own.

It looked as though a snowmageddon had stormed through while they were out. The cover was shredded to snowflakey bits all over the room. The bed itself had been divested of much of its foam.

Both dogs stood at the doorway as the couple surveyed the mess. Josh looked from one dog to the other. Ciela looked right back at him with a "You know *I* didn't do this" expression. Roadee looked at him with a piece of foam clinging to the side of his mouth.

"What am I going to do with you, Roadee?"

The basement also has a living room/rec room, where Josh and the human kids like to hang out, watch TV, and play games.

If someone leaves the downstairs bathroom door open, Roadee will tiptoe across the carpeting and get into the trash can or rip toilet paper off the roll. If the children leave a toy out—which they rarely do because they've learned their lesson—it's in grave danger.

Fortunately Roadee is Josh's shadow around the house. Roadee wants to be with him all the time. When Josh watches TV in the upstairs living room, Roadee will sometimes watch *him* watching TV.

"It's kind of creepy," Josh recently told a friend. "He just sits and stares right at me with this look."

At dinnertime, Roadee is supposed to stay far from the table, near the stairs. He usually has his favorite toy, a flexible red dog Frisbee, with him. As the family gets involved in a conversation, and food gets passed around, Roadee magically appears under the table with the Frisbee, usually folded in half like a rubber taco. He'll place it at someone's feet as if it's an offering, a trade, for a bite or two.

When Josh discovers him, he has a special phrase.

"Go to your place, Roadee."

Roadee takes his Frisbee taco and trots back to the stairs.

"Your place" does not specifically mean the stairs. It means "go somewhere farther away, please." At the dinner table, it's the stairs. In other situations, Roadee takes about twenty steps in whatever direction works, and settles in.

During a short lull in the dinner conversation, a little *click-click-click-click* is heard. Here comes Roadee again, trotting across the wood floor, the folded Frisbee in his mouth, hoping again to make a deal. Tonight it's for chicken parm. But no one trades with him.

"Go to your place, Roadee."

And back he goes.

At least for a while.

For all of Roadee's foibles—Josh describes him as "just a little quirky"—Josh knows he's worth the extra vigilance. He and the canine staff have tried to get to the bottom of the "glee pee" issue, but it appears to be firmly engrained. Josh has managed to work around it pretty well.

Roadee's shredder tendencies can be controlled by being extra watchful. Josh doesn't want the dog to have to live in his crate or be shut in a room all day on his days off. Roadee already gets plenty of exercise on his job and before work when he cuts loose outside, so more exercise is not the answer. And anyway, his energy is part of the reason he's such a good detection dog.

Roadee has many admirers in the canine program.

"I may have laughed at Roadee when he came off the trailer, but he got the last laugh," says Bill. "He's a great dog, and Josh is a great handler. One of the best. They're an excellent team."

Josh has similar words about his dogs. As with most other handlers, the superlatives flow when describing his canines.

"Both my dogs have been the best," he explains. "Ciela was the best at the EDT side when she was working. Other handlers will tell you their dog was the best but Ciela was the best. She really was the best.

"As far as the PSCO world, Roadee is the best. He really is. I have been very lucky. Both of them have been super eager to work, to please, very high drive, and I don't see 'quit' in either of them."

As the Secret Service looks at other uses for the Friendly Dog program, travel might become more commonplace. During the pope's visit, Josh and Roadee took their first road trip. It was by van, so no planes to contend with. Roadee did well and remained focused for the detection work.

Josh carefully watched Roadee in the hotel so he wouldn't eat the towels, sheets, and toilet paper. He wouldn't let him out of his sight. If Josh left the room, he shut Roadee in his travel kennel.

If air travel becomes part of the job of the Friendly Dogs, Josh hopes Roadee will handle it with the cool aplomb of Ciela.

Josh smiles at the mental image of his scampish dog flying around the world in a military cargo plane on missions to protect the president with the big boys.

"I'm just as curious as everyone else how he'd do on a plane. It would be . . ." he says, and pauses, "interesting."

CHAPTER 9

FREQUENT FLIERS

On the day after Thanksgiving 2015, exactly two weeks after the Paris terrorist attacks that left 130 people and a police K-9 dead, more than 100 in critical condition, and hundreds wounded, Jorge P. said his good-byes to his children on his way to a mission in Paris.

"Daddy, please don't go!" his son, age six, pleaded.

"It's too dangerous, Papi," his eleven-year-old daughter told him quietly. "Do you have to go?"

They'd heard about the brutal ISIS attacks through friends and at school and for two weeks had been hoping their father's upcoming trip would be canceled.

"Don't you worry about anything," Jorge told them. "Your brother will keep me safe."

He reached down and petted his Malinois, Yuri. The children rushed over to hug the dog they thought of as their sibling.

"What about Yuri? Please bring Yuri back," his daughter told him, tears brimming.

"Of course I will! I make sure Yuri is safe, and Yuri makes sure I'm safe."

He crouched down to hug his children one last time. He savored the extra long embrace.

As he walked out to load Yuri into the van, his children grabbed onto his legs, one on each. He walked a few steps with the children clinging but had to get going to Joint Base Andrews.

"OK, you guys, let go. We'll do FaceTime and I'll be back before you know it!"

The Lockheed C-5 Galaxy military transport aircraft waits in hungry-shark mode on the tarmac at Joint Base Andrews. Its nose is unhinged, pointing skyward, and its gaping mouth of a cargo hold is ready to devour whatever comes its way.

The noise from its auxiliary power unit washes over the tarmac to an adjacent parking lot where eight Secret Service EDT dog handlers have been standing by since around noon. It's been two hours, and still no sign of loading up. They're used to delays. The planes are known for them. If it's not maintenance or something mechanical, it's a crew change.

They've got plenty to keep them busy. They toss a football, talk, walk their dogs, and catch up on texts and e-mails.

Their upcoming mission will take them to Paris, where the United Nations Climate Change Conference is being held. As usual, they'll be sweeping for explosives anywhere the president will be going, from his hotel room to the conference sites. During the conference they'll work wherever they're needed to check incoming items or anything else that may need inspection.

It's a routine mission, but the recent slaughter in Paris, with vows of more carnage from ISIS, is on everyone's mind.

Earlier in the afternoon, handler Nate P. called his wife from his van to tell her he loves her. It's not something he normally would feel the need to do before jetting off with his dog. He wanted to let her know, just in case.

Scott L. is thinking about his bride. They got married on November 14, the day after the Paris attacks. The trip has been weighing on both of them, but they have faith that his shepherd, Nico, will make sure nothing happens.

Jorge was going to buy the mother of his children a surprise ticket to Paris as an early Christmas gift. He had loved the City of Light during his first Secret Service trip there and knew she would enjoy it as well. But now there was no way he wanted her walking around the streets of Paris alone while he worked—or even at his side during his downtime. She appreciated the thought and said she would be fine if he just brought her back a nice purse, some macarons, and a rain check.

Kim K. had a quiet Thanksgiving the night before with her boyfriend. With all the training she'd been doing, and then getting ready for the trip, there was no time to prepare a big meal. They picked up their cooked Thanksgiving dinner at a grocery store and reheated it.

Her boyfriend didn't let on if he was more concerned than usual. He knew she was in good hands with her dog, Astra. Even though the Malinois is trained only as an explosives detector, she is a textbook alpha dog, and he hoped this dog wouldn't take guff from anyone who tried to mess with Kim.

Kim's mother had been attempting to keep it normal, and to even appear optimistic. Kim read between the lines, though, when her mom was sending texts about every fifteen minutes in the week before the trip.

Most of the handlers here have worked with each other on overseas trips. They know each other well, trust each other, and have each other's backs. They talk about this over a greasy cardboard box of cold french fries someone ran to the dining hall to buy before it closed.

"I think that our training, instincts, and confidence in our dogs will keep us as safe as possible," Scott says. The others sharing the fries nod in agreement.

They also talk about the security plan for the Paris trip. It gives them confidence that they'll be in a strong position to succeed no matter what.

They're no strangers to flying to different countries during tumultuous times. Kim's first overseas trip with Astra was to Kiev not long after the Ukrainian revolution in early 2014. Conflict was ongoing in the eastern part of the country, and the protester camps at Kiev's Independence Square were still intact.

While the locals were welcoming, being so close to a conflict zone heightened Kim's situational awareness. Astra's too, it seemed. It may have gone down the leash. It seemed to go up the leash as well, with Kim becoming in tune with Astra's breathing, heart rate, hair stance (whether it stood up or lay normally), and what she calls her "crazy eyes."

One of the handlers at the Andrews flight line brings up the subject of Diesel, the French police dog who was sent in to search the apartment where the man suspected of orchestrating the attacks was holed up. The seven-year-old Belgian Malinois, who was going to be retired to his handler in a few months, was killed during a dramatic shoot-out with terrorists.

The hashtag #JeSuisChien (I am dog), a riff of the #JeSuisCharlie slogan born of the January 2015 Paris attacks that began at the satirical magazine *Charlie Hebdo*, had gone viral. Its presence in social media, in addition to ongoing reports of the whole Paris tragedy, reminds the handlers of how vulnerable their canine partners can be.

"It hits close to home," says Jorge. "It makes it a reality. You think about it and realize it could be your dog.

"These dogs are one, your partner, two, your friend, and three, your kid. You can't imagine losing them. You know it's a possibility, but you don't go there."

Sergeant John F. walks over to the handlers with some good news. The dog handler, who is serving as the team leader, had just secured their seats on the C-5. They're close to the steep, ladderlike rear stairs that lead down to the dogs, but not too close to the bathrooms, which tend to become ripe after a few hours. It can get cold by the stairs, but it's worth being able to have easy access for checking on the canines during the flight.

The C-5 is one of the world's largest military aircraft. Its cargo deck runs the length of the plane. At more than 120 feet long, 14 feet high, and 19 feet wide, the cargo area can transport some of the biggest military equipment. Today it will be carrying a variety of vehicles for the presidential entourage, other large equipment, and eight dogs in their travel kennels.

The upper deck seats about seventy-five passengers and crew. The seats face backward, toward the tail of the plane. There are no passenger windows, although some doors have tiny portholes. The setup can be disorienting, even to veteran fliers.

"It always feels like you're crashing when you're taking off, because you're facing downward, like you're falling," says Stew.

Air sickness can be a problem, especially if the C-5 has to refuel in midair. The Air Force flight crew often passes out airsick bags before the precision operation that looks something like a giant insect mating ritual. It can become turbulent as the C-5 gets in position and extends its nozzle into the top of the tanker air-craft. Fortunately, today's flight to Paris won't require refueling.

John confers with the plane's flight crew again and gulps a Red Bull as he heads over to the handlers. He's not worried about stay-ing up all night because of the caffeine. He manages to sleep no matter how much caffeine he drinks.

He updates the handlers with the latest. Loading probably won't start until at least 5 P.M.

If the flight keeps getting delayed, the handlers may have to make another run to the dining hall when it reopens for dinner. They could purchase a basic cold meal on the plane but prefer to pack their own. They've all brought food for the trip, but more along the lines of snacks than meals. John has a hearty supply of beef jerky to go with his Red Bulls. Kim packed along fruit bars and pretzels in her stash.

With time on their hands, some of the handlers bring the dogs out for a photo in front of the air field. A couple of the dogs want to eat each other. Astra is muzzled until she gets to a place far from the other dogs, at the end of the row.

John's dog, Ritshi, has zero aggression. If you pet him, he flops onto his back for belly rubs, much like Hurricane. John has to stop petting Ritshi so he'll sit tall like the others. In the background, the C-5's open shark mouth aims straight at them. So close, and yet so far . . .

The average EDT Secret Service dog will take 204 work-related plane trips in his or her career. Campaign years tend to be the busiest, with about thirty-six annually. But even during noncam-paign years, with some twenty-four trips annually, Secret Service dogs are among the top frequent fliers of the canine world.

In 2014, the most recent year for which travel figures are available, Secret Service dogs worked in twenty-seven foreign countries, including Belgium, Brazil, Chile, Colombia, the Dominican Republic, Estonia, France, Germany, Guatemala, Israel, Lithuania, Malaysia, Mexico, Morocco, Myanmar, the Netherlands, the Philippines, Poland, Saudi Arabia, South Korea, Turkey, and Ukraine.

Dog teams rarely have to fly in commercial planes these days. Most transport is by military planes, especially for those on presidential detail. Those in the Service often refer to them as "car planes," because they carry the vehicles that are part of the presidential entourage. While these planes are far less comfortable for handlers, they provide a much better setup for the dogs.

On C-5s, handlers can go downstairs to check on their dogs any time they're allowed out of their seats. Even though it's a cargo plane, and the dogs are on the cargo deck in their kennels, it's reassuring for dog and handler. If there's a problem, it can be addressed immediately.

C-17s are more popular with many handlers because the dogs are on the same deck as the handlers, with their kennels right in front of them. Handlers sit on bench seats facing the center of the plane where their dogs are. Some handlers bring small blow-up mattresses and stretch out on the floor of the plane.

A big drawback of the C-17 is that if even one dog goes to the bathroom, it reeks up the whole passenger area. There's no escape from the olfactory assault. Handlers try to schedule feedings so their dogs won't need to go, but when nature calls, sometimes it can't be ignored. Handlers clean up messes, but the aroma tends to linger.

The longer trips are more challenging. Fortunately they aren't usually straight shots. It recently took EDT dog handler Tim D. and his dog, Desi, thirty-six hours to fly to Myanmar from

Washington, D.C. The trip was divided into three legs: D.C. to Hawaii, Hawaii to Guam, Guam to Myanmar. They had about two to four hours between flights, so Desi got decent breaks.

Tim gives Desi a light sedative before long trips so she won't bark the whole time. Incessant barking is something that no one holed up in a C-17 with a dog needs—least of all the dog. But despite the meds, Desi is always raring to go for walks between flights.

In the past, dogs usually took commercial flights. If there was room in the cabin, they could sometimes join their handlers. Training assistant and former handler Leth O. was able to fly with his dog, Reik, right beside him several times. Reik sometimes even got to sit in a seat, and since the dog liked looking out the window, Leth would give up the window seat for his dog if he had one.

Reik would sit looking out the window until he couldn't see anything anymore, and then he'd lie down and sleep until it was time to land. "He was a great traveler," Leth says.

Usually dogs on commercial flights ended up in the cargo hold. Handlers were concerned about temperature, pressure, and everything that could go wrong when their dogs weren't with them or under their care. Worrisome as it was, no one recalls anything going seriously awry.

But flying commercial wasn't always without incident.

On a return trip from Atlanta, former handler Cliff Cusick was waiting for the plane to pull away from the gate when a man ran on and hurriedly told him that his dog had gotten loose from his kennel and was running around on the active runway.

"There's no way that could be my dog, sir," Cusick told him. "He was very firmly secured."

"I'm sorry but we will shoot your dog if we have to in order to prevent a catastrophe," the man told him.

Nice way to start a trip.

"I was scared to death," recalls Cusick, who rushed out of the plane with the man. They got to where Buddy was, and Buddy ran straight to him.

"He was so disoriented and happy to see me. The feeling was very mutual," he says.

He later found out that a baggage handler had slightly opened the kennel to pet Buddy, and he got loose.

Former handler Wes Williams's dog, Arco, pulled two getaways when he was in the cargo compartment of a commercial plane. Baggage handlers had nothing to do with his escapes. He broke loose on his own. When workers opened the cargo area, there was Arco, out of his kennel, wagging and wanting to go for a walk. Williams had to use a chain around the kennel and an extra latch to keep his dog secured after those incidents.

And then there's every dog lover's nightmare: arriving at the destination airport, and no dog showing up. In 1988 Don Racine boarded a direct flight from Chicago to Dulles. When he landed, Racine waited for his dog, but he never came.

No one knew what had become of Rex. After too long, the cargo department at Dulles got a call from the airline's San Diego cargo department. A dog in a kennel marked for Dulles was sitting there with no one claiming him. Apparently the two planes had been side by side in Chicago, and a baggage worker put the dog in the one bound for San Diego. Once they figured out the mistake, back Rex went into a plane, this time bound for Dulles.

It had been twelve hours since Racine had last seen Rex. He expected him and his crate to be a hot mess. But when his dog finally arrived, the crate was spotless. Racine opened the door to let Rex out and was about to embrace him and leash him when

Rex ran out of the kennel and charged out the door of the airport. As soon as he got outside, he relieved himself.

"He just didn't want to do it in his kennel or in the airport. He was a good dog. I can't imagine what it must have been like for him," the former handler says.

Handlers still sometimes have to take commercial flights, but it's something most wouldn't choose, even though they have more creature comforts.

"Flying commercial with your dog sucks," says Stew. "You're thinking, 'Oh God, please let them be OK,' as you sit there. The whole time you're worried.

"When you look out and they're loading your dog, it's not like, 'Well, there goes my rifle.' It's more like, 'Well, there goes my son.'"

The change to using mostly military flights came in the late 1990s, in part because of tightening security in the years after the devastating Oklahoma City bombing, according to former dog handler and unit commander Barry Lewis. The dogs were needed more than ever, and getting them back to the nation's capital after a detail was a priority. There was more control with dedicated military flights than with commercial flights and they were in synch with the president's travel. It was safer for the dogs as well.

"I wish we'd have been able to use the car planes when I was a handler," says former handler Henry Sergent. "It would have saved us a lot of headaches and a lot of worry."

Not that military flights have always gone perfectly for the dogs . . .

Stew's dog Nero did not like any kind of plane ride. The loud noises, being cooped up in a travel kennel for hours on end, and the unsettling sensation of takeoff and landing can rattle the calmest of dogs. Nero was a revered working dog—"athletically, he could do things you can't even imagine," Brian M. says—but he wasn't low-key. His amped-up temperament was a boon on the job but worked against him on planes.

To keep his Malinois from panting and barking too much during a flight from Waco, Texas, back to Washington, D.C., Stew had given him a vet-recommended dose of Benadryl a couple of hours before the flight. It usually just took the edge off, which was all Stew wanted. Nero's kennel was strapped right next to a presidential limousine—a perfect location, since the dog wouldn't be tempted to get into a barking contest with it, as he would have if a dog were his neighbor.

Stew shut the door of the travel kennel and secured it for the flight. Nero watched calmly. It was a promising start for what Stew hoped would be a short, uneventful ride home.

What could possibly go wrong?

Stew climbed the steep stairs to the passenger deck and strapped into his seat, a row away from the stairs. The C-5 taxied to the runway. The hulking plane gained momentum, and the front wheels lifted off the ground. Stew tipped slightly forward in his rear-facing seat and braced for the sharp ascent.

He heard what sounded like a yell. Somehow it pierced through the screaming engine noise. Then another. It seemed to be coming from the cargo deck. Stew let gravity push his torso forward so he was able to see a sliver of the lower deck.

He thought he saw an airman running below. Strange that someone would be running during takeoff. He leaned forward more and saw the airman bolting between the limousines. It didn't look like he was running *to* something. More like he was running *from* something.

Stew had a bad feeling about this.

An instant later he saw a familiar flash of fur.

"Loose dog!" someone yelled from below.

Stew flew into action. He undid his seat belt, and as the plane sped skyward in full takeoff mode, fought his way down the stairs against the plane's upward momentum.

"Heel!" he yelled as loudly as he could as he raced down. "Heel!"

The dog wasn't having any of that.

The C-5's engines were at full throttle, and the floor underneath Stew and his dog and the airman shook and heaved and threw off their balance. The presidential vehicles bounced in place. The airman, clad in a green jumpsuit, managed to continue evading Nero, but the dog was closing in.

Anyone who could make out the scene from the upper deck would have witnessed quite a spectacle: a man yelling and chasing a dog who was racing around presidential vehicles and chasing a man in a green jumpsuit who was now scrambling to climb up the plane's curved metal interior wall.

Stew caught up with Nero just as he was within biting range of the airman. The dog turned around to bite Stew but recognized him and stopped. Stew grabbed his dog and checked in with the airman, who was shaken but hadn't been hurt. He brought Nero back to the kennel to figure out how this could have happened.

The chrome grille door of the plastic travel kennel was open and swaying with the airplane's movement. On closer inspection, he saw that his dog had thrashed against the door so hard that the metal latches that fit into the plastic inserts for the door at the top and bottom were bent. With the mechanism compromised, the dog had sprung out like a prank snake in a nut can.

After letting the dog unwind a little, Stew got Nero back in the kennel. He wound three cargo straps horizontally around the kennel and zip-tied the door shut. The jury-rigging kept Nero in check through the rest of the flight.

After that, Stew switched to a metal Ray Allen travel kennel—just as roomy as the other kennel, but basically a dog vault. Nero never escaped again.

Years later, after Nero retired, sometimes he would dream with his paws paddling the air in an unsteady fashion. Stew wondered if he was back in the C-5, reliving the high-flying adventure of his crazy glory days.

At around 4:30 P.M., John tells the handlers they may be loading soon. Jorge walks over to his van to make sure his gear is ready to go. He unzips a large black backpack. It opens down the middle, revealing several compartments on both sides. They're marked with yellow embroidered labels, indicating which ones hold treats, leashes, first aid equipment, bags, and training aids. He likes to be organized.

One item he hasn't yet packed is his can of Lysol Neutra Air Sanitizing Spray. He hopes that if any dogs must do their business, the Rejuvenating Morning Linen scent will help make it a little more tolerable.

A few minutes later, it's finally time to start driving the vans toward the flight line.

"Everyone needs to check tires first. Please go ahead and help each other out," John says. As the vans approach the tarmac, the drivers work together to inspect tire treads for pebbles or other foreign objects that could cause damage.

The vans—emergency flashers blinking and headlights on—snake toward the flight line, going slower than the fifteen-miles-per-hour speed limit. But it's still not time to board. Instead of driving toward the C-5 to the left, the vans turn to the right, into a parking area that runs along a low, long building.

One by one, the white vans back up to the wall behind them. When they're done with the graceful four-wheel choreography, they look like eight piano keys, perfectly lined up.

A host of presidential support and protection vehicles, all black, slowly make their way to the area in front of the vans and turn around to face the C-5. It's a long process, involving what some handlers think are more vehicles than normal.

Handlers wait in their vans, walk their dogs, talk to their dogs, and watch the parade of Secret Service vehicles and personnel. Several Counter Assault Team (CAT) members gather near the vans in a circle and have a discussion. Wallets come out, and everyone passes money to a team leader. They'll be on the airplane food plan tonight.

A little after 6 P.M. the first of the presidential vehicles rolls toward the C-5. It's dark now except for the headlights and the glow from inside the C-5's wide-open front end. But the vehicles don't drive right onto the plane. They line up and wait, yet again.

The canine vans cut carefully in among the limos and SUVs and park close to the plane. The handlers will be loading their dogs and gear before any of the vehicles can drive onto the C-5. They pull their empty travel kennels aboard with the leashes they've attached—a trick that saves a lot of hassle. Most bring their roll-on suitcases and other gear at the same time.

The handlers walk up the ramp into the mouth of the shark, and down the belly of the beast to the back of the cargo deck. A pallet is waiting, and they arrange the kennels in two rows of four, right next to each other. They run off to park their vans and grab their dogs.

Kim waits as the handlers of Ritshi, Bris, and Tarzan put their dogs in their kennels in the row of kennels facing the back of the plane. Hers is the last dog to board. Astra stops to sniff Bris in his kennel, just to the left of her own. She recognizes him. They've worked together quite a bit. He's on her cool list. She moves on.

She then checks out the neighbor in the kennel to the right of hers. It's Tarzan, Nate's dog. She doesn't work with him much, and he's not yet on her short list of acceptable dogs. She barks and growls at him. Tarzan returns the greeting.

Once one dog starts, a chain reaction often follows and leads to an unpleasant racket that's difficult to quell. Kim tells her dog to knock it off, hoping to stop it before it spreads beyond Tarzan. Astra stops barking and walks into her kennel. Having no one to argue with, Tarzan lets bygones be bygones.

The kennels are strapped down and the vehicles finally start rolling up the ramp one at a time. Aircrew loadmasters tell the drivers where to park their vehicles so the weight is distributed evenly. Other crew members secure the vehicles so they stay put. It takes about ninety minutes to load everything.

The C-5 takes off at 8:30 P.M.

It touches down in Paris the next morning.

Astra, who had been quiet for the whole flight, is the first to bark once the crew starts undoing the vehicles. This inspires the other dogs to sound off.

You could choose to hear it as a bunch of dogs barking. Or you could hear it as the handlers did: *Welcome to Paris!*

It is a whirlwind trip, with dogs sweeping the president's hotel, the Le Bourget Exhibition Center, the Château de la Muette, and other key sites. During downtime, handlers check in with loved ones to let them know all is well. Some walk their dogs near the Eiffel Tower. And one shops for a nice purse and macarons.

When Jorge's children awaken on the morning of December 2, they find their father just back from Paris. They jump into his arms and bury themselves in his hug.

Yuri, who had just fallen asleep, wakes up and sees the happy reunion. He watches and wags, still lying with his head on his bed.

"Yuri!" Jorge's daughter exclaims. She and her brother run over to him. Yuri wags a couple more times, closes his eyes, and falls back to sleep in their embrace.

CHAPTER 10

INTRUDER ALERT!

There was a time when people could stroll around the White House grounds and even walk into the White House on their own without getting arrested or making headlines.

The "People's House" was highly accessible to the public for much of its history.

Thomas Jefferson wanted to ensure that the people of the new nation felt his house was also their own. He welcomed the public into the White House most days, although not early in the morning. He staged exhibitions—including a showcase of artifacts from the Lewis and Clark expedition—to draw more people into the Executive Mansion.

He even displayed two "perfectly gentle" and "quite good humored" grizzly bear cubs in an enclosure on the White House lawn for two months.

Andrew Jackson's and William Henry Harrison's presidential inaugurals resembled Executive Mansion frat parties, with scores of rowdy, drunk partygoers coming and going.

And then there was Jackson's 1,400-pound block of cheese, a

gift he decided to share with the public nearly two years after receiving it. On February 22, 1837, he opened the White House to anyone who wanted some cheese, which was placed in the foyer. It wasn't so much a chance to get to know his constituents—he was weeks from the end of his presidency. It was, quite ingeniously, one of the biggest regifting opportunities in history.

The cheese did not stand alone that day. Thousands of visitors flocked to the Executive Mansion, not put off by the ripe cheese's odor, which one observer described as "an evil smelling horror" whose potent stench reached far beyond the White House. Prominent journalist Benjamin Perley Poore wrote about the event in his *Reminiscences:*

> For hours did a crowd of men, women, and boys hack at the cheese, many taking large hunks of it away with them. When they commenced, the cheese weighed one thousand four hundred pounds, and only a small piece was saved for the President's use. The air was redolent with cheese, the carpet was slippery with cheese, and nothing else was talked about at Washington that day. Even the scandal about the wife of the President's Secretary of War was forgotten in the tumultuous jubilation of that great occasion.

It was not the end of the cheese, though. It lives on, at least symbolically. In the fictional White House TV drama, *The West Wing,* Big Block of Cheese Day referred to an annual tradition of granting White House access and attention to obscure interest groups one day a year.

The Obama administration continued the theme of opening the White House to the public through three annual, daylong Big Block of Cheese Day social media events. The public was invited

Explosives detection dog Astra enjoys some downtime at dusk near Air Force Two during a vice presidential detail in Rhode Island. *(Courtesy of Kim K.)*

Leth O. and his dog Reik traveled on protective missions to Germany, Japan, Thailand, Cambodia, South Korea, Oman, Jordan, Romania, and forty-nine states— all but Maine. Reik is now happily retired and living the good life with Leth's family. *(Courtesy of Leth O.)*

Two weeks after the November 2015 Paris terror attacks, Astra and handler Kim K. were among eight Secret Service dog teams that traveled to the City of Light for a presidential detail. *(Courtesy of Kim K.)*

The first canine class of the United States Secret Service graduated on April 30, 1976. The German shepherds had been donated or plucked from shelters. *(Courtesy of Bill Shegogue)*

President Ronald Reagan laughs at a quip made by handler Tony Ferrara, who keeps a firm grip on his 110-pound Dutch shepherd, Bart. *(Courtesy of the Ronald Reagan Library)*

Presidents and vice presidents have visited the James J. Rowley Training Center (RTC) and watched demonstrations of the dogs who protect them and their families. Here President Barack Obama listens to a brief on the canines before a demo with a tactical dog. *(Courtesy of "Stew")*

Secret Service Emergency Response Team (ERT) members typically place first overall in the patrol portion of a popular K-9 Olympics they attend every few years. Left to right, canines Baco, Jason, and Nitro worked with their handlers to bring home the "gold" at the 2015 K-9 Olympics. *(Courtesy of the United States Secret Service)*

ERT canine Spike and handler Jim S. won several top awards at the 2010 K-9 Olympics, including first in individual and team patrol. Jim's wife and children bestowed the first-place ribbon on seven-year-old Spike when he arrived home. *(Courtesy of Jim S.)*

Belgian Malinois Jason was eight years old when he competed in the 2015 K-9 Olympics with handler Shawn S., but his age didn't get in the way of placing first in the challenging obstacle course and being part of the Secret Service team that won first in patrol. *(Courtesy of the United States Secret Service)*

ERT dog handler Larry C. has been watching over the White House with his dog Maximus since 2009. "Maximus is like my own child," he says. It's a common sentiment among handlers. *(Courtesy of Larry C.)*

Above: The first time handler Sal S. brought home his explosives detection dog, Daro, the 110-pound German shepherd walked up the stairs, turned around, lay down, and sighed. From then on, this was Daro's spot. *(Courtesy of Sal S.)*

"Friendly Dog" Roadee (left) at home with sisters Bailey and Ciela. Whenever a sponge, dog bed, or anything else in the house is destroyed, all eyes turn to Roadee, who is inevitably the guilty party. *(Courtesy of Josh B.)*

Roadee takes his job of sniffing for explosives on humans seriously, but tourists who see him working outside the White House fence often chuckle and ask, "What kind of dog is *that*?" *(Courtesy of the author)*

Below: "Friendly Dogs" like Dyson go for walks for a living. Rain, shine, sleet, heat, snow, ice—they spend their work days weaving among tourists near the White House fence, focused on their mission. *(Courtesy of the author)*

Handler Nate C. has to be extra vigilant about keeping Dyson from getting too hot after the springer spaniel nearly died from a heatstroke. Nate spent almost every waking and sleeping minute at Dyson's side at the military veterinary hospital that treated him. *(Courtesy of the author)*

Jon M. offers his dog Rex a cup of water from a water cooler while sweeping a building for explosives in preparation for Pope Francis's 2015 visit to Washington, DC. *(Courtesy of the author)*

Canine program instructor Steve M. pets a potential future Secret Service explosives-sniffing dog during weeklong testing at Vohne Liche Kennels (VLK) in Indiana. *(Courtesy of the author)*

The Secret Service has a reputation for being very picky when it comes to dog selection. Here canine training assistant Shawn G. releases a candidate from the Service's dog trailer for testing at VLK. *(Courtesy of the author)*

ERT handlers and dogs train for every imaginable scenario, including rappelling down tall buildings. *(Courtesy of "Stew")*

ERT canine Jardan leaps up to bite decoy "Stew" during training at RTC. ERT handlers are pretty much guaranteed bites and injuries throughout their career, despite protective gear. *(Courtesy of "Stew")*

Secret Service ERT dogs and handlers take part in a fast-rope exercise from a hovering MV-22 Osprey. *(Courtesy of "Stew")*

Hurricane, here with handler Marshall M., became an international hero after an incident on the north grounds of the White House in 2014. *(Courtesy of Marshall M.)*

Hurricane may be able to take down the toughest bad guys, but he's also an extremely affectionate dog. During this awards ceremony he had no trouble convincing US Secretary of Homeland Security Jeh Johnson to pet him. *(Courtesy of the United States Secret Service)*

to chat with White House staff, the First Lady, senior cabinet members, and others via Twitter, Facebook, Instagram, and Tumblr. Bad cheese puns abounded. ("It's That Time of Gruyère: Big Block of Cheese Day Is Back" was the title of the 2016 event's White House blog entry.)

During the centuries between the original block of cheese and today's version, White House security became far tighter. Threats and dangers, and questions about the safety of its residents, gradually chipped away at the idea of an open house of the people and for the people. Fences got stronger. Gates became locked and fortified. A lone "watch box" for sentries built during Jackson's presidency became a security force thousands strong—including an impressive group of canines.

World War II saw the end of free public access to the grounds. Following the bombings of the Marine barracks and U.S. Embassy in Beirut in 1983, concrete Jersey barriers, later replaced by bollards, went up around the White House complex. As a result of the Oklahoma City bombing in 1995, the portion of Pennsylvania Avenue flanking the north grounds of the White House complex was permanently closed to vehicular traffic.

Until 9/11, people who wanted to tour the White House could show up during open times and walk in. Tour demand became high enough that in 1976, a booth was set up for first-come, first-served tickets.

After 9/11, access dramatically changed. The current system of applying through congressional representatives and being screened through a security process means would-be visitors have to apply at least a few weeks ahead of their intended visits.

But whether entry to the White House involved few barriers or many, there have always been people who didn't want to play by the rules.

Agents and officers have heard it all.

"You'd be amazed how many people have appointments with the president," jokes Bill. "For some reason, they're not usually on his calendar."

Some genuinely think they can walk in and tell the president what's on their minds. They ask officers or agents how they can be let in through the gate and into the White House to speak with the president. When they discover that it's not how it works, there's disappointment, sometimes embarrassment, occasionally anger.

Others don't ask. They just find a way to get in. These men and women usually make headlines now, but the White House has been dealing with such interlopers since the beginning.

In 1800, John Adams became the first president to live in the White House. It didn't take long for a deranged man to walk into the White House and threaten to kill him.

There would be no Secret Service for sixty-five more years, and it wouldn't be until 1901 that the agency began its mission of presidential protection. Still, the second president of the United States could have cried out for help and found able-bodied assistance. Instead, he sat down with the man in his office and calmed him on his own. The man, he would later note, never returned.

Tightening security through the years hasn't stopped those intent on making their way into the Executive Mansion. Some have appeared quite sane and proven perfectly harmless.

In 1930, a well-attired man strode into the White House and interrupted the dinner of President Herbert Hoover before the Secret Service apprehended him. He turned out to be a curious and intrepid tourist.

During World War II, President Franklin Delano Roosevelt

was watching a movie in the White House with some guests. "When the lights came on, a neatly dressed young man, a complete stranger, was standing next to FDR," Margaret Truman wrote in her book *The President's House*. The man asked for the president's autograph, which FDR gave to him before the Secret Service escorted him away.

The intrusions that stir the most public concern tend to involve people jumping over the fence, or crashing into it, or flying aircraft over or onto the property.

The 1970s saw some of the most dramatic breaches.

In 1974 an Army officer stole a helicopter and ended up landing it on the South Lawn after the Secret Service opened fire. On Christmas Day the same year, Marshall Fields, the son of a retired American diplomat, crashed his Chevy Impala into a White House gate. He was wearing "Arabic style clothing," according to reports, and said he was the Messiah. He wore what he claimed were explosives strapped to his body and negotiated for four hours with the Secret Service until he surrendered. The explosives turned out to be flares.

The next year, on the night before Thanksgiving, Gerald Gainous Jr. managed to scale a wall on the south grounds and evade detection despite setting off alarms. He spent between an hour and a half and two hours on the grounds and was caught only after approaching President Gerald Ford's daughter, Susan, as she unloaded photography equipment from a car.

It wouldn't be Gainous's last attempt. By the following August, he had scaled the fence three more times.

In 1976, a Secret Service officer fatally shot a cab driver wielding a three-foot metal pipe while the president was in residence.

Dennis Martin, who would go on to become an inspector with the Secret Service's Special Operation Division, is still haunted by an event that took place during the Carter administration when he was posted at the White House as a Uniformed Division officer.

"We were like human dogs. We would wait and wait and wait, and somebody would come over and you get that crash alarm at the White House and then you get this adrenaline rush and you go like a dog after him to get him.

"Back in the day when Pennsylvania Avenue was open, people would ram the fence with vehicles. The fence was reinforced in the 1970s, but a lot of people didn't realize this. One night a guy with an Oldsmobile Delta 88, he is out on Pennsylvania Avenue going about thirty-five miles an hour. This is probably nine thirty at night. There's nobody out in the street but I remember that car turned to the fence and hit it. The force catapulted the car back to Pennsylvania Avenue.

"I ran out there and pulled my gun and grabbed the guy and put him against the column and started handcuffing him. Then I heard another door open on the car. I was out there alone and there's a door opening and I see there's a little girl, maybe five years old, coming out from under the dashboard. He had brought his daughter with him. What was he thinking?

"I remember the guy saying, 'I want to see the preacher! I want to see the preacher.' He was talking about President Jimmy Carter."

The man did not get an audience with Carter, but he did get charged with destruction of property and unlawful entry. Martin still wonders what became of that frightened little girl, and what, if anything, she remembers from that night.

Each breach of the White House grounds causes the Secret Service to review security to see how it can be improved. Fence reinforcement was a result of this kind of review. If it hadn't been strengthened when the man rammed his heavy car into it, the situation could have ended very differently.

Secret Service canines have been part of the answer to bolstering White House safety since dog teams began working there in 1976. Canines have been an integral part of the security plan for decades, greatly increasing in job scope and number since the program's inception.

Handlers from the program's pre-9/11 years say the policy about how they could use their dogs on the White House property was much more conservative than it is today. They could release their dogs to apprehend intruders only under dire circumstances.

"Either I had to be in fear of my life or I needed to be able to articulate that someone else's life was in danger when that individual came over the fence," says former handler Sergent.

They never had to release a dog on the grounds to apprehend a suspect. The main job of dogs after a fence infiltration was to check the grounds to make sure the suspect hadn't left behind anything that could do harm. They also made sure no one else had charged in and hidden while officers were distracted with the other suspect.

Because the patrol and apprehension portion of the dogs' skill set wasn't being used much, in 1997, the dogs went from dual purpose to single purpose, focusing entirely on detecting explosives. Noses were in, teeth were out. At least for a few years.

But after the 9/11 terrorist attacks, and the subsequent U.S. engagement in Iraq, the Secret Service examined the frightening reality of what the White House could face at the hands of suicide bombers or other terrorists. The Emergency Response Team was tapped to beef up its presence with a program that would put badass dogs with badass ERT members outside the White House.

"The idea was that if we did encounter a suicide bomber, we could utilize this new tool to intercept the guy, and either cause a premature detonation or at least get our team more time and slow the guy down to get prepared and get in position to mitigate the threat," says Jim S.

"It's about putting pressure on the guy and making sure he doesn't harm the president," he says. "It's all for the presidents and their families."

The ERT Tactical Canine Unit began in 2003. These dogs wouldn't be trained in bomb detection at all. Their main purpose is to stop bad guys in their tracks. The dog teams, in the words of Stew, "detect [people], extract, apprehend, and deter."

Dogs are considered a less-than-lethal force. "We aren't trigger-happy," Stew says. "No one wants to shoot anyone. These dogs provide additional protection for the White House, team members, and even the suspect."

In other words, without a dog to help stop someone who looks like a threat, a lethal weapon might become the next option.

Of course, circumstances dictate how and if dogs will be used during a given situation. Anyone who comes over the fence is taken very seriously.

"Every one of our deployments could be a suicide bomber," says Stew. "We don't want to kill anyone, we're not a bunch of cowboys. When we deploy, you have to think these people are coming to take my or my protectee's life. You can't assume anyone is safe. Maybe that person who got over really is just an old woman. But she could be a diversion, or strapped with explosives."

The Secret Service walks a fine line when it comes to protecting the White House. Yes, anyone could be a terrorist. But in reality, many White House intruders or would-be White House visitors are mentally ill, and often not armed or dangerous.

Most of the prospective uninvited visitors with mental illness suffer from some kind of schizophrenic disorder—usually paranoid schizophrenia. Gainous was eventually diagnosed with this and committed to the ward at St. Elizabeths Hospital, the usual destination for such "visitors" at the time.

These men and women were known by psychiatrists and the Secret Service as "White House cases." They were usually held at St. Elizabeths for one to three weeks, with the goal of getting them properly medicated so their psychoses came under control.

Many people with paranoid schizophrenia hear voices. (Some who try to get to the White House think the voices are messages from members of the Secret Service.) They may believe they are being spied on 24/7, or that great harm is going to come to them or important people. In an effort to make everything better, they set off to get help from the most powerful person they know: the president of the United States.

"Most of those who are White House Cases consider the president a benevolent authority, and they typically come to ask for some intervention on their own behalf, or to advise or warn the President in some way," according to a 1985 paper in the *American Journal of Psychiatry*, cowritten by David Shore, MD, a top researcher in the field.

E. Fuller Torrey, MD, a research psychiatrist specializing in serious mental illnesses, says some of the mentally ill who seek an audience with the president suffer from bipolar disorder. During periods of grandiosity, they might think they have a direct link to the president, and that they belong in the White House. Others suffering from delusions may think they're being called by the president, or that the president simply must hear about an important idea or invention of theirs.

In the late 1970s and early 1980s, Torrey was in charge of the ward at St. Elizabeths where most of the White House cases ended up. Around that time, the cases numbered about one hundred per year—so many that right next to the "name" field on the hospital's standard admissions form was a yes/no box to check for "White House case."

Torrey recalls one woman who insisted she was married to President Ronald Reagan.

"She would sit across the street in Lafayette Park day after day, expecting to be let into the White House because she was the president's wife," says Torrey, author of *American Psychosis: How the Federal Government Destroyed the Mental Illness Treatment System*.

She was eventually brought to St. Elizabeths, held for a few days, put on medication, deemed relatively harmless, and released. She didn't stay on her meds and went back to being the "other" Mrs. Reagan.

The men and women who became White House cases flocked to the nation's capital from across the United States, deeply driven to see the president.

Eugene Stammeyer, chief psychologist at St. Elizabeths at the time, gave this colorful if heartbreaking description of a few White House cases to the *Washington Post* in 1977:

> They really do come barefoot, some of the time. One lady sold her blood to get here. A man lived outdoors near the Lincoln Memorial for six months, eating out of garbage cans behind restaurants, because he spent every penny he could scrounge on phone calls to the President. There was a man who brought a roll of toilet paper all the way from California to give to President Nixon because he was sure Nixon couldn't afford his own.

St. Elizabeths has been taking in White House cases almost since it opened its doors in 1855 as the Government Hospital for the Insane. The number of mentally ill inpatients peaked at seven thousand to eight thousand in the 1950s.

The introduction of the first effective antipsychotics in the mid-1950s primed the pump that would end up purging patients from hospitals over the next few decades. By the 1970s, St. Elizabeths had only about three thousand live-in patients. Today it has fewer than five hundred.

White House cases are no longer called White House cases, and they're reportedly rarely seen at St. Elizabeths. The Secret Service declines to talk about what happens now when people who appear to be mentally ill need further evaluation, but in 2014, *The Atlantic* reported that the agency transports them to one of the local hospitals where they can get an emergency psychiatric examination. They may be involuntarily committed for a short time while a treatment protocol is worked out.

The "White House cases" moniker may be gone, but there's likely no shortage of people who fit the description.

"I will be very surprised if in fact the White House cases are fewer than they were thirty years ago," says Torrey. "We now have more homeless who are mentally ill, more people in jails and prisons who are mentally ill, and the quality of public services for people with serious mental illness has deteriorated markedly. White House cases have almost surely increased as well."

Dozens of men and women have scaled the White House fence since the ERT Tactical Canine Unit began its watch outside the Executive Mansion in 2003.

At least one was a repeat offender. A man who reportedly believed his family was being terrorized and poisoned thought President George W. Bush was the only person who could help. Brian

Patterson, of New Mexico, jumped over the White House fence four times between 2004 and 2006 in an effort to meet the president, tying Gainous's attempts at entry.

An Arkansas man who jumped the fence in 2005 wasn't intent on an audience with President Bill Clinton, but rather with his daughter, Chelsea. Shawn Cox thought she still lived there (she didn't) and that he was destined to marry her.

"He insisted that Chelsea Clinton was in the White House as well as President Bush and described how former President Bill Clinton had told him that [Cox] was 'going to marry my daughter' when he had met him in Arkansas," a psychologist wrote in a court document, according to a news report. The document also stated that Cox said his head was "a cell phone implanted by Jesus."

In 2007, Catalino Lucas Diaz, a spry sixty-six-year-old man, scaled the fence and claimed he had a bomb and he would throw a missile. The Secret Service used a water cannon to destroy the package he brought with him. It contained nothing dangerous.

On the thirteenth anniversary of 9/11, a twenty-six-year-old man wearing a Pokémon hat and carrying something in his hands—which turned out to be a Pikachu doll—jumped over the fence and was quickly subdued. The man's mother said the doll was his best friend since childhood. She said he had been suffering from mental illness for years, and that he may have become despondent when his health insurance wasn't accepted where he was seeking care.

"He went to talk to the president about his insurance and health care," she said.

Among the others ending up on the wrong side of the fence since the introduction of ERT dog teams have been a Code Pink protestor who was on a hunger strike for two months, and a Japanese man wearing "military style camouflage clothing," who later said he was in the U.S. on a visa and had run out of money a couple of days earlier.

In 2014, a toddler managed to squeeze through the bars of the fence just before President Barack Obama was going to brief the press on Iraq. The brief was delayed while the matter was resolved. It didn't take long.

"We were going to wait until he learned to talk to question him, but in lieu of that he got a timeout and was sent on [his] way with [his] parents," joked Secret Service spokesman Ed Donovan.

The toddler is probably the only fence infiltrator the Secret Service hasn't been too concerned about, but it's a safe bet that someone made sure the toddler wasn't being used as a distraction for something bad going down elsewhere on the grounds.

Considering all the people who have jumped the fence since the Tactical Canine Unit started, it's quite remarkable that ERT dogs didn't need to physically apprehend anyone for more than a decade.

Dogs have been involved in stopping fence jumpers in other ways. The canine teams are trained to deploy out of their vans in an extraordinarily short amount of time. (The Secret Service asks that the number of seconds not be revealed.) They bolt to where the handler deems he and his dog would be most effective and set to work to "convince" the suspect that he or she needs to freeze and then lie down prone.

It's a team effort, with the handler yelling to the intruder that he will release his dog if the suspect doesn't cooperate, and the dog barking at the end of the leash and looking like he would dearly love to pitch in with his teeth.

On September 20, 2011, Jim sat in his van on the White House's north grounds in the middle of the day, watching the crowds at the fence line for anything suspicious. His Malinois, Spike, lay in the back, relaxing but ready for anything if called upon.

Jim and Spike had been together since 2005 and in 2010 had taken first place in the patrol competition at Vohne Liche's K-9 Olympics. But Spike was getting older and would be retiring in the next few months. Jim didn't want to think about what life would be like not having Spike at his side at work every day.

They'd had some exciting times together keeping presidents safe. He wondered if Spike would ever see any action again. He knew that Spike wouldn't mind one last exciting protective detail before hanging up his leash.

A couple of hours into their shift, Jim saw trouble. A man had swiftly scrambled over the wrought iron fence and was in a dead sprint toward the White House, dashing straight in the direction of their van.

Jim felt like he was moving in slow motion as he and Spike deployed from the van and ran toward the man. The first time he had headed off a fence jumper, without a canine, it felt like it took him an hour, instead of seconds. It's not an uncommon sensation in this kind of work.

As the man ran toward the White House, and toward him and Spike, Jim shouted for him to stop and get on the ground or he'd release his dog. The man didn't comply. No other ERT officers had arrived yet.

He wanted the guy to give up without Spike having to bite

him. But the fence jumper showed no sign of relenting. Spike barked steadily and pulled at the leash, anxious to move in.

Jim made his warning announcement again and let a few feet of line out of his hands, allowing Spike to run closer. He was going to play it by fractions of a second. He could stop the dog any time. The guy didn't know this. But when he saw the reality of this dog and those teeth, he gave up and knelt down in the grass.

Jim didn't need a leash to stop Spike. All it took was a word and the dog halted. Other ERT officers had arrived, weapons drawn in case the man decided to pull a fast one.

Spike continued to bark, front end down, hind end up, ready to help again any time he was needed.

Marshall, who was on ERT but not yet in canine, moved in to handcuff the intruder. He took extra time because as he was patting him down, he felt hard objects up and down the man's chest. He needed to assess whether these were explosives, part of a suicide vest, or something else. Fortunately they were rocks, loads of them, lining the front of his baggy jacket.

Marshall glanced over at the dog barking to his right—this dog who was so passionate about his work and had just stopped this guy in his tracks—and it hit him. He wanted to be holding the leash of a dog like Spike one day. He decided right there on the green grass of the White House that he was going to do whatever it took to become an ERT dog handler.

Spike retired a few months later. That deployment would turn out to be his last. Years later, well after Spike passed away, Jim still has a link immediately available on his cell phone. Click it and you'll see the video of the last part of the action that day, captured by a far-off news crew. It shows his partner barking with a passion and fully immersed in doing what he most loved to do.

Jim has watched it dozens of times, and it still makes him smile.

"I'm going to keep this forever," he says.

The White House perimeter fence is seven feet six inches tall with a horizontal railing running under decorative spear points, called finials, at the top. As the dozens who have breached it could attest, the fence is not all that hard to climb.

It's an issue multiple agencies would dearly love to remedy.

In the summer of 2015, the Secret Service and U.S. Park Police installed a removable anticlimb feature consisting of small, sharp spikes that fit between the finials. The spikes are temporary until there's a better way of deterring would-be jumpers, or at least slowing down anyone determined to get closer to the Executive Mansion and its occupants.

An independent panel convened by the Department of Homeland Security recommended the fence be made four or five feet taller. The rationale was given in an executive summary of the report:

> A better fence can provide time, and time is crucial
> to the protective mission. Every additional second of
> response time provided by a fence that is more difficult
> to climb makes a material difference in ensuring the
> President's safety and protecting the symbol that is the
> White House. Additionally, the ease with which
> "pranksters" and the mentally ill can climb the current
> fence puts Secret Service personnel in a precarious po-
> sition: When someone jumps the fence, they must

decide, in a split-second, whether to use lethal force on a person who may not actually pose a viable threat to the President or the White House. By deterring these more frivolous threats, a more effective fence can minimize the instances when such difficult decision making is required.

Other ideas have already been rejected. Barbed wire, a water-filled moat, and an electrified fence aren't going to cut it at the White House. Neither is a giant solid wall. The panel noted that it had confidence that adjustments "can be made without diminishing the aesthetic beauty or historic character of the White House grounds."

A *Washington Post* editorial in January 2015 noted that "the security of the president and his family must be paramount. But it's not clear that security depends on or is enhanced by all of the incremental militarization near the White House."

Many in the Secret Service believe that a beefed-up ERT canine presence could go a long way toward making the White House more secure without making it look militaristic. To that end, the Tactical Canine Unit has been tapped to increase its presence at the White House.

Whatever happens to the fence, there will probably still be those who succeed in scaling it. An enlarged welcoming committee of tactical canines will help do what no fence can do.

It wasn't until March 30, 2014, that an ERT canine put the bite on a fence jumper. It was a misty, rainy day, and the press area outside the White House was empty. The event would go largely unreported, garnering three paragraphs in an AP story that didn't note that a dog was involved.

Subsequent one-paragraph stories did mention a dog, but only with a line from a Secret Service press release, which stated that after "failing to comply with lawful orders, the subject was subdued by a U.S. Secret Service Uniformed Division K-9 unit."

After the man jumped the fence, he ran around erratically on the north grounds, evading capture and not listening to commands to stop, an ERT member would later describe. When he started running once more for the White House, the handler gave another command to halt, and when it went unheeded, he let the dog settle the situation. The dog sped toward the man, grabbed him by the forearm, and took him down.

As soon as the man was under the control of the ERT, the handler asked the dog to release his wrist.

The man was arrested and taken to a hospital for treatment of minor injuries.

The first real-life apprehension by an ERT canine happened with no fanfare. And that was fine with the ERT guys. "We're not in it for the glory," says a handler. "We just want to get the job done."

When standing among tourists admiring the White House, it's fairly common to hear comments like one from a man from Massachusetts talking with his wife.

"I think that's where that man got into the White House. I can't believe the Secret Service couldn't stop him. How could that happen?"

The Secret Service and the Department of Homeland Security have spent a long time trying to figure out the answer to that question.

Mention "the September event" to those in the Secret Service, and chances are they'll know exactly what you're talking about and wish it had never come close to happening. It's a painful embarrassment, and some take it deeply to heart.

On the evening of September 19, 2014, Omar Gonzalez, an Iraq war veteran battling PTSD, jumped over the White House fence, sprinted across the north grounds, overpowered an officer guarding an unlocked front door to the White House, and ran past a stairway that leads to where the First Family lives. (The president and his daughters had left for Camp David by helicopter from the South Lawn about ten minutes before Gonzalez breached the fence.)

He kept going and dashed into the East Room, where he was tackled by a counterassault agent. Some reports say he got as far as the doorway to the Green Room.

It was a security failure of almost the worst kind. It would have been far worse if he had been armed with something more than the Spyderco VG-10 folding knife he carried in a pocket in his pants.

"If he has [an explosive] device on him and he gets in, he controls the White House. He could have anything on him," a former high-ranking Secret Service official, speaking anonymously, told the *Washington Post*.

Gonzalez had come to the attention of the Secret Service twice that year. In July, Virginia law enforcement had found several rifles, shotguns, and handguns in his vehicle during a traffic stop, in addition to a map with a line that pointed to the White House. The Secret Service interviewed him but didn't find him to be a threat.

In August, Secret Service officers stopped Gonzalez and spoke with him after they spotted him walking near the fence on the south side of the White House with a hatchet in his waistband. They weren't aware of the earlier incident and let him go on his way after searching his car and finding nothing threatening.

Less than a month later, Gonzalez would somehow make it through several rings of protection that are set up to prevent anything like this from happening.

One of those rings included an ERT dog and handler.

Every moment of the fiasco was examined in a detailed DHS report on the incursion. The executive summary alone is several pages.

"It was one Murphy moment after another," says a member of the Tactical Canine Unit who spoke under condition of anonymity. "I didn't sleep for days after the incident.

"It hit us so hard. We were all sick to our stomach about the entire incident. It was a failure on all parts, we failed, everyone failed. It's not ever going to happen again."

Almost immediately, the ERT Tactical Canine Unit instituted a significant change in the way dogs are used. Before "the September event," there had been only one dog team stationed on each side of the White House. After, teams would never be solo again.

The program is also working on outfitting a new kind of vehicle that will make deployment times even faster than they already are, with a front-deploying system specially designed for dogs. Turning around to get a dog out of a minivan can take the focus off the suspect. The new design would not only shave a little time off deployment, but should make it easier for a handler to remain engaged with the subject.

"Good always comes from bad," says Bill. "It wasn't our finest moment, but we learned some valuable lessons."

CHAPTER 11

DRIVE

The Secret Service goes shopping for dogs in Denver, Indiana, population 471. It's an eleven-hour drive from RTC when pulling a ten-dog trailer. That's with just one quick stop and no traffic, and doesn't include getting stuck behind a horse and carriage.

A couple of the smaller roads that lead to Denver go through Northern Indiana Amish country. Scenic, yes, but to have to slow to five miles an hour when the canine selection team is so close to its destination can be painful. It's even worse when heading back to D.C. with a trailer full of barking dogs at the beginning of the trip.

"It may be for only two miles, but two miles behind a horse is forever," says Secret Service canine program instructor Steve M., who makes the trip every few months.

Denver is home to Vohne Liche Kennels, which has provided most of the Secret Service canines since the year 2000. Kenneth (Kenny) Licklider, who started Vohne Liche in 1993 after retiring from the Air Force, says the kennel has trained and/or provided dogs for more than five thousand agencies, including U.S. Army

Special Forces and U.S. Marine Corps Forces Special Operations Command (MARSOC).

During the wars in Iraq and Afghanistan, the kennels were often at near capacity. With almost six hundred dogs in the seven kennel buildings, Denver had more dogs than people for a while, and some months it still comes close.

Denver is just a couple of miles away from the larger town of Mexico. But Peru, about five miles south, is the place where most of the Secret Service instructors who select dogs go to eat and spend the night.

Peru, with a population of about 11,200, is the biggest city in Miami County. If you're a local of a certain age, you may still be pronouncing it *pee*-roo. It's no metropolis but it has a past more storied than many cities several times its size.

Depression-era gangster John Dillinger and his gang plundered weapons from a police arsenal in Peru in 1933. The deputies watched dumbstruck as the men ransacked their gun cabinets and made away with a variety of powerful weapons they'd soon use in deadly bank robberies.

In 1972 the ransom from an American Airlines hijacking was found by a farmer tending a soybean field. Another farmer, this one in a corn field, found a submachine gun used in the hijacking.

If that's not colorful enough, Peru is also the self-proclaimed "Circus Capital of the World."

"Children in Peru learn circus skills the way other kids learn soccer," notes an article in *USA Today*, which also informs that Peru is "where human cannonball is a prestigious occupation."

From the late 1890s until the 1940s, a half-dozen professional circuses, including Ringling Bros. and Barnum & Bailey, chose Peru as a place to spend winters because of its relatively central location and proximity to railroads. When they eventually pulled up stakes for good, they left behind a circus-oriented population.

Today Peru is home to the International Circus Hall of Fame Museum, the Circus City Festival and Parade, a youth circus, and the Peru Amateur Circus.

The city is the backdrop for the 2006 film *Little Big Top*, about an aging drunk whose passion for clowning is reawakened when he moves back to Peru, his hometown. One scene features the real-life Mr. Weenie, a drive-in that's hard to miss because of its logo: a giant smiling hot dog wearing a bow tie and a hat. A big yellow arrow under the happy hot dog points the hungry to the eatery, where they can get a large selection of wieners and burgers. (On Mondays customers can buy two corn dogs for $1.50.)

The Secret Service canine crews here for "buy trips" are so focused on finding quality canines that they don't know much about Peru's circus lore. But there's a reminder of it every time they come into Peru from a certain direction: a sign with PERU painted in blue, with a painted red circus tent outline and colorful flags over it. Under that, CIRCUS CAPITAL OF THE WORLD.

Beneath it all: HOME OF COLE PORTER. Who knew?

The hotel where they often stay is about as close as they come to the city's big-top reputation. The Best Western Circus City Inn features circus-themed lobby decor, including large clowns etched in glass panels that separate the lobby from the pool. Every so often a young child who is raring to go swimming sees the giant clown faces and runs away, crying.

The town is not an ideal destination for the coulrophobic.

(Vohne Liche also runs its own hotel—a former barracks—down the road at Grissom Air Reserve Base. The refurbished lodging features two-room suites, convenient for handlers who come from across the country to train with dogs. Across the street is the Red Rocket Bar & Grill. The name has a double meaning to those in the dog world, but to most visitors, a red rocket is just a red rocket.)

The Best Western is a dog-friendly hotel. A sign at the front door proclaims, WE LOVE DOGS—BRING FIDO. The Secret Service takes the hotel up on this offer on a regular basis.

During the Service's weeklong buy trips, other hotel guests are likely to see a variety of Belgian Malinois parading in and out of the lobby, past the stuffed toy lion lounging in his wooden cage topped by big toy gorillas.

The testing of the dogs is mostly done at VLK, but some of the Secret Service dog buyers find it helpful to see how the dogs react in an environment like a hotel.

"I will typically bring the dogs back to the hotel room so I can socialize with them," says Brian. "I don't just want to see them in their working environment but their social environment. It's important because these dogs are going to be living in someone's home for eight or ten or more years."

He also watches out for telltale signs of fear, shyness, or unwarranted aggression. Wanting to nosh on a pillow is one thing. (He doesn't let them and rarely turns his back for more than a few seconds.) Wanting to nosh his arm when he reaches for a water glass on the bedside table is quite another.

The demand for high-end law-enforcement and military canines greatly increased after 9/11. A declaration by the Pentagon years later that dogs are the best defense against improvised bombs sent the demand through the roof.

Before this, it wasn't as challenging to find dogs with a few years of solid training. Several dogs the Secret Service acquired in the first years of ERT were three or more years old. They still get the occasional older dog, like Hurricane. But the age and level of previous training have generally decreased as the demand has increased. Most dogs the Service now buys are about two years old.

There's always the question of whether it's better to have a dog with little to no training—a canine tabula rasa—since nothing has to be unlearned. But there is something to be said for a highly trained dog.

The increased demand means the Secret Service's intensive screening process is more important than ever. Every month or so, depending on the Service's canine class schedule, a couple of instructors, who are also trainers, hop in the cab of the Ford F-350 pickup and make the long drive to Denver.

The trailer they're pulling is rarely empty. During their week of testing at VLK, instructors can weed out most of the dogs who won't be good fits. But inevitably there will be one or two dogs who end up having to make the round-trip because of unforeseen medical or behavioral issues. Sometimes these are discovered right away. Other times, the problems can take months to discover—long after dogs and handlers have bonded.

On this trip to Denver, Steve has brought back a couple of dogs, including one with the odd name of Butyalk (pronounced *but*-yok). He had failed the Service's extensive medical testing. It's not that he wouldn't be good for other departments that demand slightly less physicality from their dogs. It's just that his hips might not hold up under the more rigorous needs of the Secret Service.

Vohne Liche has a generous return policy for the Secret Service. Dogs can be returned up to a year after they're selected. Not much fun for the dogs, but Licklider understands the Service's need to be super selective.

"They do return the dogs more frequently than others, but

they're protecting the president of the United States. We give them a lot of leeway."

Many of the dogs who make the round-trip to Indiana have had at least rudimentary training from the Secret Service and will be welcome additions to law-enforcement entities with even slightly less stringent standards.

But the ride back to the kennels probably feels extra long to these dogs—even without a horse and carriage to delay the inevitable.

Steve has been looking for Rex for a few minutes, but Rex is not where he's supposed to be. A roster gives the kennel number for the Malinois, and Steve double-checks it with the dry-erase chart that shows all the dogs and their kennel locations. The dog is not there, nor in any kennels near it.

When it comes to dogs named Rex at Vohne Liche, it can be a little confusing. The misplaced Rex is technically Rex 62. That means he's the sixty-second Rex the kennel has had so far in 2015, out of about one thousand dogs, and it's only October.

Other names aren't quite so traditional. Also present at the kennel are Wacko, Barko, Broke, Messie, and Vagany. The latter means *tough* or *rough* in Hungarian. Even though most K-9 departments try to keep the name a dog comes with, some will change a name if they're concerned about its implications. Blackie is usually switched out. Vagany only sometimes.

The Secret Service dog who won the K-9 Olympics at Vohne Liche in August was one of the rare dogs whose name was changed after the Service got him. Luke's champion ERT dog was originally named Beano. One wonders if he would have come so far if the instructors hadn't switched his name to Nitro.

Someone tells Steve that Rex 62 must be in one of the other kennel buildings and points toward a likely location. Steve walks down the long rows of steel-barred kennels searching for the one with Rex 62's name on it. The majority of the dogs are Malinois, but there are a surprising number of German shepherds, and many combinations of the two breeds. The kennel building is clean and, to say the least, cacophonous.

As he passes by, some dogs sit silently and stare, or lean their paws up on the bars and quietly reach out in what looks like a heartbreakingly stoic plea to go out and get some fresh air and hang with some people. They get good care here, but it's not set up to be an intimate kennel with lots of attention given to each dog.

Most dogs bark like mad as Steve walks by. Some spin relentlessly. A couple of the Malinois jump high, straight up, as if on invisible trampolines. One dog a few rows over bounces so high his head and torso rise above the kennel wall. Dogs have been known to fly over into other kennels, but if they have such acrobatic leanings, they're usually given a kennel with a ceiling.

Steve passes by a springer spaniel whose kennel card says "Teddy." Teddy? Steve does a double take.

He knows this dog. Teddy is one of many dogs from the first Friendly Dog class who ended up making the round-up back to VLK. The rest of the returned dogs, including Ziggy, were snapped up by other K-9 units. But not Teddy. He has been here since his return more than a year ago.

He turned out not to be the dog the Secret Service instructors had hoped he would be. He proved a bit slow for their needs. Springers aren't as in demand as other dogs, but a company in Europe has been eyeing him to do explosives detection there.

Meanwhile he stares sideways at visitors, like someone in a poker game who doesn't trust the dealer.

"Sorry, buddy, someone's gonna take you one of these days," Steve says to him and moves on in pursuit of Rex 62.

He finally finds his Rex, toward the end of a row in the middle of the building. Steve is happy to find Rex 62, and Rex 62 is happy he has been found. When he sees Steve, he barks a few times and wags when Steve steps inside the kennel. Once Steve has leashed him up, Rex pushes past the door and leads Steve by all his barking brethren, pulling hard to get out of there.

He's the last of several dogs they'll be testing in this round. Vohne Liche has selected twenty-four dogs for the Secret Service to screen this week for its next Explosive Detection Team class. The dog trailer fits ten dogs, so they do the testing in shifts.

The area for today's tests is just a few hundred yards away, but trailering them over is the most efficient way to go. After letting Rex 62 sniff the grass, lift his leg, and soak up some rays, they load him into the trailer and drive over to the edge of an alfalfa field, where they'll begin to see who among these dogs has the right stuff.

Brian has been instrumental in developing testing for all the Secret Service canine jobs. He has been with the Secret Service since 1998 and training dogs professionally since 1988.

"He lives it, breathes it," says Bill.

"There's no one greater in the canine community," says Stew of the trainer he has worked with since 2004.

Brian grew up immersed in dogs. His grandfather had a large farm on the Eastern Shore of the Chesapeake Bay, where the family hunted geese, and occasionally quail and ducks, with their dogs. Brian's dad had given him a black Lab named Apollo as his first field trial dog when he was about ten years old. But the dog wasn't cut out for the work and was too energetic for their little house, so they gave Apollo to Brian's grandfather.

Apollo thrived on the property, expending his energy running around in nature and never being much of a field trial dog. But Apollo and Brian's grandfather had a way of communicating that would influence Brian for the rest of his life.

"I remember going down and seeing him with Apollo. He would tell that dog to go grab an apple, and Apollo would run into the orchard and grab an apple. He would tell him to go get a peach, and he'd go get a peach. Same with a plum.

"I was only ten or eleven years old at the time, and he and that dog just had something special that really clicked with me. It was like an epiphany. It wasn't his training, it was the relationship and the communication that they had.

"He was in his seventies, the greatest man I've ever known, and that dog made him so happy and he made the dog so happy. I saw how that bond worked to make them understand each other," says Brian.

Not long after, Brian got a black Lab named Spunker, who was another field trial dog. She was the real deal—an outstanding competitor in trials that tested the working abilities of gun dogs, and the best canine companion Brian could have imagined.

One day when he was about seventeen, Brian was visiting his grandfather when Spunker ran into the road chasing an errant Frisbee. A car hit her and dragged her underneath for what seemed to Brian like an eternity. They raced her to a veterinary hospital, but besides patching her up a little there wasn't much they could do.

"We brought her back home and she had this huge hole in her body. She couldn't use her back legs and I tried to take care of her for a week or so but I finally admitted to myself that it wasn't going to work out. I couldn't let her suffer like that anymore.

"I wouldn't let anybody go with me. I wanted to have her put down by myself. I carried her into the van and drove to the vet with her in my lap. It was just a me-and-her thing. Like with my grandfather when he and Apollo looked at each other and understood each other, she and I had that. She knew she was getting put down. She knew something. I could just feel it, that there was a kind of giving up. That it was OK. She let me know that."

Brian can't continue with the story. It's still too much. He has been through many deaths of subsequent canine companions as well as dogs he and his handlers have worked with, but this one still rips him wide open. He understands what handlers go through when they lose their first working dog. And he understands that it can take a long, long time to get over.

After a stint in the Army as an infantry medic, he saw his first Rottweiler. "I thought it was the most amazing beast I'd ever laid eyes on," he says. He ended up adopting one from a pound. He decided to train the dog at a Rottweiler kennel in Northern California, not far from where he was working in a psychiatric hospital. At the kennel, many dogs were doing Schutzhund, a dog sport that tests dogs for the traits needed for police or military work.

"I was done. I quit work, drove up there four days a week to train. It was the greatest thing in the world to me," he says.

He ended up working full time in the world of dog training, which a decade later led to teaching some classes at the Secret Service. When a job for a Secret Service canine trainer/instructor opened, he immediately applied.

"When I got the job, I was euphoric," he says. "To be out here and see how professional everybody was, and how good the quality of the dogs was, even coming in on the bottom of the totem pole was exciting."

Many of the traits tested in Schutzhund are the ones he and the dog staff seek out on buy trips. Among them: courage, intelligence, perseverance, trainability, and drive.

Secret Service dogs have to have an additional trait: sociability. "A strong social police dog" is the term Brian uses. That piece can be the most difficult to find with high-intensity, high-drive dogs.

For ERT, for instance, the Service wants a dog who won't back down until the fight with a bad guy is over or his handler calls him off. That same dog needs to be able to quickly get on with his day and not be a crazy, fuming mess afterward. In other words, the dog needs the coveted "off" switch. ERT dogs also can't be dog aggressive, since they can work close together as a team.

Courage is one of the most important characteristics the Secret Service tests for. It's not just the ERT dogs who need it. They all do. Even the Friendly Dogs. What is it exactly?

"The Friendly Dogs have to walk on a piece of concrete in hundred-degree heat for hours a day searching thousands of people. That's not easy," says Brian. "That takes a drive and a desire to perform and takes a level of courage as well."

For EDT dogs, courage manifests in other ways.

"They have to frequently get on a military transport, land in a different country, often with a completely different climate and a very different way of living," says Brian. "That can rattle a lot of dogs. They have to be strong enough in character that when they land, they can behave as though nothing has changed. And that's not normal."

The Secret Service uses a variety of tests for courage. The testing depends on the dog's future role. They're all tested in the dark, because night duty is a fact of life. ERT dogs will have to work in a completely dark room by themselves as part of testing. In training, anything that minimizes a dog's senses can steal from their confidence. "That's where courage kicks in," explains Brian.

"That's like telling an officer, 'You're going to go into the building and we're going to put something on you to blind your eyes. Are you comfortable going in there and fighting?' That's a tough thing to ask of dogs."

A dog who's scared of the dark might bump into something and refuse to go forward. An ERT canine candidate might find the suspect but choose not to bite him, or be startled that he found him. These are issues the Service can work on up to a point, but if courage is not inherent in a dog's makeup—or as Brian likes to say, "if Mom and Dad didn't put in the courage and drive"—it's probably not going to work.

At home, Brian has an animated assortment of dogs, goats, and chickens. It's the one place he doesn't worry about animals having drive or courage. His dogs are well trained, though, and his goats listen to him pretty well. Bill jokes that even his chickens come when called.

Brian doesn't usually admit it at first, but if someone talks to him long enough, he may also mention that he has three cats. But these are not normal cats. One afternoon while he's standing around the training yard watching handlers and talking with Bill, the subject comes up.

"I'm not really a cat guy," Brian says. "I have Bengal cats."

Bill turns toward him. "Do you even know what a Bengal cat is? It's what a guy who has cats calls them when he wants them to sound cool."

Brian tells him the story of how he came to be a cat owner.

"I never had a cat in my life and then a few years ago I walk into PetSmart and there's a lady petting this cat. There were bangs in her face and the cat hauls off and bites her in the face and I said, 'That's the cat for me!' I never would have gotten the cat unless it looked like a patrol dog. I saw it apprehend the woman and that was it!"

"When you have to say *cats* with an *s,* that's when you know you're a cat guy," Bill deadpans.

"Not with Bengal cats."

A pad of lined, white paper on the tailgate of the Ford pickup truck serves as a makeshift report card for the dogs being tested by the Secret Service at VLK. The top pages whip in the strong wind that's rushing across the green field of ten-inch-tall alfalfa. If a Malinois named Herta, who hails from Holland, could read the evaluation of her afternoon's performance, she might wish the wind would rip away the page.

> *Afraid of kennel/trailer*
> *Soft mouth—would not bite toy/ball taken out by hand*
> *Possession (6)*
> *Exchange (8)*
> *Prey (6)*
> *Hunt (5)*
> *Visual out of kennel / slow to hunt / eventually found odor/*
>   *ball*

She's going to need a much better showing in the next day's stakeout, which tests for courage and drive and reactions to stress. Steve and Secret Service dog training assistant Shawn G. are pretty sure that while she's a good dog, she's not cut out for the Secret Service.

"Her head is small for her body," observes Steve, as Herta gambols through the alfalfa, looking halfheartedly for a tennis ball. "Not that that means anything."

On the fluttering report card pages, another dog's comments state that his pursuit of a tug is "nonexistent," but that he is "very social." Social is good. Not having the drive to find a toy will probably not make him a presidential protector.

Boyan, from Slovakia, rates much better.

> *Ball possession (9)*
> *Good on exchange (7)*
> *Good chase on ball (8)*
> *Great pace to problem*
> *Immediate active search/found ball*

Next up is Zigis, a Malinois from Hungary. He's wagging, jumping, and whirling around Steve as they run together to the edge of the field, attached to each other by a ninety-foot nylon lead. He throws the tennis ball and Zigis bounds for it, springing through the alfalfa. Steve lets the lead slip from his hand so he won't impede Zigis's search. In a few seconds, Zigis, ball in mouth, is circling Steve, wagging and loping with the excitement of his find.

Steve leans over and pats him playfully, cheering his find in the kind of high, enthusiastic voice these dogs love.

"Ohhhh yeah! What'd you find, buddy? You're a gooooood boy!"

Zigis revels in the praise, head high, mouth clutching the ball. Steve tries to get the ball from his mouth, and the dog resists but eventually gives it up. Steve throws the ball again.

After going through the same routine, Steve lobs the ball into the field a third time, but instead of letting Zigis run after it, he grabs the lead and jogs him back to the trailer. Zigis stares at the field in the area where the ball landed and looks up at Steve as if he can't believe this guy is going to leave a perfectly good ball in the middle of the field. Steve has him jump into his kennel in the trailer and shuts the door.

A few minutes later, Steve opens Zigis's kennel door, snaps on the lead, and lets him out. The dog pulls toward the spot in the alfalfa field where he clearly remembers the ball landed after Steve abandoned it there.

Zigis staccatos some barks, wags his tail vigorously, and bounces from side to side, bursting to find the ball. Steve lets him go. Zigis runs to within a couple of feet of the ball, as if guided by GPS. He sniffs the air, turns around, and *boom*. The ball is his again.

Steve cheers him on, and when he calls Zigis back, Zigis will not give up the ball. He has found his prey and isn't going to let this guy who doesn't know the value of a tennis ball throw it into the field and walk away from it again.

Steve likes this. He puts another tennis ball under his shoe to see what Zigis will do.

Some dogs will immediately drop the ball they're holding and paw under his shoe to try to get the ball. But not Zigis. He keeps the ball in his mouth, dives down to his side, and digs to get to the other ball. When this doesn't work, he lets go of the ball in his mouth and attacks the ground under Steve's shoe with his jaws, pushing his front paws against the earth for better leverage.

"Most dogs aren't this tenacious," Steve says. "They'll paw and scratch at it but he wants to put his mouth on it bad. Look at that!"

Steve lifts up his foot. "I'll give that to him. Look at that. That's just a nice dog."

Next up is Tek, a stunning black German shepherd with tawny paws. The Hungarian dog doesn't want to jump out of his trailer kennel, which is only a couple of feet off the ground, so Steve helps guide him out. He and Steve trot together toward the field for several steps but the dog trips on the lead and is momentarily splayed out on the cut grass. He gets up, shakes it off, and moves on.

Steve grabs a rope tug toy that's lying in the grass near the field and Tek grabs the other end. They play for a minute and Tek relinquishes the tug. He runs out a few steps and Steve throws the tug back to him. Instead of jumping to catch it, Tek flinches when it gets near, not wanting the ball to hit him in the head. Steve smiles and shakes his head.

He calls him and rubs his back quickly a few times, encouraging him with a few "good boy" comments. Pep talk over, he throws a tennis ball into the field. Tek runs into the field and trips again.

"He's a klutz," laughs Shawn, who's taking notes nearby.

Undaunted, Tek wanders around, looking for the ball. This is no hot pursuit. It looks more like he's taking advantage of being able to stretch his legs and enjoy the wind through his thick fur. A minute later he finds the ball, scoops it up in his mouth, and stands in the field until Steve calls him. He gives it back to Steve, who throws it back to the field. Tek watches the ball and then seems to forget about it as Steve takes him back to the trailer. The dog jumps in, Steve pets him a few times and shuts the kennel door.

"He's a beautiful dog. A nice dog, too," he says to Shawn, like a teacher scraping for something positive to tell parents of a C-minus student. This is not the same kind of "nice" as Zigis.

Shawn and Steve go over some of their notes on the dogs and in a few minutes, it's time for Tek to come out of the trailer again. The shepherd jumps down without assistance this time and runs with Steve toward the field.

Steve strokes Tek's dark head, which is already warmed by the autumn sun. Then he points to the field. "Go ahead!" Steve tells him in a high, happy voice, motioning for him to head out and look for the tennis ball.

Tek wags for a couple beats, then jogs into the alfalfa. Several yards in, he slows to a trot and then to a walk, sniffing here and there, then not really sniffing so much as hanging out and enjoy-ing the outdoor experience.

"Get the ball, boy!" Steve coaches from the sidelines.

This seems to get Tek back on track, and nose down, he makes his way toward where Steve had thrown the ball.

"He might be on it!" Shawn says.

He's within a couple of yards when a little yellow and black butterfly flutters up from the alfalfa and zigzags low in the air. Tek sees the butterfly and trots toward it, entranced.

His head traces its movements, and when the colorful insect flies away in another direction, Tek follows after it—not like he wants to eat it, but more like he has found a beguiling new friend. Steve lets him enjoy his time with the butterfly.

Shawn, scorecard in hand, writes "chased butterfly." Not that they would forget.

Early Friday morning, Steve and Shawn load up the trailer with the ten dogs who have impressed them the most with their prey drive, hunt drive, courage, environmental stability, intelligence, and other qualities essential to a solid EDT dog. The original pool of twenty-four dogs didn't have candidates that would meet the Secret Service's stringent standards, so Vohne Liche had provided Steve and Shawn several more to test during the week.

Whoever chooses the dogs also trains the dogs as much as they can before a new class begins, and they teach the class, too. Steve and Shawn have a lot of skin in this game and work hard to select just the right canines.

"I continually think about who we are training these dogs to protect, and the extremely important mission of these dogs," says

Steve. "The amount of responsibility that these dogs are entrusted with is pretty amazing when you think about it."

He feels good about the new recruits: Rex 62, Laila, Boyan, Fusti, Ringo, Pepe, Bolt, Athos, Ricky, and Zigis.

The dogs bark in the trailer, and the white truck kicks up a cloud of dust in the dirt driveway. Steve tunes the radio to a country music station and settles in for the long drive ahead.

CHAPTER 12

A FEW LITTLE BITES

Jim's engaging blue eyes, rugged build, and dazzling, easygoing smile make him a prime mark for the ribbing that goes on 24/7 among ERT canine guys. The fact that he also has a voice that Hollywood should put to good use doesn't help his case.

"I seriously hate you. Please get fat and darken your teeth," Stew likes to chide his fellow former Marine, who holds a master's degree, as Stew also does.

They give Jim a hard time, but they know that his looks belie a body that's battered from years on the job. He's not the only one. ERT dog handlers don't talk much about the physical toll the job takes. But when you put some of the most driven dogs together with some of the most competitive alpha males—men who will do whatever it takes to keep each other and their protectees safe—bodies are going to get beat up.

"We all go through the same stuff. We all have ailments. We all have nasty injuries and hide many of them. Yet we push on. Not to sound cliché, but we do it for the team, and not for ourselves," Jim says.

He has been bitten multiple times. Three bites resulted in

hospital visits. His old dog, Spike, had this little "quirk" in the beginning: He liked to turn and chomp Jim every time he took him off of a bite. It became so severe that Jim quit and walked out of the training yard during class one day.

"I was more pissed than anything. That stuff starts to hurt after a while," he says.

Both of his forearms were bruised and cut up. He had teeth marks and punctures up and down his arms from the dog who was supposed to become his lifelong partner and eventual best friend.

But it wasn't just Spike who got him. He was bitten by another dog in training, lacerated right down to the bone. It wasn't pretty. Fatty tissue protruded from the wound in a sickening way. He also took a nasty bite from Luke's dog, Nitro. The dog got him on the arm and wouldn't let go. Nitro didn't win first place in the 2015 K-9 Olympics for easily giving up.

Even though Jim is now an instructor and not a handler, he's still getting the occasional reminder of what these dogs are capable of doing. A dog he was recently training got him in the bicep and put two more holes in him.

"That one hurt bad," he admits.

Besides the puncture-wound scars, he has mild numbness in both of his forearms from all the trauma. All told, he has been bitten in both arms (upper and lower), both legs, the stomach, and the back. He has also had knee surgery as a result of the wear and tear that these guys put themselves through.

That's nothing, though, he says.

The biggest problems for the thirty-five-year-old are the two bulging disks in his lower neck, and the two bulging disks in his lower back. Both his neck and his back require surgery. He has known about these issues for the past six years but has refused surgery because he doesn't want to give up working with the team. Three-round cortisone injection cycles keep him going.

"My body is completely wrecked, but I usually just get the shots and suck it up," he says.

ERT canine guys are pretty much guaranteed bites and injuries, long hours, frequent overnight shifts, and more bites and injuries. But whoever makes it to this level has proven he can handle the rigors.

The challenge starts with completing general ERT school. "It's brutal," says Luke.

"Insanely tough, mentally and physically," describes another ERT member.

In Luke's class, twenty-four were selected to start the twelve-week program, and six finished. That's more than usual. Normally only about 10 to 20 percent graduate.

Team members interested in working with dogs usually have to put in three years on the Emergency Response Team before they'll be considered for the ERT's tactical canine program.

Canine school is also immensely challenging to the mind and body. Some quit once they realize what they're getting into with the powerful dogs and the rigors of the program. But those who get through training become part of a special brotherhood.

"The caliber of men on this team are not a-holes or cocky. They're highly trained and skilled and dedicated," says Stew. "Like any SWAT team or special military unit, it's a different quality of men that are awesome to be around.

"We're like brothers. We might fight, we'll definitely bust each other's balls, but we're there for each other no matter what."

When someone does get bitten or hurt, though, there's an

interesting dynamic that usually comes into play. The unwritten rules of being an injured but badass ERT canine handler go something like this:

1. No matter how much it hurts, you act like it's no big deal.
2. If you have to go to the hospital, you will refuse an ambulance if at all possible. Handlers can usually convince the EMT or paramedic at RTC that they don't need an ambulance. Someone else drives them to the hospital in a regular car.
3. If you have to stay in the hospital, guys from the team, including supervisors, will be there around the clock in their off time. You'll maintain a stiff upper lip.

Some do this better than others.

One October morning in 2013, Marshall put on the show of fortitude a little too well for his own good . . .

Marshall heard the dog before he saw him. The rustling through the woods, the cracking of twigs, the panting as Max sniffed him out in full hunt drive.

As the bad guy in this training, Marshall could have gone up in a tree, and the dog's job would have been to find him and alert his handler and the rest of the ERT members to his presence. But the idea this day was to engage the dog in a "fight," which is way more fun for the dogs than just barking, and a better use of the skills they'd use to keep on point.

Marshall hadn't donned a bite suit for this. He wore only a football jersey and sweatpants. He usually wore a sweatshirt but somehow hadn't that day. Since the dog was wearing his leather muzzle, there was no need to guard against bites, but it was always more comfortable to have some kind of extra layer.

These dogs don't seem to care if they're muzzled. When they're in fight drive and wearing a muzzle, their drive can actually be kicked up an extra notch. It's like being in a fight with one hand tied behind your back, ERT canine students are told early in their schooling. Most people would fight even harder knowing they didn't have all their tools available.

The muzzled dogs go all out, jumping on the bad guys and doing what they can to take them down and win the fight.

Sure enough, when Max found Marshall, he went full throttle on him. Marshall played along, acting like someone the dog shouldn't like—not hurting him, just agitating him, pulling on his harness, wrestling him a little, taunting him on, making Max want a piece of him.

Then in the midst of their pseudofight, something bad happened. Really bad.

Max's muzzle broke.

The dog paused. Marshall realized the horror of the situation at the same moment Max realized his own grand luck.

The men on the team were nowhere in sight. For a dog to be effective in this kind of scenario, it's important for him to be well ahead of his people. Marshall's training kicked in, and he realized the sacrifice he would need to make.

He had to pick a body part to offer Max, who was now lunging straight at him, his huge mouth open, teeth poised to puncture.

Arm? Leg? Marshall picked his forearm.

But Max chose his elbow.

"LIVE BITE!" he yelled as loudly as he could as the dog bit into his elbow and tried to pull him down to the ground. The pain ripped through his arm. The puncture wounds were bad enough, but the pressure on the bone and joint was even worse. His elbow felt like a walnut about to be cracked by the dog's mouth.

Even though Marshall knew all the commands, there was nothing he could have said to the dog to get him to release, and he knew it. The dogs are trained to stay on a bite, even if a bad guy happens to know the magic word or words.

Marshall couldn't pull the dog off physically either. Max had done the textbook perfect bite and "punched in." Punching in means the dog is holding the bite but then loosens slightly and goes in deeper to ensure a super firm hold.

The dog had bitten the perfect spot, just what he wanted, but the first bite usually lands only the canine teeth. Max then punched in to get the arm to the back of his mouth so he could really lock and hold. Max punched in twice, and the pain knifed through Marshall's body.

Marshall had the presence of mind to move with the dog and fight the instinct to rip his arm away from Max. It wouldn't have done any good and would have resulted in his flesh and other layers of his arm tearing.

In a real-life scenario, the handler would be positioned so that if a bad guy gives up, the handler would be able to quickly take his dog off the bite. Not always so in training. It was all Marshall could do to stay standing as the dog treated his elbow like a giant tug toy. He'd been bitten before, but this was a whole different class of pain.

And then, in the midst of his own private hell, he looked up and saw a sight he would later describe as being "like birds flying up, like doves of happiness." Larry C., former college football defensive back, and one of the most athletic guys on the team, was hurtling toward him.

Larry didn't have his dog Maximus with him that day and was in a better position to get to Marshall than the dog's handler was. Marshall had seen Larry run like the wind before, but he didn't know he could fly quite like this.

Larry grabbed Max by the collar and did a tactical takeoff, forcing the dog to give up.

The rest of the team reached the scene.

"How you doing, man?"

"I'm fine," Marshall said, trying to grin as rivulets of blood poured out of his left elbow. He glanced at his arm and saw his white shirt rapidly turning red. The puncture holes were too many to count. It was a hot, bloody mess. The guys looked at each other and back at him.

"Really? You sure?"

"Yeah, it's no big deal."

Inside, his body screamed with pain.

The medics at Rowley Training Center treated him and wanted to take him by ambulance to a hospital. Part of Marshall wanted to, but there was no way he'd give in to that temptation unless he were dying. It's just not how the team rolls.

Instead, the canine program manager at the time drove him in his own car to Howard County General Hospital. He talked to Marshall about anything but his injury to try to take his mind off it.

Doctors treated him in the ER, but after an MRI and examination, they realized how deep the bites were and how bad the injury was. Max had gotten him right in the elbow joint, with all its glorious complexity of bone, muscle, tendons, ligaments, and bursa sacs.

The injury was severe, but Larry's rapid response had probably saved Marshall's Secret Service career. The longer the dog was on, the worse it would have been.

Doctors suggested he go to MedStar Union Memorial Hospital in Baltimore, where world-renowned elbow and joint specialists could help him better than they could. Supervisors and instructors stayed with Marshall for hours at a time at MedStar. No matter what time it was, someone from the Secret Service was by his side.

When Stew got to MedStar later that night, he could see Marshall was in severe pain, try as he might to hide it. The nurse unwound the wrapping from his left elbow, and Stew felt a wave of nausea. Marshall had maybe twelve deep puncture wounds and a couple of dozen or so significant bite marks. It was red and oozing weird stuff, and it was on its way to swelling to the size of a large cantaloupe.

To make matters worse, Marshall had offered Max the wrong arm. He's a lefty. This was his shooting arm. Also his baseball pitching arm, but that ship had sailed a few years ago. There just hadn't been time to offer the dog his other arm.

"C'mere!" Marshall beckoned to Stew when no else was in the room. Stew leaned in close. If you happened to be passing by the room and looked in, you might have thought he was about to reveal a deathbed secret.

"I haven't taken any pain medication," he said in a low, hushed tone and quickly looked to see if anyone from the staff had heard him.

"What? Are you crazy?"

"I can't! They think we're *trained*!"

His whole life, Marshall had never taken anything stronger than an ibuprofen for his pains, which were significantly increased after joining ERT. At first he thought he could deal with the pain from the injury without painkillers and said no to the medication he was being offered.

This blew away the nurses and doctors. Word quickly got around about this big superhuman Secret Service guy who wasn't feeling any pain despite a serious injury.

"Are you the guy who's not taking any pain medications?" asked awed doctors, nurses, and aides who came to see him. He didn't want to disappoint them, much as he was starting to really want whatever they had been offering.

He heard them quietly talking behind the curtain and outside his door.

"This patient is the Secret Service guy who can't feel pain."

"Wow! I hear that blocking pain is part of the training they go through."

He really wanted something to dull the agony he was in. It gripped his whole body. But now he had a reputation to live up to. He longed for the superhuman powers they had ascribed to him.

He had already been through a couple of cleanings without it. Deep, painful cleanings, with long, cold sticks probing inches into his elbow.

"You might pass out," the nurse told him the first time.

"I'll be fine," he said.

She had him lie down, so that if he did pass out, he wouldn't go anywhere.

"How bad did that hurt?" asked Brian once the nurse had left.

"Worse than the bite."

Marshall dreaded future cleanings, which were happening every several hours.

Stew tried to talk him into accepting some pain meds.

"I can't even stand to get my teeth cleaned!" Stew told him. He had had several bad injuries himself on the job and would not think twice about accepting a little prescription relief from his doctors.

Much as he wanted to, Marshall wouldn't be convinced.

He hadn't eaten for thirty hours. He thought maybe some food would help him feel better. He'd had dinner early the previous night, raced out the door for work without having breakfast. When Max ripped into him, it was right before they were supposed to break for lunch. At the hospital he hadn't been allowed to eat in case he needed surgery. But now it was midnight and he was famished.

Stew could do one thing to help. He left and came back with two foot-long Subway club sandwiches, loaded with every topping and condiment available. When no nurses or doctors were nearby, Marshall wolfed them both down in the space of ten minutes. Stew threw away the wrappers far from his room so there would be no evidence.

Marshall tried to sleep despite his arm being raised in a traction device. He'd catch a few minutes here and there, but whenever he'd wake up, he'd see Stew's face glowing in the light of the computer as he graded papers from the criminal justice course he was teaching at American Military University.

"I wake up in this strange place and see a glowing serial killer with this weird mustache," Marshall told him. He wished he could turn to the other side and see his girlfriend, who was also staying over.

Not Max.

Of all the dogs on all the days . . .

Marshall could not believe his luck. It was his first day back in canine after eleven weeks of painful but productive physical therapy, and Max happened to be at RTC for training.

And of course, the dog needed someone to be the decoy.

The dog would be in muzzle, the decoy would not be wearing a bite suit.

This sounded a little too familiar.

This time, the decoy would be crouched in one of several small wooden hiding boxes in the training yard. Inside, the boxes smell like fresh-cut timbers, which is the only mildly pleasant aspect of being in one.

Hiding in these cramped, stuffy boxes and knowing a barking, hyped Malinois will eventually be knocking at your door to try to bite you is standard fare around here.

But it wasn't something Marshall was expecting to have to do. Not on his first day back. And not with *this* dog.

Marshall's instructor took a couple of steps closer to him.

"Let's just get this out of the way now," he said.

Marshall knew he had to do it. They needed to make sure he was OK, not scared of dogs, any dog, not even this dog.

"Nothing like getting back on the horse!" Marshall said, smiling, trying to look like it was no biggie. He donned the sweatpants and hoodie handlers often wear over their uniforms when they're decoys for muzzled dogs.

As he waited, crouching in the box, he had a lot of time to think. He hoped that this time, the muzzle would not have another freak accident. And he wondered if the dog would remember him and the taste of his flesh and blood.

"We already have top-notch guys on the team, one percenters," says Stew. "Then you give them a one-percenter dog. They're a force to be reckoned with."

The dogs of ERT are not unlike their human teammates.

They're tough, driven, resilient, have boundless energy, like to win, and keep going far after most others would quit.

Early in their training together, Luke's dog, Nitro, was doing a search about fifty yards into a tree line. As he bounded around looking for the bad guy, he jumped over a fallen tree and impaled himself on a branch.

Luke had no idea. He had seen his dog get hung up a little so he knelt down to check what was going on. By then, the dog had extricated himself and charged off to find the bad guy and bite him.

There were no outward signs that his dog had been impaled. Nitro did two more searches for bad guys and nailed them both.

A little later in the day, Luke saw Nitro licking at his belly. He went over to check him out. There was a little blood, not much. He carefully examined his dog's belly and saw what seemed to be a small hole in his abdomen.

Luke immediately realized what must have transpired earlier. He tried to keep calm as he hoisted Nitro into his van and rushed him to the vet.

The vet staff did emergency surgery and a bunch of tests. They discovered that a small branch had plunged five inches deep into the dog's gut. But he was lucky. While it tore through tissue, it had gone into a kind of dead space where there were no organs. The vet cleaned it out and did a few layers of stitching to secure everything that had been impaled.

The vet explained that Nitro hadn't bled at the time because when he hit the branch, his body had been extended for the jump over the fallen tree. When he went back into normal position, he effectively sealed it.

Nitro appeared to be sore for a few days, and Luke had to limit his dog's movements—no easy feat with a high-drive Malinois.

The dog was out of commission for close to a month. Luke figured Nitro probably would have gone back to work immediately if given the choice.

What's a little gut pain to get in the way of a beloved job?

In late 2015, an ERT handler showed up at training with some severe abdominal pain of his own. It would turn out to be appendicitis. He didn't say anything, but enough guys commented about how sick he looked that he fessed up and went home.

Later, when they learned that the doctor thought his appendix had already ruptured and he needed emergency surgery, they scrambled to find someone on the team to care for his dog until he was better. And of course, they made sure he had the pleasure of their company around the clock at the hospital.

ERT members have to regularly maintain rigorous physical training (PT) standards to stay on the team. There are the tough but less-challenging requirements back-to-back: doing fifty-five perfect push-ups in one minute, forty-eight sit-ups in a minute, eleven pull-ups, and running 1.5 miles in under ten minutes and fourteen seconds.

Then there's the operational standard, which is far more demanding. It's hush-hush and can be mentioned publicly only in the most general terms. To qualify to get on the team and stay on it, handlers and the other ERT members have to do a variety of exercises wearing full kit, since that's what they wear every day. They combine pull-ups, running, and a qualifying course of fire, both with primary (rifle) and secondary (pistol) weapons. They must score 90 percent. If they're off, they need to remediate, train extra, and repeat.

Canines are held to a standard as well. They have to run with their handlers and meet qualifying times and perform operational scenarios during the process.

Instructors are always watching for signs of dogs slowing down or having other obvious physical issues. The job takes a toll on man and beast. The average age of retirement for an ERT dog is around nine to ten years old, but it varies widely. Some go strong right to the end, others start winding down early.

ERT handler Shawn's dog, Jason, seems to be drinking his water from the fountain of youth. He's more than eight and almost as fast and strong as he was when he was young.

He was only eleven months old when the Secret Service, with some trepidation about his young age, selected him from VLK. He's the youngest dog ever selected for the Tactical Canine Unit. He's been a stellar dog. Jason first went to the K-9 Olympics in 2010 when he was almost three years old. He and Shawn took third place in individual patrol competition, and the Secret Service placed first as a team.

The ERT Tactical Canine Unit can't afford the time it takes to prepare for competition, and the time away from the job—at least not on a regular basis. So the next time the Service went to the Olympics was in 2015. Shawn was thirty-seven, Jason was eight. They were among the older competitors but placed remarkably well: fourth in individual patrol, and first in the obstacle course. They were an important part of the Secret Service team that won first overall.

The Olympics brings out the fiercely competitive spirit of the handlers, but in 2015 the competition to be chosen as one of three who would represent the Secret Service at the Olympics was just as intense—if not more so.

In the internal "qualifying rounds," winning was often a matter of split seconds, fractions of an inch. A few dogs stopped within zero feet of biting the bad guy when their handlers told them to stop. This takes incredible control developed over years of working together. Since more than one dog stopped at zero feet, the winners were determined by who got to the bad guy fastest.

"These guys would cut each other's throat for one point," says Brian.

All in good fun, of course.

When the sun is just right, and Hurricane is lying on the grass and getting belly rubs, and his mouth falls open in the relaxed ecstasy of the moment, you may catch a sparkle, a glint, a flash. On further inspection, you'll see that his four canine teeth are not bright white like his other teeth. They're a gleaming light silvery color. Titanium, to be exact.

The first day Marshall had Hurricane in the van, he discovered the dog was not fond of plastic travel kennels. (Van kennels are metal now.) Marshall had left the van in the training area to grab a quick lunch, and when he came back a half hour later, he was more than a little surprised to see that Hurricane had chewed his way halfway through the top of the kennel.

There was blood everywhere. It looked like a case for CSI.

When Hurricane had a dental visit months later, the veterinarian immediately saw that the dog's upper right canine tooth had a lot of exposed root pulp in an area of the tooth that was hard to see.

"The nerve is basically hanging out of it," Marshall explained to his supervisor. "That would make people scream."

Many dogs with an exposed nerve don't noticeably flinch when using their teeth. They just make accommodations, like chewing food and toys on the unaffected side of the mouth, until the nerve dies. But with the kind of biting work Hurricane was doing on a regular basis, there was no way he could have favored one side.

"It's like he just didn't feel or acknowledge the pain," Marshall told a supervisor with a mix of pride and empathy.

Hurricane needed a root canal and a crown, so Marshall brought him to a veterinarian who specializes in these procedures. Hurricane emerged with one titanium canine tooth.

The other three canine teeth followed soon after. They'd been chipped badly when, during a bout of separation anxiety, Hurricane took to biting the metal cage that replaced his plastic kennel. Rather than have Hurricane put under three more times as the chipping got worse, they opted to do it all at once. These teeth didn't need root canals, just reinforcements in the form of crowns.

The bedazzling titanium teeth don't bite any harder than regular teeth; they're just more durable than the teeth that had chipped away. Marshall found they collect plaque more than natural teeth do and require more toothbrushing attention than he ever thought metal teeth would.

But he loves how they look. Very badass against his dog's shiny black fur. And rather daunting, if you're the bad guy.

Sometimes it's the little bites that make the biggest impression on handlers.

Stew recalls a hot summer night wearing a bite suit in one of the small, sweltering wooden boxes in the canine yard. While waiting for a dog to find him, he saw with his flashlight that he was sharing the box with what seemed like a metropolis of spiders.

The dog could not come soon enough. He arrived, barking, and Stew popped open the door. Not thinking, he exposed his hand momentarily as he flew out to engage the dog, who took the opportunity to bite the handler's finger.

It hurt like hell, but he couldn't say anything, much less yell. It was his fault and he'd just have to suck it up. When someone noticed the injury later, Stew played it off as a simple puncture wound.

Four days later, he was on a car plane to a mission. One of the team's medics walked by and saw his hand, which was noticeably swollen.

"Hey man, you have cellulitis and a staph infection. You're going to die!" the medic said, laughing, and continued walking to his seat.

Since everyone on the team messes with each other, Stew didn't take it seriously. But then he took a good look at his hand and got concerned. It was swollen to his wrist, and blood was still oozing from the small wound. He realized he'd better see a doctor as soon as possible, but he didn't want to call out for sick leave, because that would have meant extra work for a teammate.

When they landed, he drove himself to an emergency room, where the medical staff lacerated his hand and drained it. They gave him some antibiotics and he was on his way, still operational, not missing a beat.

It doesn't always take a bite to rip open flesh. A dog's leather muzzle can pack a powerful punch during fight scenarios. While Stew was decoying for a muzzled dog one freezing winter afternoon, the dog whipped his head and the muzzle smashed Stew in the mouth.

"Uh, Stew, you might want to get that checked out," a friend on the team told him.

"Nah, send another dog!"

But the handler and other team members persisted. Stew couldn't figure out what the problem was. Sure there was some blood on his fleece jacket, but it didn't feel like anything bad. But then again, he wasn't feeling much at all on his face, because it was so cold.

He walked over to a vehicle and looked in the rearview mirror. His top lip was ripped completely in two right down the middle.

At the hospital, he didn't hesitate to say yes to whatever numbing and pain meds were offered. As the plastic surgeon in the emergency room stitched his lip, he could still feel the needle. He couldn't help but jerk every time it pushed through his lip.

"You guys are trained to be tough. This doesn't hurt, does it?" she asked.

"Mm-mm," he murmured in agreement. He took his mind off the pain by reliving the scene from the movie *Dirty Rotten Scoundrels*, where Steve Martin's character has to pretend to feel nothing as he gets whipped in the legs. It almost made Stew smile but that would have made matters worse.

Stew tries to keep perspective on the physical pitfalls of being an ERT dog handler.

"What we go through may look pretty badass from the civilian perspective, but it's not as badass as a Special Forces operator saying, 'Well, I jumped into a hot zone, rescued a hostage, killed a bunch of terrorists, and got shot in the leg.' Some of these military guys have a Superman cape underneath and don't tell anyone."

And then there are those you'd never guess had been to hell and back . . .

CHAPTER 13

THE KILLING FIELDS . . . WITH DOG

One day in late 2004, three years into his career in the Secret Service's Uniformed Division, Leth O. was called in to his lieutenant's office. He thought he must have been in serious trouble for something. When a lieutenant or captain asked to see you, it wasn't usually to pin a medal on your chest.

He sat down across the table from the lieutenant and steeled himself for whatever was about to happen.

"You're always happy coming to work. You work hard and seem to really enjoy what you do," the lieutenant said.

This was going much better than Leth had expected. He nodded appreciatively and smiled.

"I have a question I'd like to ask you," he said to Leth. "Do you like dogs?"

"I *love* dogs," Leth said, his face brightening. "I have one now. Before I came to this country, back in Cambodia I grew up with a dog. We went through a lot together. He was the best little dog . . ."

Every day, when Leth came home from school in the city of Battambang, Cambodia, his French bulldog, Dino, greeted him at the door of their little house. Dino knew the exact time to stand post waiting for his young charge, and he wagged his tail hard as Leth approached from the distance. When his boy arrived home, Dino burst with a puppylike happy dance, ecstatic to be reunited.

Other than school, the two were inseparable. Leth thought of his dog as a brother. When Leth went to the movie theater, Dino accompanied him, sitting in his own seat beside him. Dino shadowed him everywhere. Leth didn't use a leash. Dino just listened.

The family fed him condensed milk mixed with hot water, rice, a little fish, pork. He was part of the family, and he ate what they ate.

In April 1975, when Leth was nine years old, he awoke at sunrise to the sound of guns, RPGs, and chaos. Several days earlier, his father, an army lieutenant who was about to make the rank of captain, had been taken away to a high school with hundreds of other officers, with the promise that they were going to see Prince Sihanouk. He hadn't come back.

Leth brought his father breakfast two days after he had been taken away to the school. When he went back to deliver lunch, his father wasn't there. No one was.

During the course of the week, schools, banks, government offices, and most businesses were being closed down. He had no idea why.

And now, as night turned to day, here were these fighters of the Khmer Rouge guerrilla army at their doorstep. At everyone's doorstep. They shot rifles into the air. They commanded everyone to leave the city.

"You don't leave, you die!" they threatened as they pushed guns into the faces and chests of men and women.

His mother, crying uncontrollably about this sudden takeover, wanted to wait for her husband's return. Surely he'd be coming home soon. But there was no choice. The Khmer Rouge soldiers yelled through loudspeakers that the city needed to be emptied. Everyone had to leave.

Leth heard the frightened wails of neighbors, the pleading, the babies crying, the angry shouts of the Khmer Rouge soldiers. Every so often, there was the sound of a gun clearly hitting its target: someone who refused to leave. And then the piercing screams of the victim's loved ones.

The smell of smoke was growing strong as soldiers torched the homes of those who put up a fight. Leth's mother realized they had to get out, and fast.

She told Leth and his older sister to help pack their most essential belongings. There were few valuables. His mother worked as a seamstress, and his father didn't make much money in the army. Leth knew his father could have already been captain and earned more money, if not for his propensity to speak his mind. He never kept quiet when he saw leadership making what he thought were poor decisions that endangered the lives of his men, who were embroiled in the country's civil war.

Leth's mother didn't want the children to panic but needed them to act swiftly. They gathered some clothes, rice, cooking pans, and a few beloved books. His mother fashioned packs out of swaths of cloth and wrapped their possessions in them. She tucked away a few pieces of cherished jewelry, knowing there would be no use for them other than trading them for essentials. But it was better than leaving them here to be looted.

The children brought the packs over to their one-speed bicycles that were leaning against the side of the house. Leth thought his bike could be like his horse, taking him somewhere with little effort on his part, or at least bearing some of the load when he couldn't ride it.

They had no idea where they were going. They slipped their makeshift packs over their shoulders, got onto their bikes, and said good-bye to home.

As they started on their journey from this new hell to nowhere, Leth's dog trotted along, right by his side.

Three long days and nights they walked and the rain poured so hard at times that the children could barely push their bicycles through the thick mud. They had to stop often to wipe it off tires and rims.

The first night they stayed with his father's cousin. They were tired and drained and in shock. But they had to push on.

By now they knew their fate. There was no avoiding it without being killed trying. They were to essentially become slave labor in rural camps, part of the communist Khmer Rouge's radical social reform with the initial goal of creating an agrarian-based society.

Khmer Rouge leader Pol Pot had declared this to be "Year Zero"—the beginning of a new era. In short order, money was banned, family ties shredded, religion denounced, education stopped, and businesses and hospitals shuttered. Newspapers were closed, mail curtailed, and basic rights restricted.

Most people ousted from the cities were to work to help the Khmer Rouge meet its goal of tripling rice production. The fertile land of the Battambang Province, known as "the rice bowl of Cambodia," would be pushed to its limits, and beyond. So would the people.

Because Leth's family lived in the province, their journey was a relatively short one. Others marched for weeks to reach the rice-growing areas.

On the second night, they came to a small village and asked distant relatives of his father if they could stay with them even for a night. They refused. The family wanted nothing to do with them, since the Khmer Rouge was after anyone even related to a soldier. It would be challenging enough for these relatives to cover up their ties to his father, but nearly impossible if the soldier's children and wife had stayed in their home.

The relatives did let Leth's family spend the night on their rice field dam. The rain poured down and they huddled close together with their extra clothes over them. The clothes became soaked in seconds. His mother thanked God that her youngest child, a three-year-old girl, had been staying with her grandmother in a small community outside the city, where she might escape the purges.

Even in the heat of the next day, with temperatures in the upper nineties, the humidity kept their clothing from drying completely. It was hard to move, but they didn't want to stop. They needed shelter, and some food, even if it meant laboring in rice paddies for no money.

Dino, who had been walking beside the family most of the time, broke out ahead one afternoon. When they caught up to him, he was sitting in the shade of a large tree. He ran toward them barking, scrambled back to the tree, and sat under it.

They passed him by, expecting him to follow, but he just sat in the shade and barked at them. Leth knew what his dog was telling them.

You need to rest. Come here and sit with me and take a little break in the shade.

Leth explained this to his mother, and they backtracked to the tree and rested for a few minutes. When they were ready to continue their journey, Dino joined them without an argument, wagging along beside them once again.

Tens of thousands died en route to the labor camps around the country. The longer the trek, the worse the outcome. Lack of food, water, and shelter, combined with the scorching humid days, the rains, and the incessant walking, claimed the youngest, oldest, and feeblest.

The death marches were just the beginning. For the next four years, the utopian vision of "agricultural communes" would become one of the world's worst genocides. About two million—one-fourth of the population—died of starvation or disease, or were executed.

It seemed as though almost anything was punishable by death. Having an education; practicing religion; being able to speak or understand another language; being of Chinese, Vietnamese, or Thai ancestry; and even wearing glasses—a sign of intellect and education, believed the Khmer Rouge—was a death sentence. Close relatives of soldiers and even former civil servants also faced death, or at least especially cruel treatment.

Leth and his family took on other names and identities to disassociate themselves from the link to the army. "I didn't care what I was called," Leth says. "You can call me Tin Can as long as I can survive."

Only Dino kept his original name.

Leth and his family decided to tell people his father was a tricycle driver who taxied people around, and to say his mother and father were divorced. Leth felt guilty lying about his father, but he knew his father would approve.

Paranoia grew rampant. Children were bribed to betray relatives and other adults, often having no idea that even an offhand comment, no matter how innocent, might become a reason for the person's arrest and disappearance. Some children indoctrinated deeply enough with the brutal regime's ideology ratted people out, knowing the consequences.

During their years living under the Khmer Rouge, Leth's family was discovered four times by people who knew them. The family had to flee, and did so under dark of night.

The labor camp where they spent the most time was at a long-abandoned rice-processing factory. They shared the rat-infested domicile with twenty to thirty families. Everyone slept on the floor, on sheets of plastic.

Some days Leth left for the rice paddy at 4 A.M. and did not return until midnight. Twelve-hour shifts were standard, but they usually went far longer, and sometimes it was miles to the paddy.

Food was in as short supply as sleep. Workers were given the most meager portions possible for survival—a little rice in liquid was all Leth expected on a daily basis. People were hungry all the time. Starvation was rampant.

In desperation, Leth and some other children would try to catch field rats. Everything was watched, and if they were caught, the best they could hope for would be to be tied up and deprived of food for a day or two. Some were shot for the offense.

The safest time to catch rats was at night, which worked well with the nocturnal habits of the rodents. The children would steal out of the factory and find them in nearby fields using homemade lanterns made from bottles with oil.

Cooking the rats had to be done with the greatest of care, since the smell of cooked meat—whatever the source—was easy to trace in a place where food was almost nonexistent and rarely smelled of anything other than cooked rice. They would skin the rats, gut them, wash them, and cook them over a fire far from camp. If they could get their hands on herbs, especially mint, it would help kill the rat smell and taste.

Leth also collected water bugs in the rice fields whenever he wasn't being watched. Their sting burned his skin but his hunger made him not care. He would cut off their heads, clean out some part in the middle he knew he wasn't supposed to eat, and roast them on bonfires. They tasted like nothing, but the crunch was satisfying and they were a source of much-needed protein.

A friend a year older than Leth went off looking for edible vegetation one afternoon. He didn't come back that night. Two days later his decapitated body, stuffed at the neck with hay, was tied to a tree for all to see. It was a lesson to others who might attempt to think and act so freely.

In this dark time, the one light in Leth's life was his dog. Somehow Dino had managed to stay alive. He was well liked by the families. He added a little memory of home, of normalcy, of better times, to the misery. Plus he chased away the bad rats. The kind of rats in the factory were believed to be disease ridden, so they were not usually on anyone's menu.

It seemed to Leth that his dog knew what to do for survival. Dino escaped the scrutiny of the Khmer Rouge because he usually stayed in the factory during the daytime. With food so scarce, the dog fended for himself. Sometimes Leth would sneak him some of the extra rat meat if there was any. Or rice.

When Leth came back from the rice paddies, Dino would run to the door and greet him, just as he had at home. He jumped up and down and wagged with excitement at seeing that his boy was home again.

One night, Dino wasn't there to greet him. A couple of people said they'd seen him by the train tracks. With his makeshift lantern, Leth ran outside and found Dino. His lifelong friend was lying in a pool of blood, with two bullet holes in his body.

Leth wept silently. He wanted to open up and wail but he knew he would end up like his dog if he did.

He later learned that two young Khmer Rouge soldiers had used Dino for target practice. They laughed as they walked away after killing the dog.

Leth and his mother buried Dino in the yard of the factory. They said no words, in case someone would accuse them of praying.

Shortly after Dino's death, Leth was separated from his mother and sister, and taken ten miles away to another labor camp, only this one had no shelter. He was ten years old.

Separation of children from their families was common. It made it easier for the Khmer Rouge to inculcate youth with its lessons. The other children could tell from the way Leth spoke that he had a decent education for a boy his age. His father had taken his schooling seriously. He had hoped to one day send his son to France or Australia for college.

But in the camp, Leth refused to acknowledge he had any education. He acted illiterate. They tested him several times but he kept up the ruse.

Leth and the other children slept outside. A pile of leaves was his mattress. His imagination helped him get through the nights.

As he would later describe, "Fire was the light at night, wind was the music, the sky was the movie." He wished Dino could be there to watch the movie with him. He would have loved it.

When it rained, as it did for months at a time, his imagination dried up and he felt hopeless. He was sure he would not survive for long.

He would get to see his mother only rarely. One time she visited when he had a flu. She brought him some medicine she had made from a tree. He had taken it before and knew how bitter it was. He didn't look forward to the medicine, but he knew it could help. "The more bitter the taste, the faster it will cure," his mother used to tell him.

The leader of the group refused to let her give it to Leth. "Because of mothers like you pampering their children so much, that's why the children are so weak and lazy!" he yelled. Leth watched helplessly as his mother stood under a large tree, only slightly protected from the torrents, and wept.

He waved for her to leave. He didn't want her to be accused of anything.

When people were escorted away from the camps after a transgression—admitting they had an education, being caught hunting for bugs to eat, the discovery they were related to a soldier or government worker—they were often told they were being taken to a place where the slate would be wiped clean. At first, those left behind thought this meant a place of forgiveness, perhaps reeducation.

But when these people never came back, it was clear they had gone to the killing fields—the mass graves throughout Cambodia where the bodies of the executed and dead were rarely fully buried.

The lucky ones were shot. To save bullets, executions were often carried out using clubs, spades, sharpened bamboo sticks, deadly scorpions, and sharp palm tree leaves. Children and babies were sometimes killed by bashing their heads against the trunks of trees.

Young Leth was certain that with any misstep, this would also be his fate.

"Failure is not an option," Leth tells a Secret Service dog handler he's helping to train at the tactical village at RTC some thirty-six years later. It's a phrase heard a great deal among Secret Service officers and agents. And it was the same mind-set that kept Leth alive through the years of the killing fields and on the subsequent arduous journey to refugee camps in Cambodia, Thailand, and eventually the Philippines.

A Vietnamese invasion that began on December 25, 1978, eventually forced the Khmer Rouge to relinquish control and loosen its death grip on the citizens. The killing fields were over, but it's estimated that another three hundred thousand died of starvation from 1979 to 1980.

The torment was far from over for Leth and his family. On their long walk home, Leth and a friend were taking a quick bathroom break from a large group walking back to Battambang when Khmer Rouge soldiers armed with AK-47s saw them and accused them of spying. They marched them to a small house and separated the boys, bringing his friend down to the basement and Leth upstairs.

Five large men—anyone would be large to a thirteen-year-old boy who had been starved for four years—tied him up and beat him, urinated on him, and spit on him to get him to admit he was a spy. He told them he was going back home to reunite with his family but they insisted that he was a spy, that boys like him spy for the Vietnamese and that's why they were successful in the invasion.

Leth knew they were going to kill him if he kept telling the truth. And he knew they would kill him if he said he was a spy. He couldn't believe he had survived all those years only to be killed after the liberation of his country.

After eight hours, someone ran into the room and told his torturers that the Vietnamese were on their way. The men let him go and reminded him how lucky he was, "this time."

In Battambang, the family's house was in ruins. They had nothing. He and his mother and sister visited his younger sister and grandmother for the first time since 1975. It was a tearful reunion, but it didn't last long. Leth and his mother had to go off and make money to help them, and to survive.

They set out for a village a little past the border of Thailand, about a week's walk away. They had to hide from skirmishes between the Khmer Rouge and the Vietnamese, and as they got closer to the border, Thai involvement as well.

Their route took them close to some killing fields. Leth could smell the nauseating odor of decomposing bodies for a mile before reaching them. He tried not to look at the wasteland of human decay, but sometimes he couldn't help it.

He wondered if his father might be in one of these fields. He held out hope that somehow he had escaped that fate—that one day they might pass each other by and there would be a reunion like no other. Whenever he saw a man in a Cambodian army uniform, the boy's eyes hungrily scanned the face for signs of familiarity.

When Leth and his mother finally reached the border, they went a little farther into a Thai village and bought bread, noodles, and moon cakes, then walked back to the border, selling the goods there for three weeks at a time, back and forth from the village to the border. They made the long walk home with the money they made, rested, and set back out.

His older sister joined them on what would turn out to be their last trip. They hadn't brought enough provisions, and ran out of food and water on the way there. In the oppressive heat they would not survive long.

They drank water that had pooled in the footprints of elephants. They ate leaves off trees and bushes for their moisture and to try to stave off their incessant hunger.

They prayed for a miracle.

Shortly after, their path led them to a pond. It looked fairly clean. They couldn't believe their fortune. They ran in, past its muddy shore, until they were thigh deep. There, they gulped their fill out of cupped hands. Leth felt like a dried-up old sponge someone had suddenly doused with water.

As they filled their containers for the rest of the journey, Leth spotted what seemed to be a couple of floating tree trunks on the other side of the small pond. One seemed to have some bright cloth on it.

He walked over to see what it was. It wasn't until he was a few feet away that the familiar stench of death hit him. He didn't want to look but by then he was so close he couldn't help it. The logs were the bodies of a man, woman, and child, dead for days but not long enough to make them unrecognizable in gender and age.

He felt his stomach lurch and quickly looked away. He couldn't afford to lose the water his body so badly needed. He ran along the pond edge to rejoin his mother and sister. He didn't tell them about the bodies. What good would it do?

The next day brought heavy violence between the warring

factions. He and his family were caught in one of the worst gun battles yet. People everywhere around them were dying. Explosions hit so close they shook the earth under his feet.

They hid for three days and when they emerged, to their astonishment, they were picked up on the road by a relief organization. The truck transported them to the first of several refugee camps. It was the beginning of a long journey away from the torment of the past years.

Cambodia, Thailand, the Philippines, each camp got better. But there was no way for Leth to get in touch with his grandmother and sister. He hoped that if he found a country to take them in as refugees he could work hard, send them money, and eventually bring them to live with them.

They had been told their best options for a country that would welcome them as refugees were Canada, Australia, or France. They never dreamed the United States was a possibility, but in 1983 they found themselves on an airplane to Washington, D.C. An uncle had arrived in the area a year before, and a Montgomery County, Maryland, church had agreed to sponsor them.

It was a big adjustment, but Leth wanted to live the American dream and be successful enough to take care of his whole family. He already knew he had it in him to work hard. Harder than he could ever imagine a person could work.

He went to high school, learning the English alphabet with three other newcomers during his first days. To help make ends meet and start saving for the future, he took a job washing dishes in a Chinese restaurant in Silver Spring after school and on weekends. He saved up enough to get a bicycle, which he rode to work, even in the winter.

When Leth graduated from high school, he would have liked to go to a four-year college, but his focus was on keeping two or three jobs at a time. Over the next several years, he attended community colleges whenever he could. He eventually got an associate's degree in Philadelphia, and in 1998 he graduated from Widener University with a degree in criminal justice and sociology.

He did some social work with juvenile offenders and then worked several years for the Bureau of Prisons in Philadelphia and New Jersey. He was grateful for the work, but being an officer in the system was not an easy way to make a living. After a few years, he applied for work with the Secret Service's Uniformed Division.

Not long after, in 2002, he received the letter offering him a job with the United States Secret Service.

"I was so joyful I was jumping up and down like a little child. I never thought this would happen. It is the American dream for me."

At the graduation ceremony, his mother fought tears when she thought of how far her son had come, and how proud her husband would be of him. Leth was feeling emotional as well.

"Every day I go to work I am proud of who and what I am working for," he says. "I came to this country with nothing, just one small backpack, did not know a word of English. America is my country.

"I feel a deep loyalty to my country and to the Secret Service, and am very proud to protect the most powerful office in the world with my life any time and any day."

Leth has been a training assistant for the EDT program since 2013. He spent nearly nine years working as a handler with his EDT dog, a friendly Malinois named Reik. They traveled the world to protect the president of the United States, the vice president, and other key leaders.

They did their job together in Germany, Japan, Thailand, South Korea, Oman, Jordan, and Romania. They went on missions in forty-nine states—all but Maine.

In 2012, President Obama visited Cambodia. It was the first time a U.S. president had gone to Cambodia. Leth was thrilled he and Reik had been selected to be part of the canine entourage.

He had often thought about his younger sister, whom he hadn't seen since 1979. He and his mother and older sister had tried to find her and his grandmother, but there was never any response to letters or inquiries. No news at all.

He assumed the worst. He had finally resigned himself to the likely truth that his father had been killed shortly after Leth brought him breakfast at the high school. He learned that several fellow officers had been found in a killing field not far from their home.

It would not surprise him if his sister and grandmother had perished in the harsh post–Khmer Rouge years.

Leth occasionally tried to tell his American friends a little about what he had been through. He was surprised by how many couldn't believe such atrocities could happen to anyone anywhere in the world.

He saw photos in magazines or online that showed the nightmare in a way he could never describe to anyone: black and white memories of hundreds of skulls and bones in the mud, of the lines of frightened people forced to leave their homes, of the brutal conditions they endured for years. When he looked at photos like these, the heartbreak of a childhood of starvation and fatigue and fear would come rushing back to him. So would the sadness over the likely loss of his sister and grandmother.

In 2005, a freak coincidence led him to discover that his sister was still alive. Their grandmother had passed years earlier.

His sister was just as shocked that Leth and their mother and sister were still alive.

They talked on the phone regularly. His mother was so overcome that the first time she tried to talk with her daughter she could only cry.

He reunited with his sister during his Secret Service detail in Cambodia with Reik. They met in front of his hotel in Phnom Penh and instantly recognized each other. They hugged and cried. Reik had not seen his handler cry before and Leth thought the dog looked concerned. He told him it was OK. That it was better than OK.

Leth and his sister talked in his hotel room for hours. In his downtime she brought him the food he missed so much from his homeland. They caught up on the decades, and he realized just how devastated his country still was from the genocide. He vowed to do something about it.

Since then he has been sending money to provide wells for villages that have no clean drinking water. It's $200 per well, and he has made a dozen wells so far. He also sends money to his sister to donate directly to the poor, especially the elderly.

He went back to Cambodia in 2015 with the First Lady, who was there as part of the "Let Girls Learn" campaign. If he wins the lottery, he wants to build schools there.

He and his sister met again during the trip with Michelle Obama, but Reik was now retired and enjoying some well-deserved couch time at home.

Reik's retirement was a hard adjustment for both Leth and his dog. For two years, Reik walked to the front door with Leth every day as he left for work and sat looking plaintively through a nearby window for hours.

Reik, who is almost fourteen, has a retirement most humans would envy. He eats organic food, drinks filtered water, walks miles a day, gets spoiled around the clock by Leth's ninety-eight-year-old mother, and sleeps on any of a number of special beds set up throughout the large Northern Maryland house he shares with Leth, his wife, mother, and other relatives who need a place to stay.

His favorite bed is in the master bedroom. There's a chaise longue by a large window that overlooks the front lawn and street. On the chaise are two cushy dog beds. When Reik reposes on it, he looks like canine royalty.

Reik still has his paw in the game as well. Leth's daughter occasionally distributes some black powder around their yard for him. Leth gets it at a gun store as a special retirement activity for Reik. When Reik heads out with Leth after the gunpowder is hidden, the dog is always delightfully surprised. He wags as he sniffs around for the familiar scent. When he finds it and sits, Leth praises him like mad and throws him a Kong. For a few moments, they are back in it together.

He loves making his dog feel like he is the greatest dog on earth, because it's clear to Leth that he is.

Of course, there was Dino, back in Cambodia. He was the best dog, too. Leth will never forget how his hero helped save him and his family from physical and mental anguish. He doesn't know if he could have made it if it weren't for that little dog who seemed eternally happy.

Leth named his first dog in the United States after his French bulldog. This Dino was a German shepherd. When he died at age fourteen, Leth interred his ashes in a Buddhist temple. On his urn, under his name and dates of birth and death, is this simple inscription: BEST FRIEND I EVER HAD.

It took him many years before he was up for getting a dog

again. But eventually another German shepherd worked his way into his heart. This one he called Buddy. Buddy "owned the house" but didn't mind when Reik joined the family.

If Buddy had one pet peeve with Reik, it's that the law-enforcement canine could be a tattletale. When Buddy did something Reik knew wasn't quite within house rules, Reik would run and bark at Leth, who would be obliged to see what crime his Secret Service dog was reporting this time.

When he found Buddy with the shredded item or other evidence of the canine crime he had perpetrated, Buddy would glance at Leth, then look at Reik with an expression that seemed laden with disappointment at his betrayal.

"Hey, Buddy," Leth would comfort. "It's OK. What doesn't kill you makes you stronger."

CHAPTER 14

ONE HOT DOG

Two students from Italy look confused as they stare at the massive, five-story gray building with its French Second Empire architecture on Seventeenth Street NW. They glance from the building to their phone maps and back at the building. They come to the same disappointing conclusion.

"Questa è la Casa Bianca," one says to the other. *This is the White House.*

They take each other's photos in front of it, but one of them decides to ask a security guard posted in front of one of its gates, because this just doesn't seem right.

"No, this isn't the White House. It's just around the corner," she tells them, motioning with her hand to the right and backward, like a flight attendant pointing out the exit rows.

"Or you could go this way and you'll get to the other side," she says, pointing with her left arm and backward.

"Thank you! We thought this is not very white for a White House!" one of them says cheerfully. "It looks like a haunted house." His friend is already erasing the photos of what was actually the Eisenhower Executive Office Building from his phone.

The guard says it happens. Some phone maps indicate that the whole White House complex is the White House itself.

The students decide to take the guard's second suggestion. In a few minutes, they're among the crowd taking photos on the south side of the White House along E Street NW. It's a far-off view of the Executive Mansion, but a famous one, with its large fountain, lush lawn, and splendid variety of trees.

A boy about twelve years old points to a man standing with his legs apart on top of the White House. It's a Uniformed Division Countersniper Team member.

"Is that a rifle or a telescope?" he asks his father.

"He could kill someone in a split second if they look like trouble," his father tells him. "So look sharp."

A woman in her sixties asks a Secret Service officer if she can take his photo as he stands by his vehicle.

"No, sorry," he says, and smiles.

"That's OK," she says, and tells her husband, in a knowing and hushed voice, "Agents have to be very careful."

"Is this as close as we can get to the White House?" the husband asks the officer. "It looks closer in photos."

"No, sir, if you go down to that street, Fifteenth, make a left and another left on Pennsylvania Avenue, you can get closer on the other side."

"Thank you! We're from New Jersey. We don't know our way around here." The man packs away his camera, and he and his wife walk off in pursuit of a closer view.

As they reach the intersection of Pennsylvania Avenue and Fifteenth Street NW there's a sign that covers a steel barricade. It features the face of a smiling chocolate Labrador retriever, with the words CA-NINES WORKING TO KEEP YOU SAFE: PLEASE DO NOT ATTEMPT TO TOUCH OR PET THESE ANIMALS WHILE THEY ARE WORKING.

"Mommy, doggy!" a girl in an orange stroller exclaims on seeing the sign.

"Maybe we'll see a doggy like Katy's!" her mother says.

As they wheel by the Treasury Building, there's no sign of a dog.

"Look, there's the White House!" the girl's father says. "That's a big house, isn't it? That's where the president lives."

The vantage point on the north side is much closer than the south side. The man from New Jersey must be happy.

The little girl doesn't seem to care about the White House.

"Where's Katy's doggy?"

"There's a doggy!" her mother says, pointing to an English springer spaniel walking toward them, his leash held by a tall Secret Service dog handler. The dog is named Dyson, and for some reason, his head is damp.

His handler, Nate C., gently guides the dog around passersby, holding the leather leash so there's enough slack for Dyson to follow his nose. Nate moves his hand in another direction, and the dog takes his cue, walking into a small crowd.

The liver-and-white springer looks like he's simply out taking a stroll, but he's actually sniffing for scents of explosives on people. He's one of the Personnel Screening Canine Open Area (PSCO) dogs, better known as Friendly Dogs. He has the same job as Roadee but attracts slightly less attention.

Nate and Dyson walk up to the family with the toddler. Dyson gives the stroller a quick sniff, walks near the parents' legs, and moves on.

"That's not Katy's doggy!" the girl pouts.

The scent of hot dogs wafts in on a light breeze. It seems to be coming from a Sabrett hot dog vendor a few hundred feet down Pennsylvania Avenue. But the all-beef franks don't distract Dyson from his work. Whenever he comes near people, he is a dog on a mission.

The crowd is relatively light on this warm October weekday. Thirty seconds or more can pass between little groups of people. Nate stops for a few seconds, and his shadow lands on his dog. He's like a sundial. Beads of sweat collect on Nate's upper lip, but his dog is protected from the sun.

After about fifteen more minutes, another dog walks toward them. It's Roadee. Dyson and Roadee meet up, wagging, and sniff each other in the intimate fashion of dogs. It's a change of shifts, a punching of the canine time card. Roadee's in for a half hour, Dyson is clocked out for the day.

Dyson's tail is going full tilt as he speeds over to Nate's white van, across the street from the White House, on the east side of Lafayette Square. Nate opens the door and Dyson jumps in, still wagging hard.

The van is good things. The van is a couple of mini Milk-Bones the size of a pinky tip. The van is a chew toy and a deer antler. The van is a place to "chillax," as Nate says—something that doesn't come easily to this dog, who is known for his nonstop energy as well as his speed. When Dyson isn't doing his careful searches at the White House fence line, he wants to run.

Nate reaches into a compartment and pulls out a thermometer. On seeing it, Dyson lies on his side. He stares into Nate's eyes as Nate coats the tip of the thermometer with Vaseline and inserts it. Dyson doesn't even flinch, much less look at the thermometer with concern, as most dogs do in these situations. He has become accustomed to having his temperature taken in the last several weeks. It's old hat.

His temp is 101.6—well within the normal range for dogs.

"You did it, Dyson!" he says, and the dog wags again, happy to have made his handler happy.

Dyson sits near Nate and gazes with soulful eyes into Nate's once again. Nate looks at Dyson with a similar expression. There's a lot of love going on here. Far more than the end of a typical shift at the White House.

Today was their first day back at the fence line in eleven weeks. For a few agonizing days in July, Nate thought he might not ever be back here—or anywhere—with Dyson.

Nate spent a week of leave in late July 2015 installing Pergo Highland Hickory flooring in the living room of his split-foyer house. Actually, it's Dyson's house, as he sometimes calls it, because in a way, Nate and his wife bought the house for him.

They'd been wanting to upgrade from their town house for a while, and when Nate learned he was getting this energetic springer spaniel as his partner, he knew the small yard wouldn't be enough. It was adequate for their Boston terrier and Lab-Dane mix, but not Dyson.

"He runs seven-minute miles, and the only reason it's only seven is because I'm holding the leash," he told his wife.

They bought a place with a much larger yard with full-grown trees. Plenty of room for his springer to run around and retrieve balls.

While he was upgrading the flooring, he wasn't able to spend as much time with Dyson as usual, but Dyson was happy relaxing in the house with the other dogs.

On the last day of his leave, a Saturday, Nate and the dogs headed to the backyard for a game of catch. It was in the mid-eighties. The Boston terrier, not being a retrieving sort, sat this one out. But Dyson and Echo were raring to go.

After just a few throws, Dyson lay down on the other side of the yard while Echo ran around sniffing this and that. Dyson never rested during playtime. Nate knew something had to be terribly wrong.

As he raced over to his dog he heard an alarming gasping sound and realized it was Dyson, struggling for breath. In true spaniel form, the dog clenched the tennis ball in his teeth and wouldn't give it up.

Nate hoisted him up and was surprised that he didn't struggle as he usually did when he picked him up. He ran him to the bathtub and poured lukewarm water on him—not too cold, because he knew that could make this worse.

He took Dyson's temperature: 108 degrees.

He tried to quash a sense of icy panic he felt rushing through him. This could not be happening. Not to his Dyson—the dog no one else in Friendly Dog class had put on their list. He had seen his potential and the dog had lived up to it beautifully. They had a bond from the first day. There was something about the way this dog looked at him, even then.

He called the veterinary emergency number at Fort Belvoir, where the Secret Service and local military working dog handlers take their dogs for most veterinary care. For reasons he couldn't fathom, they wanted him to go there instead of an emergency clinic closer to his home. He'd have to contend with Maryland highways and go through Washington, D.C., before he got to the military installation in Fairfax, Virginia. If there was traffic, there was no telling how long it would take.

He lay Dyson in the van, on the flat surface where dogs hang out during work breaks, and blasted the air-conditioning.

This was an officer down. His partner. He turned on the siren and lights and drove as quickly as he safely could.

"It's OK, buddy, you're going to be OK," he told him, looking in the rearview mirror and trying to choke back the tears as Dyson lay prostrate.

After a while, Dyson lifted his head. Nate kept talking to him.

It was a weekend, so the traffic was light. As they neared Fort Belvoir, Nate checked Dyson and saw with some relief that he was sitting up and gazing right back at him with his large, brown eyes.

Nate prayed the worst was over.

He whisked his dog straight back to the treatment room. As the veterinary staff was taking his temperature and starting him on IV fluids, Dyson kept spinning around to try to get to the thermometer. He snapped at the vet tech—something the normally friendly, gentle dog had never done. Nate knew this was a sign things were still very wrong inside of Dyson, that his dog was in survival mode.

Dyson had to be muzzled. It's protocol at Belvoir to muzzle all military and other working dogs anyway, no matter how easy going. During prolonged stays they can be without muzzles as long as the staffers aren't doing a procedure on them.

"Most of the Secret Service dogs we see, even the ERT dogs, are very, very friendly," says Army captain Brianna S., DVM, who runs the Fort Belvoir Veterinary Center (VETCEN). "They're really sweet and come up and want to be petted and really want their muzzles off. They'll rub up against you like they're saying, 'Could you take this off, please?'"

Dyson made no attempt to take it off. He didn't have it in him.

His temp was only 102 degrees, which is within normal range for dogs. Cooling him with the lukewarm water and the air-conditioning had worked. But Brianna knew that since Dyson's temperature had been up to 108 degrees, he wasn't out of the woods.

She was worried but tried not to show Nate. There had been a two-week marathon of canine heat injuries as temperatures began their midsummer climb. Just the day before, an Army dog was rushed in by his distraught handler. The dog had no pulse, and nothing they did brought him back to life.

Like the dog who didn't make it, Dyson had heatstroke, the most serious category of heat injury. If it doesn't kill, heatstroke can result in damage to the heart, kidneys, liver, nervous system, and gastrointestinal system. The complications don't always manifest immediately.

The cooling Nate had done before leaving his house and en route probably saved Dyson from arriving DOA. One study showed that 61 percent of dogs with heatstroke died if not cooled before "presentation to a veterinarian." "Only" 38 percent of dogs who were cooled by their owners had died.

Blood work showed Dyson's coagulation times were prolonged, meaning he was taking too long to clot. A bad sign. His platelet count was low and getting lower with each check. Low platelet counts can lead to spontaneous internal hemorrhaging. He was already manifesting little purplish skin spots called petechiae, another signal that clotting is amiss.

Brianna was scared that Dyson was headed for something called disseminated intravascular coagulation (DIC), an extremely dangerous condition where the body is both bleeding and clotting abnormally. DIC often leads to death. Brianna had a professor who once referred to DIC as shorthand for "death is coming" to impart the severity of the condition.

They immediately started a transfusion to try to prevent DIC.

Nate stayed with Dyson all night, sitting or lying down on the tile floor of the treatment room, right next to him. Because of his worry, and the staff's hourly checks of Dyson's temperature and vitals, Nate was awake most of the night. He got maybe a half hour of sleep and subsisted on a couple of small Snickers bars they scrounged up.

Dyson had a dog bed, but Nate was just in the shorts and the T-shirt he'd been wearing when he rushed out of the house. With the AC on in the kennel area, it was cold, but he didn't care. He couldn't leave his dog's side until he knew he had rounded the bend.

Staff had removed Dyson's muzzle after the initial exam, once he was calmer. They didn't want anything to impede his breathing, and it was clear Dyson didn't need it anymore.

Nate stroked Dyson's head.

"You're doing good, Dyson. You're a good, good boy," he told him.

He felt frightened and heartbroken as he looked at his dog, with all the tubes and wires coming out of him. How had Dyson ended up almost dying from chasing the ball three times in the yard? That kind of activity was nothing for Dyson, who could run from morning to night and barely be winded. It made no sense.

Brianna told him it was probably the increasingly hot weather in the last two weeks combined with the fact that Dyson wasn't all that active that week and had spent more time than usual indoors. Maybe his body hadn't yet acclimated to the heat.

On Sunday, Dyson was about the same. Nate called his wife and asked her to have some food ready so he could run home, take a shower, change his clothes, and bring back something to eat and something to sleep on.

He was gone for less than two hours. When he returned, Dyson lifted his head and wagged a few beats. It wasn't his usual exuberant greeting, but his happiness registered on his heart monitor, which started beeping more rapidly as soon as Nate walked into the room.

Other than low but improving coagulation times, Dyson wasn't doing too badly. His energy was down, but that was expected. Brianna told Nate that if he kept on this track, he might be able to go home Monday.

Nate settled in for another night beside his partner. "Just one more night here, buddy, and you'll be home," he told him while lying next to him face-to-face, smoothing the soft fur on Dyson's ear. "Everybody misses you, Dyson."

Dyson sighed, and his eyes closed. Nate kept his hand on Dyson for a long time after his dog fell asleep. He just wanted to feel him breathing, to feel him alive. Mostly he wanted Dyson to know he was right there, no matter what.

Back when he was traveling around the world as part of the elite Marine Helicopter Squadron One (HMX-1) in support of the president of the United States, Nate would often see the squadron's canine teams and think how much fun it would be to work alongside a dog.

He didn't think it would ever be his career. He loved his job. He'd enlisted in the Marines right out of high school and had gone through MP school in hopes it would look good on his résumé when he one day applied to be a New York state trooper.

HMX-1 came recruiting, and out of the 350 Marines going through training at the time, they chose ten. Nate was nineteen years old the first time he wore dress blues and stood, armed, a foot away from President George W. Bush at Camp David. He saluted Bush, and Bush saluted him. It would be the beginning of an exciting, five-year Marine Corps career.

He and his crew would sometimes ride in the presidential helicopters to transport them relatively short distances when the president was not on board. (The helos, known as "white tops" because of their coloring scheme, are called Marine One only when the president is on board.) It was easier than dismantling them and transporting them by C-17 military cargo planes and then reassembling them at the destination.

A frequent route during Bush's presidency was from the D.C. area to Waco, Texas. It was a long helicopter flight, with a few refueling stops—secure stops with fuel trucks that had to be checked and cleared on the ground for safety.

Nate's main flying duty was in one of the Marine or Army support helicopters that accompany Marine One: CH-46 Sea Knights, CH-53E Super Stallions, UH-60 Black Hawks, or CH-47 Chinooks. Among the far-flung countries his job took him were Germany, Hungary, Saudi Arabia, Guatemala, and Indonesia.

At the end of his five years (when the initial Marine Corps recruiter handed him his contract, which for some reason was for five years instead of four, Nate thought, *Eh, what's one more year?!*), he had changed his mind about being a state trooper. His years based in Quantico had instilled a love of the area, and he enjoyed the idea that he was helping protect the president.

While in the Marines, he had come to admire and respect the work of the Secret Service. It was the only job he applied for toward the end of his time in the Marines.

He started his UD career in the Foreign Missions Branch and, after fourteen months, transferred to the Secret Service's bike patrol (known in the Service as "Trek patrol"). He thought of it as a modern-day cavalry unit, with officers able to get to areas of concern more quickly than those on foot, and able to go where vehicles couldn't. The physical aspect of the job appealed to the former high school soccer, lacrosse, and basketball team member.

In Secret Service bike training, the students learn how to ride down staircases on their police bikes. Nate challenged himself to ride *up* stairs as well and would practice occasionally on short sets of stairs.

Nate loved the job, the physicality, the outdoor nature of it. But almost three years into it, he saw an announcement for the new Friendly Dog program, and the dog lover in him jumped at the chance.

As exciting as HMX-1 duty had been, working with Dyson trumped it. Dyson was, of course, the best dog in the world. Nate loved everything about this dog: His cartoon character–like lightbulb moments when he sniffed an explosives odor during training. His wild enthusiasm for the work. His loving nature. His penchant for belly rubs. And those eyes . . .

Dyson didn't take his eyes off Nate as his heart fluttered at three hundred beats per minute. Nate imagined how scared his dog must be, how weak and awful he must feel. Nate himself had been feeling this way since 3 A.M., when Dyson started experiencing dangerously rapid heart rates at random intervals. He couldn't believe this was happening less than twelve hours from when he'd hoped to be able to bring him home.

They checked Dyson's blood work. His white blood cell count and liver enzymes came back abnormal, and his platelets were starting to plummet. The minimum is around 200,000 per microliter, and Dyson's crashed, down to 88,000, then 15,000, and eventually 9,000. Anything under 20,000 to 30,000 can lead to spontaneous internal hemorrhaging. Brianna thought Dyson was probably tiptoeing around the edge of this at best. His coagulation times were getting worse, too.

Nate tried to block the agonizing thought that Dyson could be dying right now because he threw the ball for him in his backyard. That he was responsible for the suffering his partner was going through.

His own chest felt tight and heavy. He tried not to show his worry, because Dyson would pick up on that. But Dyson knew him well, and Nate knew he couldn't hide anything from his dog.

Brianna and the tech on duty had been administering a constant rate infusion of lidocaine intravenously to try to control Dyson's heart rate, but had to give him an additional dose every time his heart went above 150 beats per minute. Dyson was suffering from ventricular tachycardia with ventricular premature complexes (VPCs). Lidocaine—the same agent used for numbing at the dentist—is the normal standard of care and first choice for VPCs. But it wasn't working well on Dyson.

Brianna conferred with Major Jay C., one of Fort Belvoir's clinical specialists and a boarded veterinary surgeon by trade. He suggested trying the drug procainamide, an alternative to lidocaine. It wasn't the first drug they reached for because it can sometimes cause arrhythmias to worsen. But at this point it was worth a shot.

They didn't have any in the clinic, so Brianna drove over to the base's human hospital, Fort Belvoir Community Hospital, to try to get some. She left instructions with the tech to phone her if Dyson started to get even worse.

Dyson had needed so much round-the-clock care that Brianna had slept only two or three hours since his arrival. When she met with resistance from the hospital's weekend staff, who didn't understand that this person in civilian clothes was a veterinarian who desperately needed this medicine for a patient, it took everything she had to keep it together.

This dog's life was at stake, and here she was, wasting precious time trying to convince them to give her the meds. Normally the hospital works seamlessly with veterinary staff. She knew it was just a glitch, and the people were nice enough, but it was a glitch that could end up costing a dog his life, a handler his best friend, and the president a hardworking protector.

About ninety minutes after Brianna first arrived, they gave her the procainamide. She raced back to the vet hospital.

To her disappointment, the new medicine seemed to wear off more quickly than the lidocaine, so after all that, she put Dyson back on his original medicine.

It had been hours since the tachycardia started, and Dyson was weakening. He couldn't raise his head anymore, or didn't bother.

Nate lay next to him, looking at him eye to eye. His goal was to try to keep Dyson's heart rate from spiking, and to keep him calm when it did spike. There was nothing else he could do.

At one point, Dyson's monitor showed a heart rate of 350. Dyson still did not take his deep brown eyes off Nate.

Nate stroked Dyson's side, his head, and had a talk with him.

"Dyson, it's OK if you have to go. It will be OK. Please don't suffer any more for my sake," he told him, trying not to lose it.

But when Dyson's heart rate spiked again, Nate tried to coach him through it. He wanted his dog to want to fight it. After all, Dyson was only two, and they had so many great years ahead together.

"Come on, Dyson, you can make it through this one," he said, listening for the monitor to drop back down. "It will be over soon; you'll feel better."

Dyson's "normal" heart rate since all this started was 150 beats per minute, higher than it should be, but not dangerously so. When Dyson's heart dropped back down to 150 after an episode, Nate could feel his own heart relax.

On Monday morning, with the regular staff back at the human hospital, Brianna went over and got a bunch of other supplies for Dyson. One of them was a lipid emulsion therapy, which acts as a toxin scavenger. She hoped it would help remove toxins that may have been contributing to his VPCs and tachycardia.

They administered it through a catheter into a vein. Within twenty minutes, his heart rate went down, he started having more normal beats, and the frequency of the VPCs decreased.

As the hours passed, Dyson's heart rate during his episodes gradually decreased. Gone were the 350s, then the 300s. The highs became 250, then 200.

Brianna and another vet who had come in had thought about putting a central line into Dyson to be able to administer multiple drugs and nutritional support more efficiently. It would also help Dyson because they could draw blood without having to poke him all the time. But they decided against it. It's a relatively bloody procedure, and because Dyson's platelet count was still far too low, there was concern about clotting issues.

Instead they opted to place a feeding tube in Dyson's nose. He needed to get nutrition, and he wasn't eating. He had already lost five pounds from his forty-five-pound frame.

Brianna wanted to stay with him to see him through. But the other vets and the techs insisted that, for her sake, she go home and get some rest after the marathon weekend. A vet sedated Dyson and wove the tube into his nose and down his esophagus to his stomach. Staff checked it with an X-ray to make sure the placement was right and started "feeding" him Ensure. He didn't seem to mind.

Dyson's blood work was improving. His platelets were still far too low, but they were moving in the right direction.

On Tuesday night, Nate felt for the first time like his dog was really going to make it. He had barely slept during the days and nights next to Dyson, but his fatigue was supplanted by cautious relief.

Dyson was now able to walk and would go outside to relieve himself. At first he moved lethargically. But by Tuesday night, with the feeding tube gone and eating on his own, he was strong enough to pull Nate outside.

On Wednesday, Dyson seemed almost like his old self again. He wagged when people came to see him, he rolled over to get a tummy rub, and while not as energetic as usual, he appeared to be well on the road to recovery. His platelets were at forty thousand and steadily improving, and his other blood work was back to normal.

Dyson was drinking in his usual funny manner as well. When he's excited, he'll dunk his head rapidly into the bowl. It looks like he's trying to drink the water at the bottom of the bowl. Often when he's done, he'll turn quickly and fling water everywhere. He didn't do his rousing finale at the vet's, but they would have welcomed it. Anything he did that was part of his usual repertoire made them happy.

It was time to go home—something that had seemed so close on Sunday night, and then so impossibly far a few hours later.

Brianna and the staff who had cared for Dyson were on hand with hugs and good wishes for Nate and Dyson.

"I was really scared there for a while," Brianna admitted for the first time, tearing up. "I would have been very, very upset if he didn't make it through."

Nate nodded, not able to speak because his emotions were so

close to the surface, and it was all still so raw. He got out a heartfelt, "Thank you for everything," and walked out the door, with Dyson leading the way.

The next day when he came back for a recheck, Dyson walked straight to the area where his dog bed had been, right next to the kennel. But the bed was gone. Dyson looked confused. He wanted to find his bed.

He sniffed around and found it in a pile of dog laundry in another room. He sniffed intently and stared at it.

"He's like, 'What's it doing over *here*?'" Brianna said and laughed.

She was pleased to see him looking like he was back to his old self. His platelet count was 70,000, almost double when he had left. Although it still wasn't normal, Brianna was confident it would keep increasing until it reached a healthy level. A few days later, his platelets checked out at a robust 374,000.

But it would be a long road—more than two months—before he could go back to the White House. Until then, there would be rest, and slow conditioning, building up his strength, stamina, and ability to work in the heat.

In training, Nate would have to frequently take his dog's temperature. He'd also have to get in the habit of wetting Dyson's whole body with water if it was hot out, or just his head if it was only warm.

Two of Dyson's best traits—his excitement about life and his nonstop energy—would prove the most challenging as Nate tried to keep his dog calm, especially during the increasingly hot days of August.

Nate started seeing a pattern. When Dyson was sniffing

people, which had been his regular job, his temperature was normal. But when he was learning a new task, especially when Nate cut him off leash, his excitement peaked, and so did his temperature. He got up a little over 106 degrees a few times.

Nate had to remain vigilant. He will have to for the rest of Dyson's life. Dogs who have suffered heat injuries are at higher risk for them in the future.

Since going home after the heatstroke, Dyson has been like Nate's shadow. Their bond, which was already strong, has become unbreakable—as it is with all the best dog teams. Dyson follows Nate everywhere—often even into the bathroom. When Nate showers, Dyson sits patiently between the plastic liner and the cloth shower curtain, waiting for this man who waited at his side during the worst time in his life.

While the intrepid team is working at the fence line, if you look up toward the White House, way past the fence, you may see another dog and handler. They don't look like Nate and Dyson, and they have very different jobs, but this pair also shared a defining experience. One that would turn a strong bond into a profound one . . .

CHAPTER 15

THE END OF A VERY STRANGE DAY

Hurricane is a tapper. When he wants to get Marshall's attention, he taps him with his paw. If someone is petting him and stops, he'll tap on whatever part of his or her body he can reach. He taps Marshall whenever he wants to come up for a hug.

At 7:15 P.M. on October 22, 2014, Marshall sat in his van and scanned the fence of the White House, looking for anyone who might be up to no good. He could read body language as easily as most people read books.

He had been on post on the north grounds for hours with nothing of note happening. Hurricane's amped-up demeanor was still puzzling him, and becoming slightly annoying after all these hours. But nothing distracted Marshall from keeping his eyes trained on the fence.

Tap tap tap.

Marshall felt Hurricane's paw hurriedly touching his left shoulder, like someone who urgently wanted to tell him something. Hurricane's ears were forward, and he stared toward the fence line.

For all of Hurricane's tapping, he had never once tapped Marshall while they were on post in the van.

All of Marshall's senses instantly went into high alert.

He peered through the blackness of the moonless night and saw nothing out of the ordinary. Just the usual tourists.

Tap tap tap.

"Cane, buddy—what is *up* with you?"

He scanned and something caught his eye: a figure, within a few feet of the fence, bounding toward it and flying over it like a trained athlete.

At 7:16:11, the man, wearing white basketball-style shorts and a dark, long-sleeved shirt, landed on the wrong side of the White House fence. Barely pausing, he sprang up and sprinted toward the White House.

On the Pennsylvania Avenue side of the fence, Secret Service officers rushed tourists away from the scene. If there was going to be shooting, they didn't want anyone in the line of fire.

Marshall and Hurricane had instantly deployed out of the van and were in place, ready for action. Mike and Jardan had done the same in their sector. The Emergency Response Team members without dogs had immediately organized into full tactical mode, getting to where they needed to be and issuing commands for him to stop.

But the sleek, muscular intruder didn't listen.

As he made his way toward the White House, he headed into Mike's sector. Mike had already been shouting commands to stop, warning that he'd release his dog. On seeing the dog, the man slowed but continued his forward progress.

After repeated warnings there was little choice. Mike gave Jardan the signal and the dog ran toward the fence jumper. At 7:16:36, Jardan made contact, biting him on his stomach. But he couldn't get a good bite and stay with the man.

Somehow, the thirty-foot lead had gotten caught on the end of Mike's rifle. Nothing like this had ever happened before in all the years of training for anyone in the ERT canine unit. It was the worst timing possible.

The dog reached the end of the wrapped lead, which stopped him with a jerk. He likely thought he was being given a correction by the handler, and ran back to Mike, per standard protocol after a correction. The dog didn't ask why. He just did what he was told.

Still, it finally made the man pause. At that point, Mike didn't perceive him as an active threat and chose not to send Jardan back. The man wasn't giving up; he was still shouting, but at least he wasn't making forward progress.

Hurricane watched from one side, barking and pulling, wanting to jump in and do what he had been trained to do his whole life. But this was Jardan's fight right now, and Marshall held tight to the lead.

The man raised up the bottom of his shirt. There could have been a weapon, or he could have been showing he didn't have a weapon, or he may have been trying to see or show Jardan's bite on his washboard abs. Or something else.

Mike couldn't presume to know why, and he couldn't give the guy the benefit of the doubt. He had to assume the worst. That's drilled into the team from day one of training.

The intruder continued to shout and not listen to commands.

At 7:16:51, Mike released Jardan, who raced back in.

But the man was swift and strong. Before the dog could make contact, the man kicked him in the head, hard.

Jardan may have been disoriented. Dogs don't get kicked in the head or anywhere during training. There's some wrestling, lots of yelling, some mock hits, but nothing hard. This kick to the head was a new one on Jardan. Maybe he thought it was a new kind of correction. Maybe he was disoriented. Whatever the reason, he spun around and ran back toward his handler.

No problem, because Jardan's old-school chum was poised to explode onto the scene. Marshall gave Hurricane the word.

From the outside it might have looked like an easy decision, but in fractions of a second, a career of experience had come to bear, and Marshall had calculated exactly what he needed to do. He'd been through similar scenarios in training hundreds of times, so it was automatic to go into rapid-fire analysis and action mode.

He loosened his grip on Hurricane's lead, letting it feed out through his hand as Hurricane lunged. He had to trust his dog implicitly to go for the right guy and not the teammates in front of them.

A dog with less team training could have bitten the first person he came to. But Hurricane had locked in on the fence jumper long before. This guy had kicked Hurricane's pal. Not cool. Marshall was confident that his dog could have run through a crowd of a hundred people to get to the right target.

Hurricane flew through the darkness, a black flash against the red and blue lights of the Secret Service vehicles in the background. To Marshall, he looked like a superhero leaping forward to save the day. The Dark Knight.

The president and family were in residence that evening. There was no telling if this guy was armed, what his intentions were, or if he was just a distraction for something really bad about to go down.

At 7:16:53, Hurricane made contact with the fence jumper. The dog grabbed the man's knee, sweeping his leg out from under him and taking him to the ground. A perfect bite.

But the knee was big and muscular, and as large as a Malinois mouth is, it can open only so wide. The fence jumper was able to rip his knee out of Hurricane's mouth and stand back up.

Hurricane dashed around him and came back in, leaping up and biting him on the arm. The man threw him to the ground, knelt on the lawn, pinned Hurricane down, and punched him hard—one, two, three. Powerful punches, again and again. Hurricane struggled to get loose so he could continue the fight.

The fence jumper got back up, punching Hurricane as he rose. Hurricane freed himself, skirting through the man's feet, and started in again, chasing him back toward the fence, putting the bite on when he could.

The LED lights mounted on the ERT's Knight's Armament SR-16 rifles cast small circles of light on the man. He could have given up at any time. After one bite, after two. But he kept going, so Hurricane did, too.

Hurricane was trying to get control of him, to be in the dominant position. It wasn't about biting him time after time. It was about stopping him.

Most people would have quit before the first bite. Some wouldn't give up until they felt teeth in their flesh. But ERT canine teams train for every possible scenario, and the most determined, hardy suspects—"the less-than-one-percenters"—were not foreign to Hurricane. The big difference during training is that no one was punching him.

Hurricane kept running toward the intruder, pushing him thirty yards back, to the fence line. As the man turned and faced him, Hurricane ran in for another bite and got an arm. The man punched him in the face, so Hurricane changed positions, grabbing his other arm and trying to bring him down to the ground. The guy punched again.

Jardan, barking in the distance, was champing to get back in and finish what he'd started. Mike shouted to Marshall to let him know he was sending in reinforcement.

Jardan streaked in, and at 7:17:23 grabbed onto the man's free arm.

At 7:17:25, lying faceup on the ground near the Pennsylvania Avenue fence, with a Malinois attached to each arm, he had finally had enough.

"OK, I'm done! Get the dogs off of me!" he called out.

The handlers took their dogs off the bite, staying close in case the man decided he wasn't done. A six-foot-seven ERT member—who would later go on to become an ERT dog handler—cuffed him. A Secret Service medic provided initial care, but officers had already called the District of Columbia Fire Department, whose paramedics arrived quickly and took over.

Hurricane was still raring to go. Marshall knew from training that his dog's "off" switch would take a while to reset. It blew him away that after the pummeling Hurricane had taken, his energy and drive were still so high.

But it also made sense. Marshall and the rest of ERT think of every incident as the first round out of twenty. They never believe it's over when it appears to be over. Normally Marshall immediately starts looking for what to do next. One scenario in training can go on for hours.

He trains Hurricane the same way. So even though his dog was hurt, he wanted to keep going. Round one done, maybe nineteen to go.

But as soon as another dog team infilled for him, he had to get Hurricane to the veterinarian. Even in the dark, on quick inspection with a flashlight, Marshall could already see some swelling and lacerated skin under his dog's fur. He had taken a fierce beating out there.

Most dogs would not be happy, but Hurricane didn't seem to notice. This didn't surprise Marshall either. He seemed to register pain in a different way than most dogs. There was the exposed tooth nerve before he got his first titanium canine tooth, and other incidents in training that should have stopped him in his tracks but that he just shook off. Marshall figured the adrenaline coursing through his dog's body was helping as well.

He couldn't praise Hurricane at the scene. Telling a dog in a high voice what a gooooooooo boy he is in front of a suspect is just not done. But once they got to the van, Marshall brought him to the side closer to the White House, where none of his guys could see him. He had him jump in.

He had never been so proud. It was the most incredible display of heart he had ever seen.

Hurricane reached out with his paw.

Tap tap tap.

He gave Marshall such an expressive look that he knew just what he was thinking.

Did I do good, Dad?

Marshall patted his own chest a couple of times, and Hurricane jumped up and gave him a hug. Marshall hugged him back, full of such admiration for his partner that he understood what people meant when they said their heart could burst.

"Good boy, good boy, good boyyyy!" he said, again and again, quietly, to his dog.

He knew this dog was willing to take it all the way to the end if he had to. He wouldn't let that happen for something like this. But when it hit him that his dog would have died fighting, and would have done it with gusto, he choked up.

If the president had been given the all clear to go back to the north side of the White House and had looked out a window, he would have seen a most unusual and heartwarming sight that night.

The two fully geared handlers and their muzzled dogs walked into Friendship Hospital for Animals, where the Secret Service sometimes brings dogs who need immediate attention. The few people in the waiting room stared, some with dropped jaws, at these warriors fresh from the battlefield.

A veterinary technician immediately ushered them into a room. The handlers explained that they were Secret Service and had just gotten into an altercation, and asked if their dogs could be checked to make sure everything looked OK.

A veterinarian went to work on Hurricane, who immediately flipped onto his back, tail wagging, and nuzzling her with his muzzle when she came close.

"*What* did you say he just did?" she asked as she rubbed Hurricane's belly.

Hurricane looked like someone who'd just been in a formidable fight. He was swollen wherever he'd been punched and had some cuts and significant bruising. He reminded Marshall of Rocky Balboa on a bad day. Marshall was relieved there were no obvious signs of traumatic injuries, but he was aware that sometimes conditions can manifest later. Jardan looked OK, but Mike and Marshall would be keeping an eye on their dogs for anything unusual.

When they got home that night, Marshall wanted to give Hurricane something extra special. He had never given his partner human food before but figured that if ever there was a time to make one small exception to this policy, this was it.

There wasn't much in the fridge, and the store where he could buy a steak was closed. But he knew a place not too far away that was open 24/7. Hurricane was just settling into his bed when Marshall grabbed the keys to his car.

"C'mon 'Cane! We have one more place to go tonight," he told him. Hurricane was already at the door. Like his handler, he's ready for anything anytime, and the sound of the keys meant it wasn't quite bedtime yet.

Fifteen minutes later, under the glow of golden arches, Hurricane watched closely as Marshall unwrapped two hamburgers. Marshall had never opened food so close to him before. Hurricane's eyes seemed to widen, and he stared, riveted—first at the burgers, and then Marshall, back and forth. His expression was a combination of stunned and hopeful.

As Marshall offered him the first burger, Hurricane's tail burst into a blur of bliss. He wolfed it in two bites. Marshall tore the second burger into a few pieces so Hurricane could taste it this time.

A couple of minutes later, after realizing the feast was over, Hurricane stretched slowly, sighed, and fell asleep for the ride home.

Dominic Adesanya, age twenty-three, was taken by ambulance to George Washington University Hospital, where he was treated for his bite wounds. He was initially charged with two felony counts of assault on a police officer (officers Hurricane and Jardan), one felony count of making threats, and four misdemeanor counts of unlawful entry and resisting arrest.

He appeared in federal court the next day and was charged with two misdemeanors, punishable by up to a year in jail.

His father told the *Washington Post* that Adesanya, who had once been a sprinter on the track team at Stevenson University, had dropped out of college and was battling mental illness for the past year.

He said his son was convinced the National Security Agency

and the president were spying on him with surveillance devices around their home. Adesanya was so desperate to find them that he cut through drywall.

The White House incident wasn't his first encounter with the Secret Service. He had been arrested twice in July for security violations at the White House and the Treasury Building.

His father, exhausted from dealing with his son's mental illness and the fallout from the fence jumping, broke down in tears during a video interview with the *Post*.

"He wasn't trying to harm the president. He was just going to ask for help. He's not a criminal. He's just mentally disturbed and he was just trying to talk to the president of the United States, and that's the only way he felt like he'd be able to do it."

According to a Secret Service affidavit from the October incident, after his arrest, Adesanya told investigators he would keep trying to get back to the White House until he could speak with the president.

As a result of the July incidents, he received in-hospital treatment but didn't want to stay and didn't have his prescriptions filled. He would be treated again after he jumped the fence and in 2015 would be referred to a mental health program aimed at diverting low-level offenders with mental health issues from jail to treatment.

Adesanya was not armed when he scaled the White House fence. He was not wired. He was no terrorist.

But the Secret Service couldn't know that. He was strong, fast, determined, and a formidable fighter. He had put the ERT Tactical Canine Unit to its biggest real-life test to date, and it had done its job.

As enthusiastic as the guys on the team are about their dogs stopping trouble, no one wants his dog to bite someone unless it's absolutely necessary.

"You want this guy to give up without having to bite him," says Jim. "You really don't want to have to do that. You want it to end peacefully. It's better for everybody all around.

"But at the same time if we find ourselves where the person gives us no other option, we aren't willing to risk the safety of our team members, or a protectee, to make that happen."

Dog bites hurt, but using the less-than-lethal option of dogs may have saved Adesanya's life.

In the end, fence jumpers are just a small part of what ERT trains for. Team members estimate that 99 percent of their training is geared toward a full-fledged terrorist attack.

"We have the best instructors in the world here," says Marshall. "There's nothing they haven't trained us how to handle."

Hurricane had proven to Marshall that night that no matter what goes down in the future, he has the right stuff.

"Whenever that day comes, I hope it will be me and him, front and center," he says.

When the story broke—often accompanied by a twenty-one-second video from a news crew showing Adesanya kicking and punching the dogs—the public reaction was off the charts.

It's one thing if someone tries to mess with the president. But don't mess with the dogs who protect the president.

The Secret Service public affairs team asked Marshall and Mike for photos of their dogs. They each had plenty of photos of them, but nothing that looked official. Because it was urgent, they found an office with a Secret Service flag and American flag and took their own photos with their cell phones. Marshall was glad Hurricane's black coat hid his lumps and contusions.

Public affairs tweeted separate photos of the dogs, showing them as their attentive and happy selves. They included personal details that sounded almost like brief dating app descriptions, minus the moonlit beach walks. (Jardan's name was misspelled, but he didn't care.)

> "USSS K-9 Jordan—black/tan Belgian Malinois, brown eyes, age 5, enjoys walks around White House, ready to work."
> "USSS K-9 Hurricane—black Belgian Malinois, brown eyes, age 6, enjoys playing with his Kong toy, ready to work."

Special Agent Nicole M., who works in the Secret Service's Office of Government and Public Affairs, says the tweets garnered the most significant public response for anything they've ever tweeted. Among the reactions on Twitter:

> "You go to jail if you jump the presidential fence . . . You kick A Secret Service dog I say public hanging is in order!"
> "Downsize USSS, hire more dogs."
> "@SecretService He looks a Genuine very loyal, Canine Officer. Looks strong & fabulous."
> "SecretService Beautiful boys. Big beautiful brown eyes! Strong and soulful! When the @WhiteHouse needs protecting, the K9s get it done!!!"
> "@SecretService Good job. No guns needed in this intrusion. I need these dogs."

In addition, an outpouring of e-mails, letters, and greeting cards swamped the office. And there were gifts. Gifts like nothing the office had ever received. Toys, shampoos, and containers of treats—many homemade, many gourmet—came in by the dozens.

"There were amazing gift baskets, like something you'd send your parents on their fiftieth anniversary," Marshall says. Only you probably wouldn't send your parents desiccated bison-liver treats.

The public affairs office fielded dozens of interview requests. The Secret Service does not readily trot its officers and agents out to the media, and with a case pending, the handlers couldn't even talk to their friends and families about it, much less the press.

The only people the handlers could really talk with were the other handlers, and the instructors. When Marshall, Mike, Hurricane, and Jardan showed up at RTC the day after the apprehension, the instructors were ecstatic.

Not because there was a fight. But because the dogs had found themselves in an extraordinary situation the canine staff could never replicate for them, and they had responded magnificently.

Brian was over the moon.

"It took a huge dose of courage to do what Hurricane did," he says. "You could tell that dog was going to give his life to win. He wasn't going to quit.

"It's all the training, and the dogs' relationships with their handlers. They look at their handlers and you can see how much they believe in them. They know, 'When we're together, we can win.'"

Brian and the others were thrilled that America now knew about—and appreciated—these dogs. It was like when the media disclosed that a military working dog was part of the Navy SEAL Team 6 raid on Osama bin Laden's compound in Pakistan in 2011. People suddenly realized the military uses dogs, and wanted to know all about the four-legged heroes.

It wasn't all pats on the back at RTC. There would be many dissections of the video of the apprehension, a second-by-second look at everything that went right, and a couple of things that needed improvement. The Murphy moment with the leash getting tangled on the aim point was a big one.

"We learned from this and did what we needed to do," Jim says. "We addressed the malfunction, and it won't happen again. We have passion; we live and breathe this stuff. But no matter how well something goes, at the end of the day we ask, 'What can we do better?'

"We all felt like crap after the September incident. We're alphas. We do not want to lose."

One of the improvements ERT made after that dark September day was to increase the number of dogs posted at the White House. Until then, there had generally been one dog in each area. Starting the next day, there would never be just one again.

That strategy worked perfectly the first time it was put to the test. First Hurricane with his "Put me in, coach!" enthusiasm when Jardan was temporarily out of the game, and then Jardan, who couldn't wait to go back in when his pal was getting punched again.

They were the ultimate tag team.

Marshall did not expect, and did not receive, accolades from his fellow handlers. It's all about busting chops on the team.

"Did you even get out, or did you just open the door for him?" was a popular reprise.

None of them would ever congratulate another teammate on a job well done. It doesn't work like that. They just do what they're supposed to do.

"No matter what you did, no matter how crazy it was, you

never hear another guy on your team saying, 'Good job,'" says Marshall. "It would be kind of strange."

But guys around here will begrudgingly admit, when asked by someone not on the team, that they were proud of Marshall and Mike and the positive attention the dogs brought to the program.

The timing could not have been better—not just for ERT but all of the Secret Service. A month earlier, when Omar Gonzalez managed to get over the fence and into the White House, the story and its repercussions made headlines for weeks.

Other security lapses were also in the news, and Secret Service director Julia Pierson had resigned under intense pressure and bipartisan criticism of the agency.

"We were getting crushed by the media," says an officer, who couldn't bring himself to watch the news at the time.

It was a low point.

This was the opposite.

"They are the dogs that saved an agency," a high-ranking agent told Marshall.

Hector H., deputy special agent in charge at RTC, still beams when he talks about it.

"We had been in a downward spiral with all of the negative press we'd been getting. It was a slump, with a lot of swings and misses.

"But that day that Hurricane and Jardan did their job is one I'll never forget. The next day I was driving to work with my chest out to here. I got to work and wanted to get them some steaks.

"What they did, at least for a moment, was they restored the public's belief in us. We do so many great things, but all the focus is on the mistakes. For a short span, thanks to two great dogs and handlers, we were on top of the world again."

CHAPTER 16

THE DISPATCHER CALLS

Take photos of your dog. Take lots of photos. Everywhere you go. At home. At work. Just keep a record. One day you'll be very glad you did.

The advice a seasoned dog handler gave Erica F. when she was starting on the Secret Service Explosive Detection Team made a lot of sense to her. She had spent eight years in the Army and had witnessed the bonds between soldier dogs and handlers. She had seen dozens of photos the handlers had proudly shown her of their "kids" on deployments and overseas duty.

Her Secret Service sniffer dog, Noisy, was a natural poser. The German shepherd would look right into the lens, ears alert, eyes bright. He seemed to like the attention that came with the whole photo-taking process, and especially the praise after Erica snapped a few pics.

They traveled to fifty locations by plane from 2009 until 2015, and Erica has photos from almost all of them. "I always found a way," she says.

Noisy starred in hundreds of photos, from Peru to Beverly Hills to the top of the National Cathedral—"It's a *lot* of stairs."

The stairs were nothing for Erica, an ultrarunner who has done hundred-mile runs in under twenty-four hours. And they were no trouble for Noisy either. He looked like a German shepherd and chilled like a shepherd, but he worked with the tireless spirit of a Malinois.

There's an especially colorful photo Erica loves. It's from a flower production and exporting facility in Bogotá, Colombia. Behind Noisy, bunches of vibrant carnations lie sideways, gently suspended in white cloth bundles. Noisy is staring directly at the camera. He looks effortlessly calm, but his eyes sparkle, his ears are perked, and he has an unmistakable happy smile on his face.

"He was patient, but I'm sure sometimes he was like, 'Mom, can we *not* have to take another photo?'" says Erica.

One of her favorite photos is not from their travels. She took it in their living room, as Noisy was sitting facing the window and looking out intently, but serenely, through the open blinds. He is in profile, and appears strong and noble.

But if you look closely, you can see that a strip of his front right leg has been shaved. What you can't see is that his whole underbelly has also been shaved and is healing from recent surgery.

About a week earlier, Erica had noticed Noisy's belly was distended and brought him to Fort Belvoir for a check. After an ultrasound, they discovered he had a tumor on his spleen and he was starting to bleed internally. They opened him up immediately and removed the tumor.

Erica watched the surgery through the observation glass, willing him to be OK, focusing on his breath.

If you're breathing, you're alive, just keep breathing.

She spent the next thirty-six hours at Noisy's side, her upper half in the large, floor-level veterinary kennel, her lower half on the floor. She kept vigil as they transfused him and gave him all his IVs.

When they came home, Noisy's two Jack Russell terrier "siblings" were jubilant to see him again. He wagged when he saw them doing their happy dance. They kept him company, staying near him as he slept.

Several days into his recovery, the vet called with the lab results. Very bad news, she warned. Noisy had hemangiosarcoma, an aggressive cancer of the cells that line blood vessels. Hemangiosarcoma has been referred to as "among the most challenging and mysterious diseases encountered in veterinary practice." It's not an uncommon cancer in dogs. German shepherds are afflicted by it more than most other breeds.

The vet told her there is no cure. Noisy could be gone in a matter of a few weeks.

Erica felt the floor drop out from under her.

She determined she would savor whatever time she had left with him. She took more photos and spent as much time as she could right beside him. Once, on a good day, she even brought him out to training. He had always loved his work, and she knew he must be missing it. He was almost his old self that day, wrapped in the thrill of the hunt and the joy of the reward that came with finding the scent of explosives.

Erica had hoped to get him into a study that could one day benefit other dogs with this form of cancer. But eleven days after his diagnosis, she knew it was too late. Noisy was beyond tired, his gums had grown pale, and his stomach was starting to look like it did the first time. She brought him to the vet, not knowing if he would be making the return trip.

His blood work showed something bad was going on inside again. The veterinarian gave Erica options that could keep him alive a little longer. Options that wouldn't be easy for him, including opening him up again.

Erica considered them, but only briefly. She knew anything she did to keep him going was for her, not for him. She didn't want to put him through anything else. He had been through enough.

He was tired and seemed remarkably relaxed. She couldn't fathom waiting until he was in terrible pain to let him go. She sat down next to him and bent close for a little one-to-one talk as she cradled his head in her arms.

"You've been the best dog in the world," she told him, trying to maintain her usual calm, sure composure. "But if you're tired, it's OK to go."

He fell asleep and started snoring in her arms. She felt some comfort that he could be at peace in their last moments together.

The vet and a couple of techs came in. They put a blanket under him. He was still sleepy. Erica got behind him. As they administered the drug that makes him unconscious, she kissed his head tenderly. When she was ready, they gave him the final drug.

"And then it just stops. Everything stops," she later told her husband. "And then you're just kind of sitting there, like 'What do I do now?'"

She caressed his fur, felt his skin, still warm, and cried her heart out.

She walked out alone, with his leash and a gut-wrenching emptiness.

A few days later, she was back at the White House, working as a regular Uniformed Division officer.

On the way to work, she would look over her shoulder, expecting to see Noisy there. The absence of his breathing, of his constant companionship, made the long ride from Northern Maryland a lonely one. She never realized how much she talked to him until he wasn't there to talk to anymore.

During breaks and downtime, she would often find herself

scrolling through her phone and looking at all the photos she had taken of him over the years. It sometimes made her feel the enormity of the loss even more, but mostly it was comforting to see him smiling back at her from their adventures around the world.

When she had Noisy at her side, she never minded working overtime. Whenever she was with him, no matter how hard they worked and how late the hour, it felt more like she was hanging out with a buddy. Now, no matter how friendly and empathetic her fellow officers, she felt part of her was missing.

"I'm kind of an introvert as a person, so getting to be around your buddy all the time made it so easy. When we were done with a sweep, there would always be someone to sit with," she says.

Because of the canine program's long-standing "one and done" policy, few handlers ever go back into canine. At first, Erica didn't want to even try to get another dog. She could never replace Noisy and didn't want to go through the pain of losing a working dog again.

But then a handler left to take a job at another agency, and Erica decided to apply for the vacancy. She had to submit her application just like everyone else and pass a PT test (not a problem).

The program had a dog who needed a new handler as soon as possible, and here was this handler, all trained. Erica was offered the job.

A couple of handlers who had also been given another dog after their first dog died took her aside. They told her that she'd probably want to keep a distance at first but that eventually the new dog would win her over.

"Don't worry," handler Tim D. told her. "Noisy will always have a piece of your heart no matter how much you end up loving your new dog. It'll take time, but you'll grow to love him. They have a way of invading your heart."

On a warm August morning in 2015, Erica and a black German shepherd named Kid officially started their partnership. Part of her didn't feel she was ready. The dog looked quizzically at this new person who had taken him out of his kennel at RTC.

She introduced herself.

"Hey, Kid, I'm Erica. You lost your handler, and I lost my dog, so we both have something in common. We're both kind of lost. Maybe we can help each other out. What do you think?"

He gave a wag and stood up.

She vowed not to compare Kid to Noisy too much, but it was only natural. She liked how Kid would chill out in her van. Noisy rarely did. But like Noisy, Kid was friendly and sweet.

They'd have to pass the tests all other new dogs and handlers would, so after a few days of hanging out together, grooming him, and taking him on walks, it was time to get to work. They would spend the next few weeks getting back up to speed together with the help of one of the instructors.

Around the holidays she sent an e-mail update to friends. Among the news was the latest on Kid:

"We are doing well. It always helps to get out of training and really start working and bonding together. We've taken a couple of trips together and he is adjusting well to me and my style of things. He is a really good boy and VERY smart.

"Time keeps moving on and I have to as well. Lucky for me I have another great partner to do that with. I can't wait to see the finished product."

She attached a photograph she had taken just before they finished certifying together. It shows this black furry face looking straight up at her from a heel position close at her side. His mouth is open, his tongue is hanging out, and his warm brown eyes are looking directly into the camera.

He looks attentive, friendly, and hardworking. He also seems to be a good poser.

This was not the first photo she had taken of him. And it certainly would not be the last.

"As a handler you're immortal, if that makes sense," says Tim. "And the dog is mortal. And you outlive your dog. It's the hardest part of having a dog, and the hardest part of this job."

Dogs never live long enough. It's a fact everyone who has ever loved and lost a dog knows.

"Why parrots live for eighty years and dogs only live for eight or ten or twelve makes no sense," says Brian.

By the time a Secret Service dog passes, a handler will probably have been with him or her for several years, and nearly 24/7—far more than most pets and their people. "It's like losing part of your soul," says one handler. "The best part."

Ideally, before the end, Secret Service dogs will have at least a couple of years of retirement, where they can find their inner couch potatoes. With only one exception, Brian says Secret Service handlers have always chosen to adopt their dogs when the dog retires. There's just no question.

As much as most dogs love working, they seem to fall into retirement quite happily.

Jim S.'s dog, Spike, retired in 2012 after nearly eight years on the job with Jim. Spike, a former K-9 Olympics winner, was slowing down due to old age and hip issues. The day Spike retired, Jim went to Five Guys and brought him back a cheeseburger and fries.

"You deserve this, Spike," Jim told him before handing him the canine equivalent of a gold watch. "You protected two different presidents and you did your time. Happy retirement."

All the ERT dogs are on a strict eating plan. Table scraps don't figure into their diets, much less fast food, Marshall's late-night celebration with Hurricane notwithstanding.

Spike ate it in ten seconds. Five minutes later, he went outside and threw it all up. Undaunted, he came back in and sniffed around for more of where that came from.

Spike had been a one-man dog his whole career. But three months into retirement, his loyalty had shifted to Jim's wife, who worked from home.

"I come home and I tell him 'no' about something, and he'd be like, 'Whatever!' He'd walk over to Mom, and he's like, 'You're not the boss anymore!' to me.

"It was great because my wife and kids, they just loved him so much. Then they finally had that time with him to be a pet and they didn't have to treat him like a work dog so much anymore.

"They'd sneak him treats and he got fat. They'd feed him from the table. Sometimes it made me so mad because the trainer in me said you can't do that. Then it's like, oh you know he's a home dog now," he says, and pauses. "And, yeah, maybe I dropped him a piece of steak or two myself sometimes."

Spike even got human bed privileges, but not until Jim left for work.

"Every single morning, he jumped in my spot. I got him a nice memory foam dog bed, but he'd ditch it every day to be where I'd been. Retirement was very good to Spike."

While many dogs seem to fall right into retirement, it can be rough on a handler to suddenly be working without a dog.

"Those who are out of the program always miss it," says Brian. "You always see them standing at the gate, watching and reminiscing."

Jim took a couple of weeks off before going back to work without Spike. He needed to decompress and get used to the idea that he was no longer a handler. He'd still be on the Emergency Response Team, just without a dog. He'd work alongside handlers with dogs, but in some ways, that made it more difficult.

"The transition was really rough. I felt naked," he says. "It was hard to come to work and see the other handlers working with their dogs and feeling like you're not part of that anymore.

"You do it so long and you spend so much time with this dog. I was spending more time with my dog than with my own family, traveling with him, going all over the place. He becomes a part of you. You're not just the person, you're a handler now. It's not easy to lose that. It's not just a job. It's who you are."

On the way to work one evening, Stew's ERT dog, Mike, began coughing. It sounded almost like he was trying to hack up a hair ball. Stew stopped along the road and brought Mike over to a secluded area to check him out.

Mike was hunched over and moving lethargically. Stew called him over, but Mike went the wrong way—something he never did. Mike hadn't had anything to eat for hours and hadn't been exercising, so Stew ruled out bloat. Besides, Mike's belly wasn't distended.

He called work and told a supervisor what was going on and that he needed to take Mike to the vet at Fort Belvoir. He called Belvoir and told them he was on the way. A few minutes into the drive, he looked to the back of the van and saw that Mike's stomach had swollen up. He knew Mike couldn't make it all the way to Fort Belvoir.

Stew radioed the Joint Operations Center and told them he was running code (lights and siren) because his canine partner was in medical distress. They relayed this to local law-enforcement departments.

Maryland State Police met up with him on the highway. They used their own sirens and lights when needed to help clear the way for him to rush his partner to help.

It's what they would do for any officer-down situation.

When they crossed into Washington, D.C., they were joined by the Metropolitan Police Department, U.S. Park Police, and vehicles from the Uniformed Division of the Secret Service. To those they passed, it may have seemed like they were escorting the president, or at least a significant head of state.

When they arrived at Friendship Hospital for Animals, other law enforcement had already set up a perimeter. Staffers were ready outside with a gurney. They raced Mike in. After a quick exam, the vets were afraid Mike had bloat, perhaps with gastric dilatation volvulus (GDV).

Bloat itself is a dangerous condition that affects primarily deep-chested dogs. In bloat, the stomach becomes badly distended with gas. A rapidly enlarged stomach can cut off circulation, or press against the lungs, affecting respiration.

With GDV bloat, the stomach twists at both ends, and the gas can't escape either way. The effects can be rapidly lethal.

A simple preventative operation called a gastropexy is performed on all military working dogs who weigh more than thirty-five pounds. The surgery entails making a small incision and stitching the stomach to the abdominal wall. The procedure won't prevent bloat, but it will prevent the deadlier complication of GDV.

Gastropexies aren't done on male Secret Service canines unless a dog is having surgery already and needs to be anesthetized. The Service tries to avoid anesthesia because of possible risks, so male dogs—generally unneutered—usually aren't pexied. Female dogs going under for spaying usually get the procedure since they're already anesthetized.

The exact cause of bloat isn't known, although sometimes it comes about after eating or drinking too much, or exercising too soon after eating. Mike had done neither.

The vets tried to stick a tube down Mike's esophagus to release pressure, but it wouldn't go in—a clear indicator of GDV. They jammed a needle between his ribs and Stew heard the air rush out. Mike was not sedated for this emergency procedure and moaned in agony.

They rushed Mike to the surgery. The staff had to remove a third of his stomach, his spleen, and part of his small intestine, which had all been damaged beyond repair by the lack of circulation.

Stew knew his dog might never work again. He just wanted him to live.

The setup at the hospital isn't like Fort Belvoir's, where handlers can often stay next to their dogs when they're in their recovery kennels. The staff let Stew rest downstairs on a couch, but he couldn't spend the night next to Mike.

About five times during the course of the night, someone ran down to get Stew because Mike's blood pressure was dropping dangerously low. They thought Mike might not crash if his best friend came up and talked to him.

Sure enough, when Mike saw Stew, he raised his head and looked at him, and his blood pressure immediately climbed back into a normal range.

After a few minutes, Stew would have to go back to the room downstairs. Sleep failed to come on the couch, and he thought about the bond between handlers and their dogs. Seeing Mike's pressure go back to normal without tail wagging or jumping or any physical movement to induce the reaction proved to him that these dogs feel, think, and love above and beyond any level people can comprehend.

He thought about police K-9 handlers and military dog handlers who lose it when their partner is killed or even badly injured. These handlers know this connection. It can't be defined, and there aren't really people who understand, other than handlers who have been through something similar.

About twenty-four hours after the emergency began, Mike seemed to be out of the woods. Stew decided to drive to the ERT's D.C. office to take a quick shower while Mike slept at the vet's.

His cell phone rang. It was one of the vets. She had devastating news.

"You need to get here as soon as possible. Mike has taken a sudden turn. We don't think he's going to make it."

She told Stew that Mike's stomach was basically melting where they had stitched him. She said they could do another surgery, but his chances of pulling through were not good.

Stew tried to reach his supervisors to no avail to get the OK. It didn't matter. Mike had to live. He told the vet staff he'd put it on his credit card. They told him they would take as much off the bill as possible.

As Stew was racing back to the hospital, the Service got his message and agreed to pay.

Stew arrived at the vet's after the surgery had started. He didn't get a chance to see his dog first and tell him he'd be OK, tell him he loved him and what a good dog he was. He'd save it for when Mike woke up after surgery.

He never got the chance.

An hour into surgery, a vet came out and gave him the news that Mike didn't make it. They carried Mike's body to Stew in the room where he had been waiting. This big, strong, almost invincible man leaned over Mike's body, holding him and crying uncontrollably. In his grief, he had no idea what to do. He felt more alone than he'd ever felt in his life.

Then the door opened, and in strode four ERT guys in full kit and machine guns, fresh off their shift. They surrounded him as he mourned his dog. He didn't hold back because they were there. He felt far less alone with his brothers so close at hand.

The Tactical Canine Unit needed handlers, and a few months later, Stew was offered another dog. He fought it for a long time, not wanting to have the pain of this kind of loss again. But eventually he relented.

It took him about a year to warm up to his new dog, Nero. He had been comparing everything the dog did to Mike. He knew it wasn't fair, and this dog would have been considered a great dog by anyone else. The problem was that he just wasn't Mike.

But one day Nero did something that made him laugh, and the ice broke. They went on to form a special bond during their eight years working together and Nero's three years of retirement. Stew couldn't imagine that he had once felt ambivalent about Nero the best dog in the world.

When Nero was thirteen years old, he fell suddenly ill. He wouldn't go up the stairs, and the normally food-loving Mal wasn't eating.

Stew took him to his personal vet. After Secret Service dogs retire and are adopted by their handlers, they're considered pets, and the Secret Service no longer pays medical expenses or sends them to Fort Belvoir.

The veterinarian discovered that Nero had a massive tumor

that was pushing up against his stomach and spleen. He told Stew his dog had no chance of survival no matter what, and that he was probably in a great deal of pain.

Stew called a fellow ERT handler. "I didn't bring him here to put him down," he told him in shock, trying to contain his grief. "I just wanted to see why he wouldn't come up the stairs."

He didn't want Nero to suffer any more than he already must have. Since Nero was sedated for the diagnostic X-rays, he made the agonizing decision to let him go.

Before euthanizing Nero, the staff set him on a blanket and laid him on the floor of an examination room so Stew could spend some time with him. He lay next to him for an hour, telling him all the things he wanted him to know. He wished his idol, James Taylor, could be there and sing Nero into his final sleep with "Sweet Baby James."

When he felt as ready as he could be—not ready at all, really— he gave a nod, and the vet and a couple of techs came in and administered the lethal dose.

Stew lay on the floor next to his dog and sobbed. He didn't try to contain his grief. It was like Mike all over again, but even worse.

They had spent years working together, had many memorable adventures, and now his retired, old dog was a beloved fixture in his home. And suddenly he was gone. Stew didn't want to leave, didn't want Nero to be taken by the staff to a back room. But he couldn't stay there with him forever.

He said a final good-bye and left the room. As he opened the door, he saw, lined up against the wall of the hall, four of his guys from ERT. This time they were in civilian clothes. They had come in on their day off to be with him. One had driven two hours.

He had a fleeting moment where he wished he hadn't let his

grief overcome him after Nero died, because they surely heard him. But he knew that as hard as the ERT guys are, they know this bond, and understood.

They told him they would carry Nero to the back room themselves and stay with him until he was processed and everything was OK.

"It's all right, Stew, you go. We won't leave him," they told him.

That these men had his back during his darkest hour helped make the loss a little less devastating.

Barry galloped joyfully around the grassy front yard after his bath on a warm summer afternoon. He loved baths, but he especially loved what happened after baths if the weather was right.

He ran a couple of laps and then burrowed into the waiting arms of his handler, Bill Shegogue. Beaming at his dog's bliss, Shegogue toweled him off briskly, and the German shepherd bucked with happiness, bulleting off again for another round of "wheelies," as Shegogue called his old dog's puppylike antics.

Half a minute later, Barry sped back to Shegogue for more toweling. He wagged his tail so hard that the whole back half of his body wagged with it. His damp, dark fur glistened in the sun as he ran off again in wide circles.

Shegogue and Barry had worked together in the Secret Service for almost seven years, and Barry had retired only a month earlier because his arthritis was slowing him down. Shegogue looked forward to making his dog as happy as possible during his retirement years. This was just the beginning.

Barry cantered back to Shegogue for more towel time. Shegogue, who was crouched down, embraced him in the towel and dried him some more as Barry wagged and panted. The corners of Barry's mouth were drawn up in what Shegogue knew was his version of a smile. When Barry was extra happy, he smiled like this.

And then as he held him in his arms on the perfect summer day, Shegogue felt Barry's body go limp. For a moment he let himself think his dog was just suddenly tired. But when he felt the weight of his dog in his arms, he knew. He had lost Barry. Just like that, in the middle of his reverie. No pulse, no breathing. But still with a little smile.

He rushed him to the local vet. They told him he had been felled by a massive heart attack.

If ever there was a good way to die, this was it. But the blow of its suddenness was incapacitating for Shegogue. Eighteen years later, his eyes still well up when he talks about it.

> *You lived and died a life only meant for the fearless and strongest and finest of American heroes, and you were one of them; and you wore the Badge of the Very Elite . . . Rest and Play in Peace, K9 Maxo. Angels will sing for you now.*
>
> —Posted on the "Officer Down Memorial Page" for Secret Service EDT dog Maxo on March 7, 2013

On January 26, 2013, a dog named Maxo became the first Secret Service canine to die in the line of duty.

Maxo was a young, energetic Malinois. He and his handler had trained together for four months and had been operational for ten months. Maxo was an affectionate dog, a leaner. Everyone who met him instantly liked him.

Their future was bright, with years of fun and work ahead. The latest adventure was a trip to New Orleans on a protective mission for Vice President Joe Biden.

But as they were sweeping a parking garage for explosives, Maxo fell from the sixth-floor roof of the garage.

It was a freak accident, involving the Mal's unending exuberance, a leash that got torn away from the handler, and a collar that popped off the dog's neck. Maxo was rushed to a veterinary emergency hospital but didn't survive.

His death ripped his handler apart. It's terrible enough when a dog dies from an illness, or in the line of fire. But when it's an accident, even if there's no wrongdoing, the burden of the guilt can be incapacitating.

The military has been contending with its dogs nearly flying off roofs or out of buildings—and sometimes actually going over—for a long time. During predeployment training at Yuma Proving Ground in Arizona, handlers are reminded of the dangers of not having complete control as their dogs search the top of a mock "Middle Eastern" compound. Still, some break away and head for the edge in pursuit of a Kong, or just because they're such high-drive dogs that they'll take any opportunity to run.

It even happens on deployment. One day Marine Staff Sergeant Kristopher Knight's dog, Bram, was walking around the roof of a compound in Iraq when the Kong he was clenching in his jaws dropped and bounced to the ground.

Bram decided to follow it. His fall was only eighteen feet, but Bram was relegated to light duty for three weeks.

On February 4, fifty mourners, mostly from the Secret Service but also several outside agencies, gathered for a memorial service for Maxo at a military base that's the administrative headquarters for the Service's Explosive Detection Team.

The team shares space with the element that stores and services the armored fleet for the Secret Service. Maxo's memorial was held in one of the garage bays where the limos are. Two limos were used as backdrop, along with pipe and drape, so it no longer looked like a garage. There were rows of seats and a podium set up in front for the speakers.

After a call to attention, placement of the urn and flag, and a heartbreaking canine prayer read by a handler, unit commander Captain Barry Lewis stepped up to the podium. A former handler himself, he knew the pain of losing a canine partner. (In his homage that follows, the name of the handler has been removed out of respect for his privacy.)

> *Ten months. Ten months is not a long time. But then again, these were dog months. It's amazing what good work a dog can achieve in such a short time. That is what we should remember today. All the good work Maxo did in his relatively short career.*
>
> *[Handler], today we will present you with some mementos. Photos, poems, the flag that covered Maxo on his ride from Andrews Air Force Base back to this building. Maybe not right away, but in time you will pull them out and proudly share them with . . . family and friends. You will talk about all the places you traveled as a team and all the work he did. And maybe with fellow handlers you will compare whose dog, at times, could be the biggest knucklehead.*
>
> *As you know, last year was a campaign year. The Canine Unit, like every Secret Service entity, was challenged by what they were asked to do to support the protective mission. Canine Maxo did his part in helping the unit meet our responsibility of explosive detection.*
>
> *I want to share what Maxo accomplished in ten short months:*

Crisscrossing the country, Maxo and [his handler] traveled on twenty-eight separate protective details to provide protection for the president and vice president.

An additional twenty-five separate protective missions for the president, vice president, and foreign heads of state were conducted by them here in the Washington, D.C., area.

The out-of-town details included the United Nations General Assembly in NYC, the Democratic National Convention, the Republican National Convention, and cities and towns from Florida to Nevada. Just a couple of months ago Maxo and [his handler] made the long trip to Thailand to provide coverage for the president.

The most recent in-town detail was the long day known as "the inauguration where Maxo helped secure the parade route."

In ten months, Maxo saw more of the country and the world than a lot of dogs see in a career. And of course that doesn't even take into account the work done every day at the White House and other permanent areas of responsibility.

[Handler], that is something you and the unit should be proud of today. That is what we should remember.

Last week I paid a visit to our class currently going through training. They are about three weeks into their seventeen-week course.

I asked a few of the students who they thought the best dog was so far in the class.

I heard two or three different names. Not what I was looking for, but they figured it out pretty quick. By the time I left they knew the answer.

"My dog." The right answer is, "My dog is the best dog."

[Handler], we don't have to tell you that Maxo was the best dog.

The handlers in attendance knew what he meant. Every dog *is* the best one as far as their handlers are concerned. Handlers brushed away tears as they thought of their own dogs, of the mortality of these partners who would forever define them.

It's a tradition for law-enforcement officers who die in the line of duty to be called one final time by dispatch. During this "last call," police radios at the funeral or memorial are tuned to a frequency, and the dispatcher calls for the deceased officer three times with his or her call signal.

Upon hearing no response, the dispatcher says that the officer has arrived at the final assignment and that the officer's shift is over forever, or words to that effect. There may be a mention of heaven, and how the officer will be missed by all.

Maxo's version of this tradition was broadcast on the radio of one of the canine vans with its emergency lights on. A handler who had previously been a dispatcher made the call.

In the silence that followed the last call, even the most experienced, toughened officers wept—some more silently than others.

Most Secret Service dog handlers who have lost a dog still have their partner's ashes, no matter how long ago the dog passed away. Some plan to be buried with the ashes.

They also inevitably have some memento they will never let go. Often, a favorite ball. Anything the dog loved, or wore, becomes cherished. Even the fur around the house that used to drive them crazy becomes a poignant reminder.

Jim's dog Spike had two happy years of retirement before the onset of kidney failure. Spike died at home, in the arms of Jim and his wife, on Valentine's Day.

Spike's ashes are tucked away in a place where they can't be disturbed. So is his collar. Jim let his son have Spike's choke chain, and his son hung it on the wall of his bedroom. Photographs of Spike, including a collage some of the ERT guys put together, are displayed throughout the house.

Spike's leash, the leather one he was issued in 2003 when he and Jim went operational, hangs near the front door. Jim would set it there every day when they arrived home from work, and would grab it every morning before heading out.

Once Spike retired, the leash was placed there indefinitely. It is not to be used for any other dog.

Seven months after Spike retired, Jim went back into the dog world as an instructor for the ERT canine program.

"Being an instructor is truly probably the greatest thing I've ever done in the Secret Service," says Jim. "And losing Spike was probably the hardest thing I've ever gone through. It was harder than losing family members. It really was. I don't even know how to explain it.

"I think it's probably why I'm apprehensive to take another dog, because I know at some point I'll have to go through that again. It's overwhelming but at the same time I feel like I would be trying to replace Spike, and that's just something I don't want to do.

"Dog guys get weird," he says with a resigned smile.

Brian marvels at all the handlers who have forgone promotions within the Uniformed Division so they could stay with their dogs.

"It's a common theme," he says. "For most handlers, having that dog, that partnership, that relationship, is the most important thing to them, as important as their families. You would not believe the things they sacrifice for the love of their dog."

CHAPTER 17

THIS IS FOR YOU, DOG

M arshall and Mike never imagined they would be hanging out on a red leather couch with their dogs at their feet in a VIP dressing room at the Daughters of the American Revolution Constitution Hall. The auditorium, the largest in Washington, D.C., has played host to Bob Hope, Aretha Franklin, Frank Sinatra, the Dalai Lama, Harry Belafonte, Isaac Stern, Walter Cronkite, Elton John, and dozens of other world-famous people.

The spacious dressing room features a lighted theatrical vanity mirror for doing makeup—something the handlers were hoping to avoid. They'd been waiting for two hours for a photo shoot they were invited to do with their dogs, and so far no one had come in wielding makeup brushes. At this point, they were feeling pretty confident about not having to powder their noses.

Hurricane and Jardan had been sleeping most of the time, except when Hurricane needed a dose of affection from Marshall. Then the dog would sit up, lean into Marshall's leg, and wag expectantly, brown eyes gazing up hopefully.

If that didn't work, there was always the *tap tap tap*.

Theater staff checked in with them frequently, making sure they were all OK, that there was nothing they needed. Some exercised great caution, knocking on the door several times as a heads-up to the dogs, then cracking the door to see if it was safe before entering—and even then, staying close to the exit just in case.

Hurricane would usually look up and wag. But his friendly manner didn't assuage the fear of some staffers, who were not expecting these dogs to do much other than bark and growl.

"Oh no, he's looking at me and his ears are up and he's wagging. Is that bad?"

"No, he's fine! He's happy," a bemused Marshall would respond.

The handlers were told to be there at 10 A.M., November 3, 2015, for the photo shoot. The (DHS) Secretary's Awards were taking place, and Marshall and Mike were told that Jeh (pronounced *jay*) Johnson, secretary of Homeland Security, thought it would be nice to get photos with the dogs and handlers at some point during a break in the action.

Marshall had met Johnson at a holiday party the previous year, when Secret Service director Joseph Clancy invited Marshall as his personal guest—one of only three. Being invited was a big enough deal. (Clancy could bring only Marshall or Mike, and Mike graciously said his friend should go.) But when Johnson stopped by their table and wanted to hear all about the apprehension of the fence jumper on October 22, Marshall was astonished—and only too happy to talk about Hurricane and Jardan.

Now here they were a year later, about to get their photos taken with the big boss of the behemoth DHS and, most likely, Clancy. Marshall and Mike looked sharp in their black battle dress uniform pants, black boots, and black, long-sleeve tactical shirts. One arm bore a patch with the ERT motto, *Munire arcem*.

The handlers thought it was a little unusual that they had to get there before the ceremony started. After an hour, one of them jokingly brought up the idea that maybe they were getting an award. But they agreed this is something they would have been told about.

About two and a half hours after they got there, a woman with a headset knocked and opened the door. "All right, guys, you're up!"

The handlers muzzled the dogs, per Secret Service regs, and followed her out.

"You guys really have no idea why you're here? Nobody told you?" she asked as she led them down a series of snaking corridors.

Marshall and Mike glanced at each other with widened eyes and raised eyebrows. They heard an amplified voice that grew louder as they walked.

They rounded a corner and realized that the ceremony was not over. They heard Johnson saying something about the Secret Service but could not see him from their vantage point off stage right. But they could see the audience, which seemed to be engaged in the secretary's story.

Marshall felt a surge of adrenaline course through his body. Flat-out adrenaline, like the minute before a fight.

"You want to go first, don't you?" asked Mike, who was in front of him.

"Hell yeah, I do!" said Marshall, and they traded places.

"Tell us now what it is?" Marshall asked their guide.

"When I give you the word," she said, "walk up the stage toward the secretary."

This was no photo shoot.

They waited in the wings and listened as Johnson continued his speech:

Virtually every day, somebody in the Secret Service is doing something, an act of bravery, of valor, willing to step in the line of fire, willing to put themselves in jeopardy. I wanted to talk about two individuals in particular of the United States Secret Service who I want to see acknowledged here today. These are two members of the Secret Service who have never before been acknowledged for their heroism.

On October 22, 2014, the White House complex security personnel were alerted to a perimeter breach where an intruder had jumped the fence line at the White House. As part of the North Grounds Emergency Response Tactical Team, this team immediately deployed to neutralize the situation. The suspect who had jumped the fence had no intention of stopping. But these members of the United States Secret Service made sure that the intruder did not get far.

The actions of these Emergency Response Teams and members highlighted the selflessness and the bravery and the tactical proficiency and professionalism that we see every day at the United States Secret Service. One in the line of duty was badly injured in the course of stopping the intruder.

Would you come out, please? Ladies and gentlemen, would you please welcome Hurricane and Jardan, along with their partners and trainers . . .

Marshall laughed when he realized the twist, and was glad that the secretary had put the dogs first. The woman with the headset gave him the nod, and he and Hurricane strode out, followed by Mike and Jardan. The dogs heeled on their right sides and wagged as they walked across the stage.

The audience cheered, and Marshall saw they were rising from their seats. A standing ovation. His adrenaline spiked again. He wondered how Hurricane was feeling about this.

Marshall and the secretary reached out to shake hands. Hurricane had stopped between them and was looking up at their grasped hands above his head. The dog glanced quickly from one hand to the other and back, like he was watching a rapid-fire Ping-Pong game. Anyone who knew this dog knew he hoped one of those hands was going to pet him.

The secretary leaned down and pet Hurricane on the head, and then used both his hands to stroke Hurricane's shoulders. Hurricane stood right next to the secretary and surveyed the audience, looking out first to his left, then slowly to his right. The heavy seven-sided glass awards—the Secretary's Award for Valor—were handed to Marshall and Mike.

Johnson gave Jardan a friendly pat on the head, and everyone lined up for a photograph. There would be a photo shoot after all. The event coordinators had just neglected to mention the rest.

Marshall had Hurricane sit at his right side, and the dog leaned against his leg, staring up at him and the glimmering award.

Then something caught Hurricane's attention. He seemed to realize that about a foot to his right there was this nice secretary guy who had been petting him only moments earlier, and that his left hand was just hanging down doing nothing.

Not one to pass up an opportunity for affection—and always one to create an opportunity for it—Hurricane reached his nose up to Johnson's hand and nuzzled it swiftly a couple of times. His head moved in a sweeping gesture that made it clear he wanted the big boss to pet him again.

Marshall saw this in his peripheral vision and wished he could have warned the secretary. "With Hurricane, there *is* no one-time pet." You pet him once, you're his friend for life.

Johnson instantly complied with Hurricane's request, petting him with one hand while the photographer snapped several photos. Hurricane stared up at Johnson, looking into his eyes.

In the photos, it looks like true love.

Photo session done, the audience applauded again, and Johnson stepped back to clap for the teams and wrap up the ceremony. Hurricane was still looking up at Johnson and seemed surprised that his new friend had backed up and stopped petting him.

Determined to remedy this situation, Hurricane reached his head way back to try the same maneuver that had worked before—a couple of spirited nudges with his nose and a "come hither" beckoning gesture with his head—but he couldn't quite reach the secretary.

He was hungry for some more loving, so without missing a beat, Hurricane shifted his attention to Marshall. But with the weighty award in one hand and the leash in the other, it was all Marshall could do to shake hands again with everyone. There was no way he could pet his dog now without the DHS's highest recognition for extraordinary acts of valor crashing onto the stage floor.

Hurricane would just have to wait. There would be no shortage of petting and embraces backstage.

Like most of the highly competitive ERT members, Marshall likes to break records. The kettlebell record became his while he was still in ERT school. But it was not a pretty sight.

This was before they were allowed to wear gloves. Marshall did so many snatches with the fifty-three-pound kettlebell—259 snatches by the end of the ten minutes—that his calluses tore off, and his entire hand was one big, open wound. "It was disgusting," he says. The judge had to stand off to the side because when

Marshall swung the kettlebell forward, blood sprayed out in front of him from between his fingers every few reps.

He once broke the Special Operation Division powerlifting record. At the gym at ERT's headquarters near the White House, team members have to lift a total of 1,000 pounds doing a bench press, squat, and dead lift. When Marshall arrived on the scene, the record was 1,245. He worked hard until he not only beat the record, but annihilated it: 415 pounds bench, 500 squat, 515 dead lift, for a most impressive total of 1,430 pounds.

But the powerlifting test doesn't count unless competitors can still get sixteen out of sixteen on the Secret Service PT test afterward, to show they completed the feats of strength without sacrificing any stamina. Marshall nailed it but was glad when it was behind him.

He prides himself in keeping super strong and, like his ERT brothers, thrives on the competition. Most of the guys go well beyond the training standards for ERT.

During one dead-lifting competition Marshall overdid it. His back wasn't feeling so great after. Wearing forty to sixty pounds of gear ten hours a day didn't help the pain. The same handler who refused meds after having his elbow ripped apart by a dog reluctantly decided it might not be a bad idea to look for some relief from the pain.

He saw a doctor, who recommended two options: some rest and rehab to let the healing happen on its own over time while he was on light duty, or an anti-inflammatory steroid shot and immediate rehab so he could continue to work at full capacity, not even missing a day.

Marshall couldn't imagine the rest-and-rehab option, which could take weeks. He wanted to work, not sit around. But more important to him was Hurricane. When Marshall was recovering from the bite to his elbow, he couldn't help but feel bad for his dog.

Every morning Hurricane had woken up with his hopeful, excited, "Are we going to work today? Are we? Are we?" look. Normally Hurricane would have waited until Marshall was dressed in his uniform to get excited about work, but after his handler hadn't worn his uniform for a few days, he seemed willing to believe that Marshall might be going to work in a tank top and shorts.

While Marshall's elbow was healing, Hurricane didn't do much at all. Marshall knew how hard that had to have been for a dog with his drive. He couldn't even take Hurricane on runs, because his arm was in a sling the first few weeks, and after that the arm was always wrapped up, and he didn't want to irritate it.

He would throw the Kong when he could, but because Marshall is a lefty and was injured on his left elbow, he could almost see Hurricane's dismay when he watched "my weak-ass throws with my right arm. He had to have been wondering, 'Why am I getting these weenie throws from this guy?'"

Other than these disappointing twenty minutes a day, Hurricane did nothing much for months. Marshall and Hurricane had to recertify when they returned to work.

He didn't want to put his dog through a long downtime again just because of some intense back pain. And he didn't want to take any chances that his dog could temporarily be given to someone else.

So rather than hang out with his dog at home for a few weeks while he let the inflammation settle down on its own, he bit the bullet and got the injection.

The needle looked to be about the size of a baseball bat in the image Marshall watched on a screen as he lay on his stomach on the X-ray table. The doctor had already injected some contrast dye and now he pushed the giant needle in from the side of his back all the way into the epidural space in his spine. As the doctor slowly, painstakingly injected a few milliliters of epidural steroid solution, Marshall focused on one thought.

This is for you, dog.

It was a phone call he didn't expect to get for another year or two. Maybe ever.

The previous year Marshall had applied to become an agent in the Secret Service. It's typically a slow process, with many hurdles to have to clear, even for those making the transition from the Uniformed Division.

Marshall had tried to time it so that if he got an offer, it would come in around the time Hurricane could be retiring. He knew he might not be given another working dog because of the one-and-done policy, and he was pretty sure he wouldn't want another dog so soon after Hurricane retiring anyway.

As much as his whole life revolved around his love of ERT work, especially with Hurricane, after nine years at the White House, and seven of those on ERT, he figured he might be ready for a new challenge and a change of scenery as an agent in a field office when Hurricane retired.

But the time came much sooner than he expected. In late November 2015, he got a phone call with the offer to become an agent. If he accepted it, he would have to report to class in two weeks. He knew he might never be offered the opportunity again if he turned it down. He was honored to have the offer but explained about his dog and asked if he could have a little time to make the decision.

There was a big chance that if he accepted the offer, Hurricane would not be retired and would go to a new handler. The dog wasn't quite seven years old and had a lot of work left in him. And Hurricane had proven himself to be a great dog—the kind of dog the Secret Service would want to hold on to.

Marshall asked some of the bosses downtown what Hurricane's fate would be if he accepted the job. They couldn't give him a definite answer. Much as they empathized with his predicament, they told him they definitely couldn't guarantee he'd get to keep him.

Even if he had the chance to keep Hurricane, he knew it would be for selfish reasons.

"He loves to work," he told a friend. "The instructors tell you all the time as much as you think your dog loves you, they love to work a hundred times more."

Yet somehow that didn't seem quite true with Hurricane. Sure, his dog thrived when working. And maybe he would trot off happily with another handler who could provide him the chance to do what he loved.

Marshall didn't think so, though. He and Hurricane had something pretty special. They were almost part of each other, inextricable from one another. He felt that way, and he had an inkling Hurricane did, too.

As he was weighing what to do, he thought he noticed that Hurricane seemed a little sad, a little quieter, just blue. Marshall felt Hurricane knew something had happened that could tear them apart. He figured it was just going down the leash, but then again, there was that whole crazy fence jumper day . . .

Sometimes Marshall would look at Hurricane and almost hear what he was thinking:

Are you going to give me away?

Friends urged him to make a list of pros and cons. He didn't have to.

Even if the only item in the list of cons was that Hurricane might not get to retire and stay with him, it wasn't an option.

"If you came up to me with a bag with a million dollars cash and asked me to pass his leash to you, when it came down to it, I wouldn't be able to do it," he explained.

He had a feeling that if someone made a similar offer to Hurricane, he would do the same.

As he was about to dial the agent to let him know his decision, he looked over to Hurricane, who was sleeping near the front door. Hurricane looked up and wagged.

"Hurricane," he said with a smile. "No regrets. This is for you."

ACKNOWLEDGMENTS

Tap tap tap . . .

The dog who had alerted his handler to a White House intruder by tapping on his shoulder was now tapping on my leg. I was in the middle of an interview with Marshall M. at Rowley Training Center, and as far as I could tell, there was no significant incident his dog could possibly be trying to convey to me.

But it depends on your perspective. And apparently it was significant to Hurricane that he hadn't been petted for a good fifteen minutes while there were free hands around. Since I take notes with only one hand, and my other was only occasionally around my coffee cup, it was a hand that was mostly going to waste.

Tap tap tap.

I reached down to pet him. His tail wagged so heartily against the carpet that when I listened to the audio recording of the interview weeks later, I momentarily thought it was the sound of a muffled hammer in the distance. He threw himself on the ground, belly up, and locked in on me with his deep brown eyes.

Who could resist? Of course I gave him a most enthusiastic belly rub. I owe him a lifetime of belly rubs for what he did on the night of October 22, 2014, and for his contributions to this book.

He and I have gotten close over the months of getting to know his story. He now refers to me—so Marshall tells me—as "Auntie Maria." I could not be more proud of my nephew.

Nothing can compare with how proud Marshall is of his canine partner. Whenever he talks about Hurricane, he beams, he glows, he smiles, he laughs, he is the picture of joy. "I don't care about me being in the book. I just want the world to know about Hurricane," he'd frequently tell me.

Marshall spent dozens of hours helping me get the details of their stories and answering my seemingly endless questions. His passion for anything Hurricane-related never waned over the months. I am deeply grateful that this smart, funny, badass, quick-thinking, deeply devoted dog handler entrusted me to tell the world about his buddy (and him!). Grazie, Marziale!

Leth O. also spoke with me at length, and over many months, about his heartrending story. I never imagined when I set out to research this book that I would be writing about someone who went from the nightmare of being a child under the Khmer Rouge to the dream of being a man who protects American presidents. It was not easy for him to dredge up the horrors of the camps and the killing fields, but he hoped that by recounting the memories, more people would be aware of the genocide and its lasting effects on Cambodia. Leth, thank you for going through all this with me. I look forward to more delicious Cambodian meals with your family.

I owe a debt of gratitude to all the other current handlers and instructors who shared their knowledge and their stories with me. "Stew," Jim S., and Brian M. went above and beyond to help me with many aspects of the book. And Brian B., Brian W., Dante C., Daryl G., Erica F., John F., Jon M., Jorge P., Josh B., Kevin H., Kim K., Larry C., Luke K., Nate C., Nate P., Sal S., Shawn G.,

Shawn S., Steve M., and Tim D. are also deeply dedicated and utterly passionate about what they do.

I truly believe that every handler I spoke with—and probably every handler I didn't get a chance to interview—has the best dog in the world. That's the way it should be. The canines of the Secret Service deserve deep respect for their hard work, fortitude, courage, and enthusiasm for their job: from Roadee—one of the most colorful canine characters I've ever met—and his soulful colleague Dyson to the most badass K-9 Olympic champions like Nitro and Jason.

Captain Brianna S., who runs the Fort Belvoir Veterinary Center (VETCEN), works hard with her staff to keep these dogs healthy. She was invaluable in helping me understand the smallest details of Dyson's dire condition. Her three painstaking reviews of the chapter about Dyson's medical emergency to make sure I got everything right were tremendously helpful.

Lead instructor Brian M. captains a stellar ship over at the Rowley Training Center. Brian, your grandfather would be proud of you.

Special Agent Bill G. was at my side for initial interviews with each handler to make sure the handlers and I stayed away from information that could jeopardize OPSEC. He also accompanied me to many Secret Service canine locations around Washington, D.C., and to Indiana so I could observe a "buy trip." He was already extraordinarily busy, but he handled the added responsibility with aplomb, humor, and a quick wit. Bill, thanks for all your time and your support throughout. I can hear you say it now: "It's all good!"

The United States Secret Service doesn't often agree to work extensively with book authors. During the months while I awaited the agency's decision, I tried not to get discouraged but didn't want to get my hopes up either. Special Agent Brian L., of the Office of Government and Public Affairs (GPA), had liked the idea of the book from the beginning and kept me posted the best he could about the progress as it worked its way up the ladder. It was a happy day in July 2015 when he called to give me the good news.

Special Agent Nicole M. was the GPA liaison assigned to me for the duration. I watched in awe as she juggled multiple urgent media inquiries while calmly helping me gather information, or going with me to locations I would not otherwise have access to, like the Andrews flight line. I greatly enjoyed the time we spent together and appreciate all the work she put into fielding my myriad requests.

Other helpful Secret Service agents include Special Agent Yvonne D., who made it possible for me to witness how Secret Service canine teams helped secure the area where Pope Francis was to make his first public appearance of his three-city tour; and Special Agent Hector H., who contributed some excellent quotes and a spirit of conviviality whenever he joined the conversation.

In the summer of 2014, a few months before my book *Top Dog* was to be published, I was coming up with possibilities for my next book. I knew just enough about Secret Service dogs to put them at the top of my list. One day, as luck or fate would have it, I found myself on a boat with Clint Hill, the former Secret Service agent who was in the presidential motorcade when President John F. Kennedy was assassinated. He is the one you see in the famous, heartbreaking photo after he had leapt onto the presidential limousine and was shielding Jacqueline Kennedy and the president, who had just been shot. Clint was on the boat with his talented and gracious book coauthor, Lisa McCubbin, who has penned three bestsellers with Clint.

I got to talking about books with the Secret Service legend, and I asked if he happened to know anything about the Secret

Service canine program. To my delight, Clint not only knew about it, but he happened to be good friends with Bill Livingood, who was instrumental in its inception. He said if I decided to pursue the book, he'd try to put me in touch with Bill.

A few months later, a White House fence jumper made his way into the White House itself, getting past multiple rings of security, including a dog team. The month after that, two Secret Service dogs bravely apprehended a fence jumper who punched and kicked them in his attempts to break away and get to the White House. I talked with Stephen Morrow, the editor for my other two books at Dutton, and he was interested in having me pursue the book.

I contacted Clint, who connected me with Bill Livingood. When the Secret Service eventually approved the book and I flew out to Washington, D.C., to begin my months of in-person research, Bill and I met twice over lunch. He struck me as one of the nicest, most down-to-earth, humble, kind, helpful people I'd ever met. Everyone who knows him seems to feel the same way. He opened the door to the fascinating history of the canine program. A deeply heartfelt thank-you to Clint, Lisa, and Bill for helping me gain access to this important aspect of the book. And a tremendous additional thanks to Clint for offering to write the Foreword after reading a galley version of *Secret Service Dogs*. What an incredible honor it is to have his words introduce this book.

The time I spent with everyone involved in earlier years of the Secret Service canine program was fascinating. No one had ever interviewed them about their experiences, so there was almost nothing written about the history of dogs in the Secret Service. This is no longer the case thanks to these men, who still feel a deep pride in the program: Bill Shegogue, Cliff Cusick, Ray Reinhart, Freddie McMillon, Henry Sergent, Wes Williams, Dennis Martin, Barry Lewis, and Thomas Quinn.

When author Steve Kettmann learned the subject of my book, he told me about an incident regarding Barbra Streisand and a Secret Service canine who had come to sweep her property for a Clinton Library fund raiser. He kindly gave me permission to quote part of the entertaining anecdote directly from his book *What a Party!*, which he coauthored with Terry McAuliffe, former head of the Democratic National Committee.

And speaking of fund raising for presidential causes, I raise a toast to the West Coast couple who wished to remain anonymous but was happy to have a key staff member tell me of their experiences with Secret Service dogs sniffing around their magnificent home. I also wish to thank Steve Branch, archivist at the Reagan Presidential Library, for locating the photo of President Reagan with Marco and all the other dogs and handlers.

This is my third book with Dutton executive editor Stephen Morrow. I thrive on his enthusiasm and his sense of story, and greatly value his keen eye and ear for words. Plus it's fun to work with him, regardless of the challenges we may face. I couldn't ask for a better editor. This is the first book I've done since Stephen's editorial assistant, the talented and hardworking Adam O'Brien, came on board. I've enjoyed what he has brought to the project and expect him to have a bright future in the field. My editorial team included crack copy editor Kristin Roth. I am in awe of—and grateful for—her incredible eagle eyes.

Agent Carol Mann has once again been there from when a book idea was just a twinkle in my eye. She is quite selective when it comes to my book topics and always pushes me to aim high.

Several friends helped me in wonderful, tangible ways during the research and writing of the book, either through providing me delectable and soul-saving food in the last and most grueling days of my tight writing deadline (Jacquie Steiner, Sally Deneen, Tammi Goldstein) or showing me hospitality when I was far from home for long stretches during the research (Catherine Oenbrink, Scott Eyman, Lynn Kalber, Debra and Tom Targett, Bob and Mollie Dady, Richard and Michelle Leiby, Justin Breitschopf, Marius Daugirdas, and my new friends, Airbnb hosts Cheryl and Didi).

A most heartfelt thank-you to Bowie State University communications major Winona W., who drove me back to my lodging from a remote train station after a long day of research on a cold, rainy night when my car was missing and my phone was on the blink. (Winona: As we discussed on that rainy ride, the Secret Service needs people like you. Show this to recruiters at the next Secret Service job fair!)

My ever-patient, understanding rock of a husband, Craig Hanson, and our daughter, Laura Altair Hanson, held down the fort admirably in my long absences and also when I returned and was spending up to eighteen hours a day sequestered in my writing cottage.

And then there is Gus, my five-month-old yellow Lab, who is snoring loudly at my feet as I write this. He has a special story involving a soldier named Kory Wiens and his beloved yellow Lab, Cooper, who didn't make it back from their deployment in Iraq. I will save Gus's background for another time and a more appropriate venue. He is a smart, loving, good dog who brings me laughter and great happiness every day. I know it's early in the game, but I do believe he may have the makings of the best dog in the world . . .

SOURCES

All interviews in this book took place between April 2015 and May 2016. From August through December the interviews were largely in person, on the scene in the Washington, D.C., area and other locales where the United States Secret Service canine teams venture. Otherwise, interviews and information gathering from sources took place by phone, Skype, e-mail, Facebook messages, and texts.

In addition to the following sources, I read several other books and dozens more articles and gathered information from websites. Those ended up being more for background, whereas the sources here had a direct bearing on the information in *Secret Service Dogs*. I also spoke with several other Secret Service personnel for background information only.

CHAPTER 1
Interviews with Marshall M., Brian M., Bill G.

CHAPTER 2
Currency News. "It's a Dog's Life." Banknote 2003. February 4, 2003. https://www.hitpages.com/doc/6353217529053184/2#pageTop.

Federal Reserve Board. "The Use and Counterfeiting of United States Currency Abroad, Part 3." September 2006. http://www.federalreserve.gov/boarddocs/rptcongress/counterfeit/default.htm.

Interviews with Kim K., Bill G., Brian M., Nicole M., Hector H., Marshall M., "Stew," Brian B., Brian W., Kevin H., Jorge P., Erica F., Josh B., Nate C.

Mandelblit, Bruce. "Dogs Detect Counterfeit Dollars." *Newsmax*, October 27, 2006. http://www.newsmax.com/Pre-2008/Dogs-Detect-Counterfeit-Dollars/2006/10/27/id/684608/.

Mandelblit, Bruce. "These Dogs Have a Nose for 'Funny Money.'" *Crimezilla*, February 18, 2010. http://www.crimezilla.com/2010/02/these-dogs-have-a-nose-for-funny-money/.

CHAPTER 3

Gilmartin, Kevin M. "Hypervigilance: A Learned Perceptual Set and Its Consequences on Police Stress." In *Psychological Services to Law Enforcement*, edited by J. T. Reese and H. A. Goldstein. Washington, D.C.: U.S. Department of Justice Federal Bureau of Investigation, 1986. http://emotionalsurvival.com/hypervigilance.htm.

Interviews with Jim S., "Stew," Luke K., Shawn S., Larry C., Sal S., Brian M., Marshall M., and Bill G.

Schneier, Bruce. "Living in a Code Yellow World." *Schneier on Security,* September 24, 2015. https://www.schneier.com/blog/archives/2015/09/living_in_a_cod.html.

Smith, Betsy B. "Do You Have a Life Outside Law Enforcement . . . Really?" *PoliceOne,* February 29, 2008. https://www.policeone.com/patrol-issues/articles/1666423-Do-you-have-a-life-outside-law-enforcement-really/.

CHAPTER 4

Interviews with Tony Ferrara, Bill Livingood, Dennis Martin, Bill Shegogue (and his wife), Cliff Cusick, Thomas Quinn, Freddie McMillon, Ray Reinhart, Henry Sergent, Wes Williams, Barry Lewis, and Jan Boyer.

CHAPTER 5

Interviews with Jon M., Loren S., Yvonne D., Nicole M., Bill G., Kim K., Brian M., and Marshall M.

Ministry of Foreign Affairs of the People's Republic of China. "Xi Jinping Returns to Beijing After His State Visit to the US and Attendance of Series of Summits Marking the 70th Anniversary of the UN." September 29, 2015. http://www.fmprc.gov.cn/mfa_eng/zxxx_662805/t1304139.shtml.

Nakamura, David. "For U.S. Secret Service, a Presidential Pat on the Back After Challenging Week." *Washington Post,* September 29, 2015. https://www.washingtonpost.com/news/post-politics/wp/2015/09/29/for-u-s-secret-service-a-presidential-pat-on-the-back-after-challenging-week/.

Nakamura, David, and Peter Hermann. "Pope's Visit Will Produce Largest Security Operation in U.S. History." *Washington Post,* September 18, 2015. https://www.washingtonpost.com/politics/popes-visit-will-produce-largest-security-operation-in-us-history/2015/09/18/642ca250-5d47-11e5-b38e-06883aacba64_story.html.

Schmidt, Michael S., and Jim Yardley. "Pope Francis, 'People's Pope,' Is Security Teams' Headache." *New York Times,* September 22, 2015. http://www.nytimes.com/2015/09/23/us/protecting-pope-francis-means-being-able-to-stop-on-a-dime.html?_r=0.

Uhrmacher, Kevin, Richard Johnson, and Denise Lu. "Higher Horsepower: An Illustrated 215-Year History of the Popemobile." *Washington Post,*

September 21, 2015. https://www.washingtonpost.com/graphics/local/
2015-papal-visit/popemobile-illustrated-history/.

CHAPTER 6

"Barney Bites Reporter." YouTube video, 1:49. Posted by "Kherman54." November 6, 2008. https://www.youtube.com/watch?v=9myqGe_B2vE.

Berenson, Tessa. "Man Arrested for Plot to Kidnap the Obamas' Dog." *Time*, January 8, 2016. http://time.com/4173044/obama-dog-kidnap -sunny-bo/.

Interviews with Bill G., Daryl G., "Stew," Dante C., Luke K., Jon M., Brian M., Brian B., Freddie M., Cliff Cusick, Marshall M., Jim S., and Leth O.

Kim, Eun Kyung. "Jenna Bush Hager: Former First Dog Barney 'Was a Real Jerk.'" *Today*, December 5, 2013. http://www.today.com/pets/jenna -bush-hager-former-first-dog-barney-was-real-jerk-2D11697960.

McAuliffe, Terry, and Steve Kettmann. *What a Party! My Life Among Democrats: Presidents, Candidates, Donors, Activists, Alligators, and Other Wild Animals.* New York: Thomas Dunne Books, 2007.

Shabad, Rebecca. "Man Arrested in Plot to Kidnap One of the Obama Family Dogs." *CBS News*, January 8, 2016. http://www.cbsnews.com/news /man-drove-weapons-filled-truck-to-d-c-to-kidnap-one-of-white-house -dogs/.

Zauzmer, Julie, and Spencer S. Hsu. "Man in Alleged Plot to Kidnap Obama's Dog Arrested on Weapons Charge." *Washington Post*, January 8, 2016. https://www.washingtonpost.com/local/public-safety/man-drove-a-truck -filled-with-weapons-to-dc-to-kidnap-obamas-dog-authorities-say/2016/01 /08/0296bf20-b626-11e5-9388-466021d971de_story.html.

CHAPTER 7

Goodavage, Maria. *Soldier Dogs: The Untold Story of America's Canine Heroes.* New York: Dutton, 2012.

Interviews with Hector H., Bill G., Barry Lewis, Jon M., Henry Sergent, Nicole M., and Jorge P.

Swarns, Rachel L. "Who's Minding Bo?" *New York Times*, April 28, 2009. http:// thecaucus.blogs.nytimes.com/2009/04/28/whos-minding-bo/?_r=0—About Dale Haney.

CHAPTER 8

Interviews with Steve M., Bill G., Brian M., Josh B., and Nate C.

CHAPTER 9

Interviews with Jorge P., Nate P., Scott L., Kim K., John F., "Stew," Nicole M., Tim D., Leth O., Cliff Cusick, and Wes Williams.

CHAPTER 10

Associated Press. "66-Year-Old Man Jumps White House Fence." *Washington Post*, March 16, 2007. http://www.washingtonpost.com/wp-dyn/con tent/article/2007/03/16/AR2007031601037.html.

Associated Press. "White House Fence Jumper Was Looking for Chelsea Clinton." *Fox News*, December 9, 2005. http://www.foxnews.com/story /2005/12/09/white-house-fence-jumper-was-looking-for-chelsea-clinton .html.

Blitz, Matt. "The Unbelievable Story of the Guy Who Jumped the White House Fence Four Times." *Washingtonian*, November 27, 2015. http:// www.washingtonian.com/2015/11/27/gerald-gainous-jr-white-house -fence-jumper/.

Chaplin, Gordon. "The White House Cases." *Washington Post*, October 2, 1977. https://www.washingtonpost.com/archive/lifestyle/magazine/1977/10 /02/the-white-house-cases/73a8ffda-9e8a-47a8-8778-19c2dfa63a8f/.

CNN Wire Staff. "Male Suspect in Custody After Jumping White House Fence." *CNN*, September 20, 2011. http://www.cnn.com/2011/09/20/us /white-house-fence-jumper/.

Committee on Oversight and Government Reform. "Chaffetz and Cummings Request Briefing on Plans to Enhance White House Fence." Press release, December 22, 2014. http://democrats.oversight.house.gov/news/press -releases/chaffetz-and-cummings-request-briefing-on-plans-to-enhance -white-house-fence.

Crowe, Kenneth C. "He Wanted Better Health Care." *Times Union*, September 16, 2014. http://www.timesunion.com/local/article/Rensselaer-man -id-d-as-Pokemon-White-House-fence-5756522.php.

Editorial Board. "Raising the White House Fence Could Mean the Removal of Unsightly Restrictions." *Washington Post*, January 17, 2015. https:// www.washingtonpost.com/opinions/raising-the-white-house-fence -could-mean-the-removal-of-unsightly-restrictions/2015/01/17/c8cad694 9aa8 11e4 a7ee 526210d665b4_story.html.

"Fan Carrying a Stuffed Pikachu Jumps Over White House Fence & Gets Arrested by Secret Service!" YouTube video, 1:41. Posted by "Denzell Dior." September 12, 2014. https://www.youtube.com/watch?v= HDGmLKZtGB8.

Feinman, Ronald L. *Assassinations, Threats, and the American Presidency: From Andrew Jackson to Barack Obama.* Lanham, MD: Rowman & Littlefield, 2015.

Garber, Megan. "The (Real) Story of the White House and the Big Block of Cheese." *Atlantic*, January 21, 2015. http://www.theatlantic.com/politics /archive/2015/01/the-real-story-of-the-white-house-and-the-big-block -of-cheese/384676/.

Grimes, William. "A House Tour: Yes, That House." *New York Times*, May 2, 2012. http://www.nytimes.com/2012/05/03/garden/touring-the-white -house.html?_r=0.

Gross, Andy. "White House Fence Jumper Omar Gonzalez Sentenced to 17 Months in Prison." *NBC News,* June 16, 2015. http://www.nbcnews .com/news/us-news/white-house-fence-jumper-omar-gonzalez-sentenced -17-months-prison-n376461.

Hartmann, Margaret. "The 7 Weirdest White House Security Breaches." *New York,* September 30, 2014. http://nymag.com/daily/intelligencer/2014 /09/weird-white-house-intruders-security-breeches.html#.

Horwitz, Sari, and Spencer S. Hsu. "U.S. Capitol Checkpoints Return, as Do Complaints." *Washington Post,* November 17, 2004. http://www.washing tonpost.com/wp-dyn/articles/A54774-2004Nov16.html?nav=rss_nation /nationalsecurity/homeland.

Interviews with Bill G., Jim S., "Stew," Fuller Torrey, Hector H., Marshall M., and Dennis Martin.

Jacob, Matthew, and Mark Jacob. *What the Great Ate: A Curious History of Food & Fame.* New York: Three Rivers Press, 2010.

Keneally, Meghan. "How the White House Is Taking Cues from 'The West Wing.'" *ABC News,* January 20, 2015. http://abcnews.go.com/Politics /white-house-taking-cues-west-wing/story?id=28356909.

KOAT-TV. "White House Fence Jumper Has N.M. Ties." April 10, 2006. http:// www.koat.com/White-House-Fence-Jumper-Has-N-M-Ties/6099562.

Labaree, Aaron. "The Psych Ward for People Who Broke into the White House." *Atlantic,* October 25, 2014. http://www.theatlantic.com/health /archive/2014/10/when-voices-tell-you-to-visit-the-president/381780/.

Lang, John S. "Many 'White House Cases' Detained by Secret Service." *Daytona Beach Morning Journal* (Associated Press), April 26, 1971. https://news .google.com/newspapers?nid=1873&dat=19710426&id=y00fAAAAIBAJ &sjid=j9EEAAAAIBAJ&pg=938,7107692&hl=en.

Leonnig, Carol D. "White House Fence-Jumper Made It Far Deeper into Building Than Previously Known." *Washington Post,* September 29, 2014. https://www.washingtonpost.com/politics/white-house-fence-jumper -made-it-far-deeper-into-building-than-previously-known/2014/09/29 /02efd53e-47ea-11e4-a046-120a8a855cca_story.html.

Leonnig, Carol D., and David A. Fahrenthold. "New Details in Fence-Jumping Reveal Failures in Security Rings Around White House." *Washington Post,* September 23, 2014. https://www.washingtonpost.com /politics/new-details-in-fence-jumping-reveal-failures-in-security-rings -around-white-house/2014/09/23/043518ea-434a-11e4-b47c-f5889e061e 5f_story.html?tid=a_inl.

Leonnig, Carol D., Spencer Hsu, and Annys Shin. "Secret Service Reviews White House Security After Fence-Jumper Enters Mansion." *Washington Post,* September 20, 2014. https://www.washingtonpost.com/local /crime/secret-service-reviews-white-house-security-after-fence-jumper -enters-mansion/2014/09/20/23df4f6a-40e0-11e4-b03f-de718edeb92f _story.html.

Mejia, Paula. "Rogue Fence Hopper Makes It Inside White House Doors, Misses Obama by Minutes." *Newsweek,* September 20, 2014. http://www.newsweek.com/rogue-fence-hopper-makes-it-inside-white-house -doors-misses-obama-minutes-272000.

Melanson, Philip H. *The Secret Service: The Hidden History of an Enigmatic Agency.* New York: Basic Books, 2005.

Miller, Laura. "It's That Time of Gruyère: Big Block of Cheese Day Is Back." *Whitehouse.gov,* January 8, 2016. https://www.whitehouse.gov/blog /2016/01/08/big-block-cheese-day-back-again-gouda-time.

Niiler, Eric. "The White House Needs a New Fence (No, a Moat Won't Work)." *Wired,* May 11, 2015. http://www.wired.com/2015/05/white -house-needs-new-fence-no-moat-wont-work/.

Poore, Benjamin Perley. *Perley's Reminiscences of Sixty Years in the National Metropolis: Volumes I and II.* Philadelphia: Hubbard Brothers Publishers, 1886.

Presidential Pet Museum. "Grizzly Bears at the White House." March 30, 2014. http://presidentialpetmuseum.com/pets/thomas-jefferson-grizzly -bears-white-house/.

Saenz, Arlette. "Metal Spikes Installed on White House Fence in Latest Security Renovation." *ABC News,* July 1, 2015. http://abcnews.go.com /Politics/metal-spikes-installed-white-house-fence-latest-security/story ?id=32163777.

Shore, David, C. Richard Filson, Donald S. Rae. "Violent Crime Arrest Rates of White House Case Subjects and Matched Control Subjects." *American Journal of Psychiatry* 147, no. 6 (June 1990): 746–50.

Shore, David, C. Richard Filson, Ted S. Davis, Guillermo Olivos, Lynn DeLisi, and Richard Jed Wyatt. "White House Cases: Psychiatric Patients and the Secret Service." *American Journal of Psychiatry* 142, no. 3 (March 1985): 308–12.

Shore, David, C. Richard Filson, Wayne E. Johnson, Donald S. Rae, Peter Muehrer, Daniel J. Kelley, Ted S. Davis, Ivan N. Waldman, and Richard Jed Wyatt. "Murder and Assault Arrests of White House Cases: Clinical and Demographic Correlates of Violence Subsequent to Civil Commitment." *American Journal of Psychiatry* 146, no. 5 (May 1989): 645–51.

Smith, Melodi. "Toddler Causes Security Breach at White House, Delays Obama Address on Iraq." *CNN,* August 8, 2014. http://www.cnn.com /2014/08/08/politics/white-house-toddler-breach/.

Torrey, E. Fuller. *American Psychosis: How the Federal Government Destroyed the Mental Illness Treatment System.* New York: Oxford University Press, 2014.

Treatment Advocacy Center. "Deinstitutionalization." Accessed February 2016. http://www.treatmentadvocacycenter.org/a-failed-history.

Trex, Ethan. "Andrew Jackson's Big Block of Cheese." *Mental_Floss,* accessed January 18, 2016. http://mentalfloss.com/article/27228/andrew-jacksons -big-block-cheese.

Truman, Margaret. *The President's House: 1800 to the Present: The Secrets and History of the World's Most Famous Home.* New York: Ballantine Books, 2003.

United States Secret Service Protective Mission Panel. "Executive Summary to Report from the United States Secret Service Protective Mission Panel to the Secretary of Homeland Security." December 15, 2014. https://www.dhs.gov/sites/default/files/publications/14_1218_usss_pmp.pdf.

Walshe, Shushannah. "Protester Arrested After Jumping White House Fence." *ABC News,* June 26, 2013. http://abcnews.go.com/blogs/politics/2013/06/protester-arrested-after-jumping-white-house-fence/.

Well, Martin. "Apple Core Tossed over White House Fence Triggers Brief Concern." *Washington Post,* November 21, 2015. https://www.washingtonpost.com/local/public-safety/apple-core-tossed-over-white-house-fence-triggers-brief-concern/2015/11/21/8e2e86e4-90d3-11e5-acff-673ae92ddd2b_story.html.

White House. "Big Block of Cheese Day Is Back." YouTube video, 2:05. Posted by "The White House." January 16, 2015. https://www.youtube.com/watch?v=ex_jJlv5HKk.

"White House Gate Jumper Arrested." *NBC Washington* video, 1:02. September 20, 2011. http://www.nbcwashington.com/news/local/Man-Arrested-at-White-House-130236828.html.

CHAPTER 11

Ackerman, Spencer. "$19 Billion Later, Pentagon's Best Bomb Detector Is a Dog." *Wired,* October 21, 2010. http://www.wired.com/2010/10/19-billion-later-pentagon-best-bomb-detector-is-a-dog/.

Andrews, Evan. "10 Things You May Not Know About John Dillinger." *History,* August 4, 2014. http://www.history.com/news/history-lists/10-things-you-may-not-know-about-john-dillinger.

Biography.com Editors. "John Dillinger Biography." Biography.com, accessed December 11, 2015. http://www.biography.com/people/john-dillinger-9274804.

Higgins, Will. "Small Indiana Town Embraces Its Circus Identity." *USA Today* (via *Indianapolis Star*), July 12, 2013. http://www.usatoday.com/story/news/nation/2013/07/12/small-indiana-town-embraces-its-circus-identity/2511657/.

Interviews with Steve M., Shawn G., Brian M., Bill G., Kenneth (Kenny) Licklider, and Brian B.

"See the Famous Circus City Festival." Pamphlet. Peru, Indiana.

CHAPTER 12

Interviews with Jim S., Luke K., "Stew," Marshall M., Larry C., Brian M., Bill G., Brian B., and Shawn S.

CHAPTER 13

Fletcher, Dan. "A Brief History of the Khmer Rouge." *Time,* February 17, 2009. http://content.time.com/time/world/article/0,8599,1879785,00.html.

Heuveline, Patrick. "The Demographic Analysis of Mortality Crises: The Case of Cambodia 1970–1979." In *Forced Migration and Mortality,* edited by Holly E. Reed and Charles B. Keely. Washington, D.C.: National Academies Press, 2001.

Interviews with Leth O. (and his mother and wife), Bill G., and Brian M.

Lockhart, Meghan. "In Remembrance of a Tragic History." *Cambodia,* accessed October 3, 2015. http://www.roch.edu/course/doors2cambodia /cambodia._khmer_rouge.html.

Mail Foreign Service. "Khmer Rouge Torturer Describes Killing Babies by 'Smashing Them into Trees.'" *Daily Mail,* June 8, 2009. http://www .dailymail.co.uk/news/article-1191601/Khmer-Rouge-torturer-describes -killing-babies-smashing-trees.html.

Peace Pledge Union Information. "Cambodia 1975: The Genocide." Accessed September 21, 2015. http://www.ppu.org.uk/genocide/g_cambodia1.html.

Rungswasdisab, Puangthong. "Thailand's Response to the Cambodian Genocide." Cambodian Genocide Program, Yale University, accessed September 20, 2015. http://gsp.yale.edu/thailands-response-cambodian-genocide.

Taylor, Adam. "Why the World Should Not Forget Khmer Rouge and the Killing Fields of Cambodia." *Washington Post,* August 7, 2014. https:// www.washingtonpost.com/news/worldviews/wp/2014/08/07/why-the -world-should-not-forget-khmer-rouge-and-the-killing-fields-of -cambodia/.

CHAPTER 14

Gorgels, A. P., A. Van den Dool, A. Hofs, R. Mulleneers, J. L. Smeets, M. A. Vos, and H. J. Wellens. "Comparison of Procainamide and Lidocaine in Terminating Sustained Monomorphic Ventricular Tachycardia." *American Journal of Cardiology* 78, no. 1 (July 1, 1996): 43–46.

Heseltine, Johanna, and Anthony P. Carr. "Overcoming the Diagnostic and Therapeutic Challenges of Canine Immune-Mediated Thrombocytopenia." *Veterinary Medicine* 102, no. 8 (July 2007): 527–538.

Interviews with Nate C., Brianna S., and Brian M.

Marshall, Melissa. "Heat Stroke: Diagnosis and Treatment." *DVM 360,* August 1, 2008. http://veterinarynews.dvm360.com/heat-stroke-diagnosis-and -treatment.

Powell, Lisa L. "Canine Heatstroke." *NAVC Clinician's Brief,* August 2008. http:// www.cliniciansbrief.com/sites/default/files/Canine%20Heatstroke.pdf.

CHAPTER 15

Bui, Lynh, Keith L. Alexander, and Justin Jouvenal. "Latest White House Intruder Wanted to Talk to President About Spy Devices, Father Says."

Washington Post, October 23, 2014. https://www.washingtonpost.com
/local/crime/latest-white-house-jumper-had-similar-incident-in-july-had
-mental-evaluation/2014/10/23/c4f28df0-5ac0-11e4-8264-deed989ae9a2
_story.html.

di Marzo, Marina. "Dominic Adesanya, White House Fence Jumper, Sentenced." *NBC Washington,* July 2, 2015. http://www.nbcwashington
.com/news/local/Dominic-Adesanya-23-Accused-White-House-Fence
-Jumper-Sentenced-311492071.html.

Edelman, Adam. "White House Intruder Dominic Adesanya Forcibly Removed
from Court After Breaking into Hysterics During Hearing." *Daily News,*
October 27, 2014. http://www.nydailynews.com/news/politics/white-house
-intruder-dominic-adesanya-forcibly-removed-court-article-1.1989003.

Fox 5 DC. "Raw Video: Man Apprehended After Jumping White House
Fence." YouTube video, 0:24. Posted by "Fox 5 DC." October 22, 2014.
https://www.youtube.com/watch?v=onz4cfILHJU.

Hsu, Spencer S. "Md. Man Who Jumped White House Fence in October Gets
Six-Month Term." *Washington Post,* July 2, 2015. https://www.washing
tonpost.com/local/crime/md-man-who-jumped-white-house-fence-in
-october-gets-six-month-term/2015/07/02/b9d5ef8a-20f3-11e5-bf41
-c23f5d3face1_story.html.

Interviews with Marshall M., Bill G., Brian M., "Stew," Jim S., Brian B., Nicole M., and Hector H.

Rayman, Noah. "White House Fence Jumper Charged with Felonies After
Kicking Dog." *Time,* October 23, 2014. http://time.com/3533798/white
-house-fence-jumper-charged-police-dogs/.

Reuters. "White House Fence Jumper Dragged Screaming from Court After
Judge Rules Him Mentally Incompetent to Stand Trial." *Daily Mail,* October 27, 2014. http://www.dailymail.co.uk/news/article-2810083/Ac
cused-White-House-intruder-dragged-court-ruled-incompetent.html.

United States Secret Service. Internal footage from fence jumper apprehension.

U.S. Secret Service Twitter account (@Secret Service). Tweets about Hurricane
and Jardan. October 23, 2014. https://twitter.com/secretservice/status
/525379371029508096 and https://twitter.com/secretservice/status
/525378389658841089.

CHAPTER 16

"Bear's Final Call—Police Dog Honored by APD." YouTube video, 0:56.
Posted by "Katy Moore." January 10, 2014. https://www.youtube.com
/watch?v=PL-kDwftRBE.

Canine Cancer. "Hemangiosarcoma." Accessed February 10, 2016. http://
www.caninecancer.com/hemangiosarcoma/.

"Final Call—Vernon Matt Williams and Diogi." YouTube video, 2:20. Posted
by "Abcde0987." October 6, 2006. https://www.youtube.com/watch?v=
vwpBDO2hs4Q.

Interviews with Erica F., Tim D., Brian M., Jim S., "Stew," Brianna S., Bill Shegogue, Barry Lewis, and Leth O.

"K9 Jethro's Last Call." YouTube video, 5:57. Posted by "lilmisslucky13." January 5, 2016. https://www.youtube.com/watch?v=EAQIasQ-7Ic.

Officer Down Memorial Page. "ODMP Remembers K9 Maxo." Accessed February 12, 2016. https://www.odmp.org/k9/1498-k9-maxo.

University of Minnesota Animal Cancer Care and Research Program. "Hemangiosarcoma." Accessed February 10, 2016. http://www.cvm.umn.edu/accr/research/modianolab/cancerinformation/hemangiosarcoma/home.html.

CHAPTER 17

Interviews with Marshall M., Brian M., and "Stew."

U.S. Secret Service. "2015 DHS Secretary's Awards—November 3, 2015." YouTube video, 4:20. Posted by "US Secret Service." December 3, 2015. https://www.youtube.com/watch?v=E6pA5q7EqcM.

FROM *NEW YORK TIMES* BESTSELLING AUTHOR

MARIA GOODAVAGE

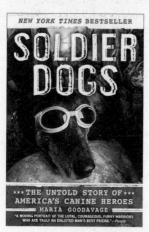

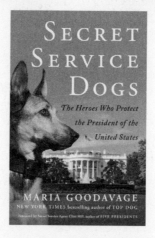

"A wonderful account and history of these unsung heroes
at work every day to make the world safer."
—*Library Journal* on *Secret Service Dogs*

Penguin
Random
House

DUTTON